W9-BSO-630

ALSO BY THE AUTHOR

Smoking Typewriters:
The Sixties Underground Press and
the Rise of Alternative Media in America

BEATLES VS. STONES

JOHN McMILLIAN

SIMON & SCHUSTER

New York London Toronto Sydney New Delhi

Simon & Schuster
1230 Avenue of the Americas
New York, NY 10020

First Simon & Schuster hardcover edition October 2013

Designed by Joy O'Meara

Manufactured in the United States of America

1 3 5 7 9 10 8 6 4 2

Library of Congress Cataloging-in-Publication Data is available.

ISBN 978-1-4391-5969-9
ISBN 978-1-4516-1238-7 (ebook)

For my parents

CONTENTS

The test of a first-rate intelligence is the ability to hold two opposed ideas in the mind at the same time and still retain the ability to function.

—F. SCOTT FITZGERALD

SOUNDTRACK

(Recommended)

The Beatles
"Shimmy Shake" (2:28) (*Live at the Star Club*)

Bo Diddley
"Pretty Thing" (2:48)

The Shirelles
"Will You Love Me Tomorrow?" (2:43)

The Beatles
"Love Me Do" (2:22)

The Rolling Stones
"Come On" (1:48)

The Beatles
"I Wanna Be Your Man" (2:00)

The Rolling Stones
"I Wanna Be Your Man" (1:49)

The Beatles
"Yesterday" (2:03)

The Rolling Stones
"As Tears Go By" (2:45)

Bob Dylan
"Girl from the North Country" (3:22)

The Kinks
"See My Friends" (2:50)

The Byrds
"Bells of Rhymney" (3:35)

The Animals
"We Gotta Get Out of This Place" (3:17)

The Beatles
"Drive My Car" (2:28)

The Beatles
"Norwegian Wood (This Bird Has Flown)" (2:05)

The Rolling Stones
"Paint It, Black" (3:22) (stereo album mix)

The Rolling Stones
"Stupid Girl" (2:55)

The Rolling Stones
"Let's Spend the Night Together" (3:36)

The Beatles
"All You Need Is Love" (3:47)

The Rolling Stones
"We Love You" (4:35)

The Rolling Stones
"Street Fighting Man" (3:16)

The Beatles
"Revolution" (3:21)

The Beatles
"Hey Jude" (7:11)

The Dirty Mac
"Yer Blues" (4:39) (*Rolling Stones Rock and Roll Circus*)

Yoko Ono
"Whole Lotta Yoko" (5:03) (*Rolling Stones Rock and Roll Circus*)

The Rolling Stones
"Sympathy for the Devil" (8:52)
(*Rolling Stones Rock and Roll Circus*)

INTRODUCTION

In the summer of 1968, Mick Jagger attended a birthday party in his honor at a hip, new Moroccan-style bar called the Vesuvio Club—"one of the best clubs London has ever seen," remembered Tony Sanchez, one of its proprietors. Under black lights and beautiful tapestries, some of London's trendiest models, artists, and pop singers lounged around on huge cushions and took pulls from Turkish hookahs, while a decorated helium-filled dirigible floated aimlessly around the room. As a special treat, Mick brought along an advance pressing of the Stones' forthcoming album, *Beggars Banquet*, and when it played over the club's speakers, people flooded the dance floor. Just as the crowd was "leaping around" and celebrating the record—which would soon win accolades as the best Stones album to date—Paul McCartney strolled in and passed Sanchez a copy of the Beatles' forthcoming single, "Hey Jude" / "Revolution," which had never before been heard by anyone outside of the group's charmed inner circle. As Sanchez remembered, the "slow thundering buildup of 'Hey Jude' shook the club," and the crowd demanded that the seven-minute song be played again and again. Finally, the club's disc jockey played the next song, and everyone heard "John Lennon's nasal voice pumping out 'Revolution.' " "When it was over," Sanchez said, "Mick looked peeved. The Beatles had upstaged him."

"It was a wicked piece of promotional one-upsmanship," remembered Tony Barrow, the Beatles' press officer. By that time, the mostly good-natured rivalry between the Beatles and the Stones had been going on for about four years. Although the Beatles were more commercially successful than the Stones, throughout the 1960s the two groups nevertheless competed for record sales, cultural influence, and aesthetic credibility. Teens on both sides of the Atlantic defined themselves by whether they preferred the Beatles or the Stones. "If you truly loved pop music in the 1960s . . . there was no ducking the choice and no cop-out third option," one writer remarked. "You could dance with them both, but there could never be any doubt about which one you'd take home."

Initially the rivalry was strongest in England. The Beatles began inspiring mass adulation among young teenage girls in the spring of 1963, but it soon became apparent that the group's invigorating music and seductive charm worked on adults as well. The Fab Four couldn't quite win over *everyone*—they were too unusual for that—but conventional wisdom held that the Beatles were a wonderful tonic to a society that was finally ready to shed the last vestiges of Victorian Era restraint. Their effect on British popular culture was said to be salutary, pitch-perfect, and perfectly timed.

The Rolling Stones provoked a different reaction. Pale and unkempt, they did not bother with stage uniforms, and they were not often polite. Instead of laboring to win the affection of the broader public, they feigned indifference to mainstream opinion. Musically, they favored American electric blues—an obscure genre in England that was championed by adolescent males as well as females, and that was most suitably performed in dark 'n' sweaty, smoke-filled rooms. Those who were faint of heart, or who enjoyed a prim sense of propriety, knew to stay away from the Stones. Adults regarded them as a menace.

That is one of the reasons that the debate over which band was better, the Beatles or the Stones, was freighted with such deep significance. To say that you were a Beatles fan was to imply that (just like the Fab Four) you were well adjusted, amiable, and polite. You were not a prig, necessarily, but nor were you the type to challenge social conventions. For the most part, you conformed. You agreed. You complied. When you looked upon the world that you were bound to inherit, you were pleased.

To align with the Rolling Stones was to convey the opposite message. It meant you wanted to smash stuff, break it and set it on fire. "The Beatles want to hold your hand," journalist Tom Wolfe once quipped, "but the Stones want to burn down your town."

Fans registered their loyalty in readers' polls conducted by music papers such as *New Musical Express* and *Record Mirror*. Whenever one group displaced the other at the top of the music chart, the news ran under a screeching headline, as if the Beatles and the Stones were football rivals or opposing candidates in a high-stakes election. People also tended to be deeply entrenched in their opinions. Beatles fans were often so devoted to the group that they would hear nothing against the Beatles. Youths who were in thrall to the Stones tended to be equally intransigent; they simply would not abide any criticism of their idols.

It is sometimes said that the "rivalry" between the Beatles and the Stones was just a myth, concocted by sensationalizing journalists and naïve teenyboppers. In reality, we are told, the two groups were always friendly, admiring, and supportive of each other. It is doubtful, however, that their relations were ever so cozy or uncomplicated. The two groups clearly struck up a rapport, but that never stopped them from trying to outperform each other wherever and however they could. And as most people understand, emulous competition rarely nourishes a friendship; more often it breeds anxiety, suspicion, and envy.

It is little wonder, then, that in some respects the Beatles and the Stones simply could not help but act like rival bands. Ensconced in West London, the Stones fancied themselves as hip cosmopolitans. They were obsessed with a particular style of "cool"—which they associated with reticence and self-possession—and so they were bemused by the Beatles' amiable goofball shtick: their corny repartee and their obvious eagerness to please. Furthermore, the Beatles came from the North Country: the industrialized and economically depressed region in England that the young Stones had always assumed was a culturally barren wasteland. Not only were they wrong about that, but like most Merseysiders, the Beatles were sensitive to even the hint of condescension. That may help to explain why when the two groups were first getting acquainted, the successful Beatles sometimes seemed to lord it over the Stones.

Before long, however, the Beatles began to feel stifled by their cuddly, mop-top image, and they envied the Stones for their relative freedom of movement. The Beatles may also have been rankled as the Stones gained greater credibility with the "right" types of fans: discerning bohemians, as opposed to hysterical teenyboppers. Of all the Beatles, John Lennon especially hated to have to stifle his personality the way he often did. Later, he would be annoyed by the way that underground newspapers portrayed the Stones as left-wing political heroes, while the Beatles were associated with the hippies' soft idealism.

The Beatles and the Stones also represent two sides of one of the twentieth century's greatest aesthetic debates. To this day, when people want to get to know each other better, they often ask: "Beatles or Stones?" A preference for one group over the other is thought to reveal something substantial about one's personality, judgment, or temperament. The clichés about the two groups are sometimes overdrawn, but they still retain a measure of plausibility. With some qualifications, the Beatles may be described as Apollonian, the Stones as Dionysian; the Beatles pop, the Stones rock; the Beatles erudite, the Stones visceral; the Beatles utopian, the Stones realistic.

None of the other famous dueling paradigms—say, in literature, painting, or architecture—tend to draw people into conversation like the Beatles and the Stones. How could they? The Beatles and Stones were popular artists of unprecedented magnitude; their worldwide record sales are by now uncountable.

Obviously the two groups shared a great deal in common; so too did their fans. Had he lived long enough, Sigmund Freud—that master of unmasking human motivations—might have understood the Beatles-Stones debate in terms of "the narcissism of small differences." "It is precisely the minor differences in people who are otherwise alike that form the basis of hostility between them," Freud wrote. Nevertheless, it is the opposing qualities of the Beatles and the Stones—which are widely known and well understood—that make comparison irresistible. Chances are, if you're reading this book, you already have an informed opinion about which group was better.

Moi-même, I don't try to adjudicate the question here. Many others have already done so and anyhow, I'm not a rock critic; I'm an historian. In this joint biography, I've merely juxtaposed the Beatles and the Stones, examined their interrelations, and shown how their rivalry was constructed. That is not to say that I don't hold a preference for one group over the other (of course I do), but rather that it is outside the purview of this book.

Besides, when rational criticism prevails, *both* groups are lauded. When they were in their prime, the Beatles and the Stones were *both* irreducibly great. Is that to repeat a dogma? Sure. But that doesn't make what they accomplished any less remarkable. Somehow, the young men who made up the Beatles and the Stones managed not only to find each other, but also to burnish their talents collectively. Both groups melded and alchemized into huge creative forces that were substantially greater than the sum of their collective parts. They came of age during one of the most fertile and exciting periods in the history of popular music, and they exerted a commanding presence.

That, anyhow, is my own view. And I know I'm not alone. Marianne Faithfull, who dated Mick Jagger in the late '60s, recalled the evening that I mentioned earlier, when members of the Beatles and the Stones turned up at that trendy nightclub and showed off their latest creations for all their friends: *Beggars Banquet*, and "Hey Jude" and "Revolution." "Vesuvio closed a couple of weeks later," Marianne said, "but the feeling in the room that night was: aren't we all the greatest bunch of young geniuses to grace the planet and isn't this the most amazing time to be alive? And I don't think it was just the drugs."

CHAPTER ONE

GENTLEMEN OR THUGS?

If you wanted to measure the distance between what the Beatles and the Rolling Stones were *really* like, before they became famous, versus the heavily mediated, highly stylized images they projected to their fans, you might seek the perspective of someone who not only knew both groups, but who also knew exactly what they were up to when they went about crafting their public personas. That person would be Sean O'Mahony, a successful London-based publisher who frequently wrote under the *nom de guerre* "Johnny Dean." In August 1963, O'Mahony began putting out *The Beatles Monthly Book*, the group's fan magazine (usually known simply as *The Beatles Book*). By December, he was selling about 330,000 *Beatles Book*s each month. Then in June 1964, he launched the similarly minded *Rolling Stones Book.*

These were both official fan magazines, and naturally, before O'Mahony was awarded the rights to publish them, he had to win each group's trust and affection.

He met the Beatles for the first time in May 1963, when they appeared at London's Playhouse Theatre to record some songs for the influential BBC radio program *Saturday Club*. "As soon as I shook hands with John, Paul, George, and Ringo, I realized this wasn't going to be one of their jokey encounters with the press," O'Mahony recollected. Instead, the group peppered him with questions and suggestions. "Editing their magazine meant that they would have to admit someone new to their inner circle," he explained, "and put up with me in their dressing rooms, recording studios, homes—in fact, virtually everywhere they went." Since O'Mahony was already acquainted with the Rolling Stones' managers—Andrew Loog Oldham and Eric Easton—the sussing out process would not have been as formal, but presumably he had to reassure them as well.

Though the Beatles and the Rolling Stones regularly appeared in all of the British music periodicals (*Melody Maker*, *Record Mirror*, *New Musical Express*, *Disc*, *Music Echo*) as well the nation's teenage pop magazines (*Boyfriend*, *Jackie*, *Fabulous*, *Rave*, *Valentine*), O'Mahony operated from a special vantage: awarded the sole and exclusive rights to publish their profit-oriented fan magazines, he became thickly intertwined in a socio-professional relationship with Epstein, Oldham and Easton, and the groups they managed. Whatever O'Mahony's private knowledge or feelings, his acquiescence was complete. In 1964, when journalist Michael Braun released his book *Love Me Do!*—a gossipy account of his travels with the Beatles during the first flush of Beatlemania, which rather contradicted the group's "squeaky clean" image—its publication was not even mentioned in *The Beatles Book*. Nor was O'Mahony eager to reveal that John Lennon was married, since Epstein feared that that knowledge would adversely affect the band's popularity with teenage girls. When publishing photos of the Beatles, O'Mahony often turned to retouch artists who would fix any splotches or blemishes on their faces, thereby making sure they were "the sort of pictures Brian wanted fans to see."

In other words, O'Mahony in this period closely resembled a Madison Avenue flack. Whatever inside information he had, he would never have wanted to print anything truly revelatory about John or Paul, or Mick or Keith or Brian. Instead, his magazines were merely platforms; they were meant to promote the Beatles and the Rolling Stones' carefully considered "brands" meticulously.

Many years later, though, when he had no need to belie his true feelings, he summed up the two groups this way: "The Beatles were thugs who were put across as nice blokes, and the Rolling Stones were gentlemen who were made into thugs by Andrew." Like many summations, this one may be a little too neat. But it's much closer to the truth than either band would like to have admitted during most of the 1960s.

• • •

"Thuggery" is of course a moral category, not a socioeconomic one, but much has been made of the fact that, however sunny their dispositions, the Beatles emerged from dreary old Liverpool, a declining industrial seaport that was pummeled by the German *Luftwaffe* during World War Two. Diversely populated, but largely consisting of the descendants of Irish refugees, Liverpool's hub teemed with roughhewn seamen and grimy pubs, and was almost completely lacking in refinement. Owing to some measure of pride, obstinacy, and self-deprecation, many Liverpudlians self-identified as "Scousers," but elsewhere in England, the term was applied purely with derision. By contrast, the Stones came from the outskirts of London. Though hardly affluent, on the whole they grew up a bit more comfortably than the Beatles, and in Britain's class-riven society, the distinction mattered enormously. "We were the ones that were looked down upon as animals by the Southerners, the Londoners," John Lennon remembered.

Given the scarcity and hardship that afflicted all of England in the immediate postwar period (to say nothing of the difficulties of drawing class distinctions), it is important to put the differences between the Beatles' and the Stones' backgrounds in careful perspective. A good treatment of the Beatles' origins can be found in Steven D. Stark's *Meet the Beatles: A Cultural History of the Band that Shook Youth, Gender, and the World.* Yes, Stark points out, the Beatles came from downtrodden Liverpool, but John, Paul, and George all resided in the city's leafy suburban districts, on the "good side" of the Mersey River. (Only

Ringo came from central Liverpool; he was born in a ramshackle row house in a notorious neighborhood called the Dingle.) Lennon was the sole Beatle who was fortunate enough to grow up in a home with indoor plumbing, but that is not quite as remarkable as it might seem, since fewer than half of British homes had indoor toilets in that period. And while Paul and George were both raised half a mile apart in state-subsidized "council houses," their quarters carried none of the stigma attached to American-style housing projects. Their homes got very cold in the winter, but they still compared favorably to the lodgings of many working-class families at that time.

Many years later, George's older sister, Louise, quibbled with the perception that their family was so rough-and-tumble poor. "My father drove a bus, and Mom looked after us at home," she said. "Occasionally she would take a job at about Christmas time . . . but we never thought of ourselves as poor or anything. Afterward you read these stories about The Beatles growing up in slums and all this kind of stuff. . . . [But] we had a good, warm, friendly family life." And in one of his final interviews, Lennon stressed that his childhood hardly resembled "the poor slummy kind of image that was projected in all the Beatles' stories."

Naturally, when the Beatles were growing up, they all endured the UK's rationing of food and petrol. Fresh eggs, fresh milk, and juice were hard to come by. All four Beatles would have walked and played amidst bombed-out buildings and charred rubble left over from the war. The dazzling array of consumer goods and leisure opportunities that so many American teens enjoyed during the booming 1950s would have been completely foreign to them. But by the standards of their day, only Ringo—who in addition to being poor, was afflicted by two major childhood illnesses—suffered real deprivation.

Growing up, the Rolling Stones were also familiar with rationing and wartime rubble, but they were better off than the Beatles. Brian Jones, the group's charismatic founder and early leader, came from an upper-middle-class home in Cheltenham; his father was an aerospace engineer and church leader. Mick Jagger was from Dartford, Kent; his well-educated father was an assistant schoolmaster and college phys ed instructor, and his mother was a hairdresser (an occupation that carries a bit more prestige in England than in the States). According to the Stones' official 1965 biography, Jagger was raised in a climate of "middle-class 'gentility.'" His three-bedroom childhood home had a name (Newlands), and when he was young his family vacationed in Spain and St. Tropez. Keith Richards likewise came from Dartford. After briefly attending the same primary school as Jagger, his parents migrated to a drab, cheaply built council estate, but they never gave up their middle-class aspirations. In response, Richards cultivated what he later described as "an inverted snobbery." "One was proud to come from the lowest part of town—and play the guitar too," he boasted. "Grammar school people were considered pansies, twerps." Only the Stones' two peripheral members, Bill Wyman and Charlie Watts, were solidly working class: Bill's dad was a bricklayer, and Charlie's drove a truck. But in spite of England's strict class hierarchy, whereby sons typically marched lock-step into the same types of professions as their fathers, both young men could afford to be fairly optimistic about their prospects by the time they joined the Stones: Watts was working as a graphic designer, and Wyman held a department store job while playing bass semiprofessionally.

Furthermore, the Stones came from Southern England, and the Beatles from the North. Differences between the two regions were stark. Writing in 1845, Benjamin Disraeli described Northern and Southern England as "Two nations between whom there is no intercourse and no sympathy," and a hundred odd years later, the situation had hardly changed. "To Londoners," Steven Stark writes, "Liverpool seemed almost like the frontier—impertinent, emotional, and a lot less important than the capital city, which was considered the center of almost everything the establishment considered English." Liverpool actually may have had a more robust music scene than London, but as fledgling musicians with thick Scouse accents, the Beatles knew the odds were stacked against them. "With us being from Liverpool," Harrison remembered, "people would always say, 'You've got to be from London to make it.' They thought we were hicks or something."

George was correct: initially, the Beatles were seriously disadvantaged by their origins (maybe even more than they realized). Certainly Decca executive Dick Rowe—aka "The Man Who Turned Down the Beatles"—had Liverpool on his mind after he heard the group's audition tape in early 1962. It's not that he thought the Beatles were *bad*, but with limited resources, his company had to make a choice: they could sign the Beatles, or they could go with Brian Poole and the Tremeloes. Many years later he explained that his unfortunate decision had rested, at least in part, upon the fact that Brian Poole was from London. That meant that his staff "could spend night and day with Brian at no cost to the company, whereas Liverpool is a long way away. You've got to get a [steam-powered] train. You've got a hotel bill to pay. You don't know how long you're going to be up there. And London is so very strange about the north of England. There's sort of an expression that if you live in London, you really don't know anywhere north of Watford. So, you see, Liverpool could have been Greenland to us then." Mick Jagger's old flame Marianne Faithfull likewise confessed that geographic prejudice against the Beatles was rampant among her charmed circle of friends. "We looked at them as being very provincial, very straight, sort of a little behind the London people," she said. Only later did she conclude that that attitude was "very patronizing and not really true."

• • •

Of course it would be unfair, and even stupid, to draw too much from this—to infer that the Beatles were "thugs" or that the Stones were "gentlemen"—based upon where they came from. More relevant is the knowledge that growing up, three of the four Beatles were known troublemakers, and the charismatic John Lennon was easily the group's most loutish member. On that last point, the historical record is so unequivocal that it is almost unseemly to delve into the details. Going all the way back to primary school, Lennon is remembered as a garden-variety delinquent—the type of kid who would pocket the change he was instructed to deposit in the church collection box, and pilfer from his aunt's handbag. He would hitch free rides on the bumpers of tram cars, steal cigarettes and then sell them, pull down girls' underpants, vandalize phone booths, set stuff on fire, act the clown in class, skip detention, gamble, pick fights, and arouse fear in others as he and his friends tooled around on their bicycles. He was, by his own admission, the "King Pin" of that age group, and many years later, an erstwhile neighbor could only remark, "Running into John Lennon and his gang in Woolton on their bikes was not an enjoyable social encounter."

Lennon continued in this vein when he attended the Liverpool College of Art, where, according to biographer Ray Coleman, "His work, erratically presented, was the last thing [his teachers] worried about." Instead, they fretted about his incredible capacity for causing trouble. Armed with a caustic wit, Lennon could be spectacularly cruel; one classmate remembered, "He was the biggest micky-take I've ever met. He picked on all kinds of characters in school, whatever their backgrounds, and tried to find some way of laughing at them." For some inexplicable reason, anyone who was physically afflicted, whether by disability or injury, was especially likely to be targeted by Lennon. Drinking only seemed to exacerbate his meanness, and according to his first wife, Cynthia, "he had a very small capacity before he became aggressive." With women, Lennon was a notorious cad. He was obnoxiously possessive of whomever he dated, yet rarely faithful to anyone and disparaging of those who were too timid to go to bed with him. His best childhood friend, Pete Shotton, explained that Lennon "came to be regarded, by all but his small circle of friends, as thoroughly bad news. Even I sometimes worried that he seemed destined for Skid Row."

Of course, Lennon had many appealing qualities as well. It was not unusual for him to show flashes of the warmth and sensitivity that he would later become well known for, and his friends always reckoned that his obnoxious behavior was merely his way of camouflaging his pain and vulnerability. Though Hunter Davies's authorized biography of the Beatles implies that Lennon may have had a happy childhood, in fact he had a terrible one. His father, Alf, abandoned him when he was very young, and later his mother, Julia—always a bit of a floozy—left him in the custody of his aunt Mimi and uncle George (the latter of whom died unexpectedly in 1955). As a young teenager, Lennon began reconnecting with his mother, but the rapprochement was confusing, to say the least: In 1979, Lennon recorded an audio diary, which surfaced in 2008, in which he reminisced about a time he'd laid in bed with his mother when he was fourteen. Somehow, he touched her breast, and then he wondered about trying something more. Then when Lennon was seventeen, Julia was struck and killed by an errant driver. "It was the worst thing that ever happened to me," Lennon said. "We'd caught up so much, me and Julia, in just a few years."

In losing a parent, Lennon had something in common with Paul McCartney, whose mother Mary died from complications of breast cancer surgery when he was just fourteen. His choirboy looks notwithstanding, Paul likewise sometimes engaged in aberrant teenage behavior, though nothing to rival Lennon's. He would merely play hooky and steal trifling things, like cigarettes, and on one occasion he may have helped steal some valuable audio equipment from a local church. Later, McCartney seemed chagrined about his uninspiring values: "All I wanted was women, money, and clothes," he said. According to one biographer, "Without question one of young Paul's greatest natural attributes was his smooth sense of diplomacy and persuasive charm. Apprehended red-handed perpetrating any number of naughty boyish pranks . . . he generally managed to weasel his way out."

The youngest Beatle, George Harrison, likewise managed to stay clear of any real trouble when he was growing up, in spite of being incredibly laxly supervised. "They let me stay out all night and have a drink when I wanted to," he said of his parents. "That's probably why I don't really like alcohol much today. I'd had it all by the age of ten." Still, George embarked on a classic anticonformist, teenage rebellion trip, stubbornly disobeying his teachers, altering his school uniform, slicking his hair back with gobs of pomade, and tramping through Liverpool in blue suede shoes. "From about the age of thirteen, all we were interested in was rock 'n' roll," remembered one of his friends. Of the four Beatles, Ringo is the only one whose childhood reputation seems unblemished by any dubious activities. Whether this speaks to his affable good nature, or his instinct for self-preservation, is hard to know. The hoodlums who prowled around the Dingle operated on a whole different order of magnitude than, say, John Lennon's bicycle gang. It was the type of place, Ringo recalled, where "You kept your head down, your eyes open, and you didn't get in anybody's way."

Ringo also was not with the Beatles during most of their trips to Hamburg, Germany (though he, too, regularly performed there, as the drummer for Rory Storm and the Hurricanes). Still, Beatles scholars agree that the Hamburg experience was formative. Forced to adhere to a brutally demanding schedule, that is where they honed their individual skills, matured into a tightly knit unit, and were introduced, via the beautiful photographer Astrid Kirchherr, to the haircuts that evolved into the mop top. Hamburg is also the place where the Beatles—consisting of John, Paul, George, drummer Pete Best, and bassist Stu Sutcliffe—enjoyed an almost unimaginably debauched lifestyle of drink, women, and pills punctuated occasionally by violence (though Pete refrained from the pills, and Stu shied away from the women except for Astrid). If a few music-industry insiders in the early 1960s regarded the Beatles as "thugs," their sojourns in Hamburg—where they held residencies at four different nightclubs over a twenty-eight-month period—are part of the reason why.

Hamburg bears some similarities to Liverpool—both are seaports, home to migrant communities, that endured strafing attacks during World War Two, and the two cities even share the same line of latitude (56 degrees North). But the St. Pauli district, where the Beatles played, made Liverpool's roughest neighborhood, Scottie Road, seem almost tranquil. St. Pauli may even have been the most stereotypically "sinful" place in the world. All of the clubs the Beatles played—the Star-Club, the Kaiserkeller, the Top Ten, and the Indra—were on or around the Reeperbahn, the street known to Germans as *die sündige Meile* (the sinful mile). It teemed with strippers, prostitutes, petty criminals, and the worst types of itinerants who intermingled in brothels, sex clubs, and dark and grotty bars controlled by mobsters. The Beatles, meanwhile, ranged in age from seventeen to twenty when they initially visited Hamburg, and for the first time in their lives, they had a wee bit of money in their pockets. It was a recipe for mayhem.

As performers, the Beatles were famously encouraged to "*mach shau*" (put on a lively show), and when they were jacked up on amphetamines and saturated with beer—as was often the case—they had little trouble generating excitement. Though merely a bar band at this point, specializing in American rock 'n' roll numbers from the likes of Chuck Berry, Little Richard, Fats Domino, and Carl Perkins, they played faster and harder than most of their peers, and their inspired performances quickly helped them to earn an intense following. With his open-legged stance before the microphone, Lennon was an especially physical presence, and he is said by biographer Philip Norman to have sometimes gone "berserk" in Hamburg's clubs, "prancing and groveling in imitation of any rock 'n' roller or movie monster his dazzled mind could summon up. The fact that their audience could not understand a word they said provoked John into cries of *'Seig Heil!'* and 'Fucking Nazis!' to which the audience invariably responded by laughing and clapping." Other times, Lennon would pass out drunk behind a piano, leaving the others to play without him. A 1962 bootleg recording documents a performance at the Star Club where Lennon sung the lyrics to "Shimmy Shake" as "shitty shitty," and Paul introduced "Besame Mucho" as "a special request for Hitler." The entire band ate, drank, and smoked on stage, and occasionally they found themselves throwing furniture around while staging mock fights. Once, Lennon played in his underwear, with a toilet seat around his neck. Locals sometimes referred to them as the *verrüchte* Beatles (the crazy Beatles). And of course, the Beatles outfitted themselves in leather gear from head to toe.

Sex in Hamburg was easily obtained for the handsome Beatles—far more so than in England—and their attitude toward it was unembarrassed. Pete Best claims that the band regularly took to partner swapping, and that each member averaged "two or three girls each night," depending on their stamina. Even if he's exaggerating (as seems likely), his bandmates have confirmed that they regularly brought women back to their cramped quarters for late-night romps. "It was a sex shock," McCartney explained. "We got a very swift baptism of fire into the sex scene. There was a lot of it about and we were off the leash." Lennon put the matter a bit more forthrightly: "Between the whores and the groupies our dicks all just about dropped off."

Amid all of these chaotic indulgences, dangerous undercurrents of violence pulsed through Hamburg. Many of the waiters and barmen in the clubs the Beatles played doubled as professional criminals; the whole lot of them carried switchblades, truncheons, and lead-weighted saps. Sometimes, as the Beatles were packing up their gear at the end of a long night, patrons who'd run afoul of the waiters would still be lying half dead on the floor. In other instances, bar fights became so riotous they could only be quashed with teargas, which of course sent everyone (Beatles included) pouring out of the club, crying and wheezing. "Virtually every night at the Indra some poor bastard was either bottled, knifed, or worse," Lennon recalled.

Usually the Beatles merely witnessed the horrific violence, but on a few occasions they acted like common roughnecks. Some of their worst behavior may have been accentuated by the fact that they grew accustomed to gobbling slimming pills called "Prellies" (Preludin). Now off the market, these little blue pills could loosen a person's inhibitions, keep him awake, and put him seriously on edge. In one legendary incident, Paul and Stu *schau gemacht* (made a show) when they fell into fisticuffs during the middle of a set. Another time, while playing cards in their flat above the Star-Club, John drunkenly struck someone upside the head with a beer bottle. "Within seconds the fellow [Lennon struck] had gotten up and knocked the hell out of John, pasting him all over the flat," remembers a friend. "And all of us stood there and let him do it, because we agreed that you don't go round hitting people on the head with bottles and expect to get away with it." A long-circulating rumor holds that when he was especially sozzled, Lennon would sometimes find a perch from which to urinate on the heads of nuns who passed by on the streets below. In another despicable episode from his Hamburg career, Lennon once proposed that the Beatles should mug a drunken sailor they'd just met. Paul and George proved too timid to execute the plan, so John and Pete were left to attack the tipsy mariner on a dark corner, at which point they got more than they bargained for: their victim retaliated with a fierce volley of punches and then whipped out what the two Beatles thought was a pistol. In fact, the sailor's gun only shot teargas pellets, but it was enough to send two assailants scrambling for their lives.

Whenever the Beatles returned to Liverpool clubs and dance halls, they brought a little bit of Hamburg with them. "They liked us because we were kind of rough, and we'd had a lot of practice in Germany," said Harrison. "There were all these acts going 'Dum de dum' and suddenly we'd come on, jumping and stomping. Wild men in leather suits." An early fan described them as "raw. . . . They were always in their leather jackets, Cuban heels, and their hair everywhere. It was so different from the run-of-the-mill groups at the time with their suede-collared jackets and matching colors, all blues and yellows." Liverpool disc jockey Bob Wooler remembered Lennon "commanded the stage . . . the way he stared . . . and stood. His legs would be wide apart, that was one of his trademarks. And of course it was regarded as being very sexual. The girls up front would be kind of looking up his legs, keeping a watch on the crotch, as it were. It was a very aggressive stance that he adopted." The group continued taking Prellies and Purple Hearts (supplied by Paul's girlfriend, who stole them from a pharmacy she worked at), and when the band played lunchtime engagements, Lennon would banter sarcastically with the audience—especially with those who worked in nearby offices. " 'Shurrup, you with the suits on,' became a regular Lennon message," one biographer said. "He mocked them for taking 'regular jobs.' " And since the enthusiasm that the Beatles stimulated in teenage women sometimes elicited an inverse response from Merseyside's tough young men, the Beatles still got into the occasional brawl. According to Best, George was too puny for real fighting, and sometimes called for rescue, but "John . . . was always ready to have a go." After Stuart Sutcliffe died from a brain hemorrhage in 1961, an autopsy found an indentation in his skull, and some have speculated that the trauma might have occurred when a group of Liverpool teddy boys attacked him earlier that year.

When Brian Epstein saw the Beatles for the first time, at Liverpool's Cavern Club in late 1961, they were much improved since their first Hamburg engagement, almost two years prior. For all their louche behavior, the Beatles still maintained a brutally demanding schedule in Germany. (In one year-and-a-half stretch alone, they are thought to have played 270 shows, clocking in more than 800 performance hours.) Epstein saw the Beatles as a four-piece band (Sutcliffe having recently left, to be replaced by McCartney on bass), and soon Ringo would take Pete Best's perch behind the drums. But the group was very different back then from the one that most people recognize today as "The Beatles." Before they were catapulted to fame, they lived very roughly, sleeping around, popping pills, drinking a lot, and occasionally getting into fights. When they weren't attired in matching leathers, they dressed slovenly. Their reputation was not based upon any recorded work, but rather on their kinetic live performances. Led by a charismatic frontman who was known to greet even fans with practiced arrogance, they projected a thoroughly disreputable, slightly dangerous aura. British music journalist Chris Hutchins described them this way: "The Beatles when they lived in Hamburg were what the Stones became."

• • •

In his capacity for making mischief and harming others, Brian Jones, the Rolling Stones' founder and guitarist, was no slouch. His background, however, was altogether different from Lennon's. Both of Jones's parents were university educated, and Jones was himself a talented student; at age fifteen, he got nine O-level passes in the General Certificate of Education (the British national subject exam) and entered the sixth form (the optional and selective last two years of school in England). "He was a rebel . . . but when examinations came, he was brilliant," remembered one childhood friend. Brian's mother, Louisa, wistfully recalled that young Brian "sometimes talked of becoming a dentist, and we were all behind him—especially when he did so well at school." Jones also showed youthful athletic promise, and growing up in Cheltenham—a ritzy but dull spa town that Keith Richards once described as "an old ladies' resting place"—he learned how to comport himself in a respectable manner. He had a stable home life, and very early on his parents recognized and encouraged his prodigious musical talent.

According to Brian's beleaguered father, Lewis, the onset of his son's problems with authorities struck abruptly, and forcefully, when he was about seventeen or eighteen—not long after he'd taken up the alto sax and become consumed with improvisational jazz (especially as practiced by Charlie Parker). "He started to rebel against everything—mainly me," said Lewis. When Brian was confronted about his disorderly behavior at school, which led to at least two suspensions, his father lamented that Brian was "terribly logical about it all." "You want me to do the things you did," Brian explained. "But I can't be like you. I have to live my own life"—a life that in short order would mean leaving his studies behind, drifting about, flirting with poverty, and evading adult responsibilities.

In 1959, when Jones was seventeen, he was expelled from Cheltenham Grammar School after his fourteen-year-old girlfriend became pregnant and declined to have the abortion that Brian had assiduously lobbied for. This was the first of at least several (some have claimed *five*) "illegitimate" children. The following year, a one-night stand led to another woman's pregnancy. Then in 1961, after making his way through several low-wage vocations (shop assistant, deliverer of coal, bus conductor, apprentice at the local housing office), Brian made a young woman named Pat Andrews pregnant. She likewise carried the baby, apparently with the understanding that, given the mores of the time, as well as Brian's personal reassurances, he would soon marry her.

He did not. Instead, he beat his way to London to work in an optician's office, forcing Ms. Andrews to track him down, baby and belongings in tow, and demand that he take them in. It would be difficult to describe the shame this must have brought upon Brian's family. After the optician job, Jones worked at a department store from which he was fired for theft. Later he would leave the employ of a record store, and then a newsstand, after committing the same offense at both places. "Brian was totally dishonest," remembered Ian Stewart, the Stones' regular keyboardist.

When the opportunity arose, he could also be a world-class bully. Keith Richards recalled how Brian used to torment their insecure, sycophantic roommate Dick Hattrell:

> *Within two weeks Brian took him for every penny, and he conned Dick into buying him this whole new Harmony electric guitar, having his amp fixed and getting him a whole new set of harmonicas. Dick would do anything Brian said. It was freezing and the worst winter. Brian would say, "Give me your overcoat," and he gave Brian his army overcoat. "Give Keith the sweater,"*

> *so I put the sweater on. "Now you walk twenty yards behind us," and we'd walk off to the local Wimpy Bar. "Stay there. You can't come in. Give us £2." Dick would stand outside this hamburger joint, freezing. Brian would invite Dick to lunch and the three of us would go to what we considered a really good restaurant, and have a hot meal, which nobody could afford, of course! Then we'd just walk out and leave Dick with the bill.*

One winter evening, Brian even locked Hattrell out of the house, forcing him to pound on the front door for hours, begging to be let back in, "by which time he'd turned blue." Worst of all, according to bandmate Bill Wyman, "One night Brian punched [Pat Andrews] in the face and she ran home with a black eye, crying. A few hours later, Brian, the true romantic, arrived outside her home, throwing pebbles up at her window and shouting his apologies. They were quickly reunited."

Philip Norman, the Stones' best biographer, observed that when "Brian fixed anyone with his big baby eyes and spoke in his soft, lisping, well-brought-up voice, it was impossible to imagine the chaos accumulating behind him." Someone else called him a "Botticelli angel with a cruel streak." His genteel background and, at times, shy and quiet persona masked an incredible capacity for harming others. In its own way, Jones's softness must have been just as disarming as Lennon's impish humor and quick wit. Though rarely as outwardly aggressive as Lennon, he clearly shared some of Lennon's capacity for antisocial behavior. But when we examine the backgrounds of the other future Rolling Stones, we find very little to suggest that they were destined to become the archetypal "bad boys" of rock 'n' roll.

As a teenager, Michael Jagger was accustomed to middle-class creature comforts, and he even had the means to become a regular mail-order customer of Chess Records, the famous Chicago blues label. "I never got to have a raving adolescence between the age of 12 and 15," Jagger explained, "because I was concentrating on my studies . . . but then that's what I wanted to do, and I enjoyed it." About the notorious teddy boy subculture, which anyhow was on the wane by the time he was old enough to participate, Jagger said he "wasn't particularly impressed." It is true that at around age fifteen, he began fashioning an insubordinate sort of attitude—his academic performance slipped as he became interested in girls and rhythm 'n' blues, and his love of sports gave way to less salubrious habits, like beer and cigarettes—but never was he at any risk of failing out of Dartford Grammar School (the rough equivalent of a selective American high school). In fact, he passed seven O-levels, entered the sixth form, and was admitted into the prestigious London School of Economics, where he blended in perfectly and began laying plans for an elite career in politics or business.

About Keith Richards, one must resist the temptation to make too much of the fact that he was, literally, a choirboy. In 1953, at age nine, he even had the honor of singing in Westminster Abbey at Queen Elizabeth II's coronation. When he was twelve, though, he was sent to the lowly regarded Dartford Tech, and in 1959, school officials expelled him for truancy. By this point, Keith was styling himself in dark glasses, pink socks, and black drainpipe trousers, and carrying his guitar everywhere, slung over his back. "Rock and roll got me into being one of the boys," he recalled. "Before that I just got me ass kicked all over the place. Learned how to ride a punch." His next stop was Sidcup Art College—a tax-subsidized training school of last resort for people like Richards who, it was hoped, might be able to acquire some kind of marketable skill in the realm of commercial art. Instead, Richards found himself surrounded by many other alienated and vaguely bohemian musicians. It was at Sidcup that Richards made his first forays into recreational drugs (amphetamines and painkillers), but according to a biographer, he was not then regarded as a degenerate or a major troublemaker, but rather as a "free-spirited . . . pest," blessed with a quick wit.

Nor did Charlie Watts or Bill Wyman arouse any great fury as young adults. In fact, Watts was considered "the most stylish young man" at his advertising agency, "wearing charcoal-colored trousers and good quality sweaters when he did not wear a suit." According to a friend, "Charlie's concession to joining the Stones was taking his tie off at gigs." Furthermore, around the time he hooked up with the Stones, his premier interest was not in rock or blues, but jazz. Bill Wyman also did not share the same musical interests as Jones, Jagger, and Richards when he joined the Stones; instead of R&B, he'd been playing "white rock 'n' roll" in the Cliftons; but as he wrote in his memoir, "The major difference between the Stones and me when we met mattered even more than the music. I was a young family man with a wife, a nine-month-old child and a day job." Wyman was also about six years older, on average, than the rest of the Stones.

It is true, though, that early in the Rolling Stones' saga, when Brian, Mick, and Keith all lived together, they seemed to deliberately slum up their Edith Grove flat in an attempt to fashion bohemian lifestyles. "The place was an absolute pit which I shall never forget," wrote Wyman. "I've never seen a kitchen like it—permanently piled high with dirty dishes and filth everywhere. They took a strange delight in pointing out the various cultures that grew in about forty smelly milk bottles laying around in mold and on congealed eggs." They lobbed disgusting gobs of spit onto their own walls and let rubbish accumulate everywhere. What little heat they had emanated from an electric coin meter, but sometimes it was so cold they stayed in bed all day. A single, bare light bulb hung from the ceiling, and even food was scarce. "I never understood why they carried on like this," Wyman later said. "Although Keith came from a working-class background, Brian and Mick were from well-to-do families. It could not have been just the lack of money that caused them to sink." Instead, he concluded there was a voguish quality to their behavior; they must have been afflicted with some kind of "Bohemian Angst."

The image the Stones later embraced, then, was not entirely a surprise. People remember that although Mick Jagger was always interested in achieving financial success, he was also a skilled poser. Even before he joined the Stones, he'd traded in his given name, Michael, for the more laddish-sounding Mick, and he was known to switch easily between his proper London accent and a faux-Cockney tongue that might have fooled someone into thinking he was from the East End. But beyond this, and with the partial exceptions of Brian Jones (whose sociopathic tendencies were not immediately discernible), and Keith Richards (whose unruly demeanor really wasn't all that unruly), we don't find anything in the backgrounds of the future Rolling Stones to suggest that they would one day arouse such tremendous fear and indignation. No one would have expected them to become antiestablishment icons—objects of tabloid fury and rough justice from the courts.

In fact, the very idea that Stones would soon become synonymous with debauchery and rock 'n' roll excess—first across the British Isle, and then the world—would have seemed preposterous to the band in its earliest incarnation. When the "Rollin' Stones" began performing together in July 1962 (consisting of Brian, Mick, Keith, Dick Taylor on bass, Ian Stewart on piano, and Tony Chapman on drums) they didn't fancy themselves as rock 'n' rollers, but rather, as R&B purists. They specialized in covers of black American artists like Howlin' Wolf, Muddy Waters, and Bo Diddley, which they performed while sitting down. Someone who caught the Stones early on described them this way: "They seemed accomplished and rather like art-school nice guys, no posturing; they were almost like jazzers. . . . They were gauche, naïve, friendly, and generally without any charisma, they were just doing their music." Bill Wyman said something similar. When he got in league with the Stones in December 1962, he of course recognized Brian's and Mick's naturally projected sex appeal, "but on stage they were keen on projecting the *music.* Selling themselves as sexy pop stars had not crossed their minds."

"R&B was a minority thing that had to be defended at all times," Jagger recollected. "There was a kind of crusade mentality." By contrast, rock 'n' roll seemed weak—artistically compromised and commercially corrupted. A substantial portion of the Stones' audience consisted of bohemians and intellectuals, many of whom were men, and it wasn't difficult to perceive a measure of snobbery in the Stones' attitude, which seemed calculated to draw a distance between themselves, and what Jagger called "waffly white pop." "But I mean there's always going to be good-looking guys with great haircuts," he added. "That's what pop music is about."

• • •

Brian Epstein was twenty-seven when he discovered the Beatles, and until then, he'd never expressed any interest in pop management. In fact, when he was sixteen, he carefully crafted a letter to his parents in which he surveyed various careers that he'd decided he was *not* interested in—business, law, the ministry—before announcing that he'd finally realized what he wanted to do: he would make his fortune designing dresses. Given his extraordinary interest in fashion, it might not have been a bad path, but Brian's father—the well-to-do son of a penniless immigrant, known for his serious mien and tenacious work ethic—was horrified at the notion. He'd have preferred, first, that Brian stay in school, but his unhappy son had been such a chronic underachiever that he resolved instead to steer him into the family business: retail furniture. Surprisingly, Brian quickly began showing acumen as a salesman; he spent hours arranging the furniture displays in the windows, and he always showed up for work immaculately dressed. As a young man, his biographer posits, he may even have been "Liverpool's best-dressed bachelor. His thick hair was styled at the Horne Brothers salon, his clothes came from the top tailors, and he found himself popular among girls," even though he was secretly gay (homosexuality being illegal in England until 1967). As hobbies,

Epstein took up foreign languages (Spanish and French), and he immersed himself in Liverpool's theater community.

In the late 1950s, Brian's dad launched NEMS (North End Music Stores) and hired his son to run the record department. Brian was a demanding, fastidious boss, and his regal bearing could rub some people the wrong way. He insisted that his employees should always look their very best, and that they address every potential customer as "sir" or "madam"—even the four particularly disheveled lads in jeans and leather jackets who were always dropping by in the middle of the afternoon to listen to records but rarely to purchase any. "They used to drive us crackers," an employee said about the group she later discovered was the Beatles. Often they were looking for "way-out American music" that was not in stock.

Epstein had a policy of ordering any record that a customer asked for, and in late 1961, he was briefly stumped when requests started trickling in for a new single called "My Bonnie," supposedly by "the Beatles." Brian searched hard for the record, but it simply didn't seem to exist in any of his ordering catalogues. Finally, he was able to determine that the disc people were seeking, which was recorded in Germany, was actually put out by the English singer-guitarist Tony Sheridan, who had merely used the Beatles as a backup band. What's more, the Beatles weren't properly mentioned on the record; instead, they were listed as the "Beat Brothers," because the company that produced the single thought "Beatles" sounded too much like *peedles*, German slang for "penis." Nevertheless, Epstein ordered twenty-five copies of "My Bonnie," which sold out in a day. Then he ordered fifty more discs, and very quickly they, too, disappeared from his record bins.

Epstein usually claimed that this was the fated episode that brought the Beatles to his attention and piqued his curiosity so much that he decided to attend one of their lunchtime engagements at the Cavern Club (which happened to be only about a three-minute walk from his store). This could be so, but it's hard to believe. Since July 1961, the Beatles were regularly featured in Bill Harry's *Mersey Beat*, a music newspaper that Epstein not only distributed at NEMS, but that also featured his own record reviews. Even though Brian's personal tastes were more for Mozart and Shakespeare than rock 'n' roll, it seems likely that the enterprising record store manager would have at least recognized the name of one of Liverpool's most popular bands—especially since they played regularly just around the corner.

In any event, it was on November 9, 1961, that Brian and his trusty personal assistant Alistair Taylor ventured down the stairs into the Cavern, where they saw the Beatles for the first time. "Inside the club it was as black as a deep grave, dank and damp and smelly and I regretted my decision to come," Epstein later wrote in his memoir, *A Cellarful of Noise*. The Beatles, though, impressed him incredibly favorably. He was "fascinated" by their "pounding bass beat" and "vast engulfing sound," and he could not help but notice the charged enthusiasm of their audience, which numbered about two hundred. He was also struck by the group's rough exterior and devil-may-care attitude. "They were not very tidy and not very clean," he remembered. "They smoked as they played and ate and talked and pretended to hit each other. They turned their backs on the audience and shouted at them and laughed at private jokes." Some have speculated that it might have been exactly this behavior—the Beatles' scrappiness—that Epstein found *most* attractive. Though Epstein was as dapper and debonair as they came, sexually he went for "rough trade"—tough, unpolished, working-class greaser types. But Taylor sharply disputes the notion. "This accusation has been put up so many times," he complained. "It's bullshit. He signed the Beatles because they impressed us."

As for the Beatles, it's clear why they went with Epstein. First, as John Lennon put it, "he looked efficient and rich." Second, Epstein was the type to think *big*, and big is how the Beatles were beginning to think as well. Though devoid of pop management experience, Epstein worked evangelically on the Beatles' behalf, championing them to music industry insiders with measures of loyalty, pride, passion, and grit that were exceptional by any standard. Numerous sources suggest that the old story about Brian meeting an audience of nonplussed record executives and angrily blurting out, "The Beatles are going to be bigger than Elvis Presley!" is probably true. He *really did* go about saying that. But before that could happen, Brian always maintained that his boys would have to clean up their act. Except for on one slightly infamous occasion, when he was probably very drunk, Epstein would not dare try to interfere with the Beatles' music, but as their manager, he worked closely with them on their presentation. As a result, he was finally able to exercise some of his longstanding creative and theatrical impulses. "Brian wanted to be a star himself," producer George Martin speculated. "That was the essential part of Brian. He couldn't do it as an actor, and now he was able to do it as a man who was a manipulator, a puppeteer, if you like. He loved this role of being the power behind the scenes."

The Beatles went along with Brian's desire to tidy up their performance, not because they ever wanted to get into spiffy suits, but because they gradually became convinced that he was right. "It was a choice of making it or still eating chicken on stage," Lennon remarked. Still, their metamorphosis did not happen overnight: first went the leather jackets, and then the jeans were replaced with smart-looking trousers. "After that . . . I got them to wear sweaters onstage," Brain recalled, and only afterward, "very reluctantly," did they begin wearing their trademark grey collarless suits, which were inspired by Pierre Cardin. (Eventually the Beatles' main tailor, Dougie Millings, would make about five hundred garments for the group.) Meanwhile, Epstein had his secretary type up memos spelling out exactly what the Beatles must not do: They must "stop swearing on stage, they must stop joking with the girls, they must stop smoking or carrying cans of Coke onstage," and so forth. Even some of their offstage behavior was regulated. For instance, it was fine if they smoked, but only filtered cigarettes. Harsh, unfiltered Woodbines, or rollies, were considered *déclassé* and strictly prohibited. The Beatles were instructed to trim their guitar strings and to bow deeply from the waist after each number. "He was a director. That's really what he was," Paul said about Brian.

Eventually, Lennon came to despise the Beatles' anodyne image, but it's not clear when that began to happen. Derek Taylor, the Beatles' press officer, dismissed Lennon's "posthumous, wise-after-the-event" objections to the Beatles makeover. "They didn't mind at the time," he said. "They were making more money that way." When the Beatles were filmed for the very first time—on August 22, 1962, at the Cavern Club, for a Granada TV program called *Know the North*—Harrison recalled, "It was really hot and we were asked to dress up properly. We had shirts, and ties, and little black pullovers. So we looked quite smart. . . . and John was into it!"

But Lennon remembered feeling differently: "there we were in suits and everything. It just wasn't us." Even though they played old standbys, like "Some Other Guy" and "Kansas City" / "Hey Hey Hey Hey," Lennon said "that was where we started to sell-out." Cynthia adds that when Epstein began sprucing up the Beatles, John was always differently minded than the others. "Paul was keen on the changes and George was happy to accept them," she recalled. "But it wasn't easy for John. When Brian asked them to wear suits and ties, John growled for days. That was what the Shadows—the group John most despised—did." Still, knowing Lennon's ambition, one gets the impression he would have had the group dress up in clown suits if he thought it was necessary.

Later on, though, when the Stones showed it was possible to become very successful while acting like hooligans, Lennon became a little annoyed. "He always believed the Stones had hijacked the Beatles' 'original' image," said Chris Hutchins, who was friendly with both bands. Without the Beatles, Lennon reasoned, the Stones never could have gotten away with so much. "Brian Epstein made them behave, conform, perform, wear suits, be polite, [and] made them do Royal

Variety Shows," Hutchins noted. "That really left the field open for Andrew to say 'Fuck that, the Stones don't do that.' As Lennon so correctly observed, Brian left the way open for the Stones to occupy a very large vacancy."

• • •

It may say something about Andrew Loog Oldham's ego, as well as the richness of his life, that in the first of his three memoirs, nearly two hundred pages breeze by before he describes his first exposure to the Rolling Stones, which happened at the Crawdaddy Club in Richmond, Surrey, on a Sunday night in April 1963. Nevertheless, he narrates the occasion in nearly mystical terms; it was not only pivotal, but epiphanous. "I'd never seen anything like it," he said. "All my preparations, ambitions and desires had just met their purpose. . . . Everything I'd done up until now was a preparation for this moment. I saw and heard what my life, thus far, had been for." At the time, he was nineteen years old and still living with his mother.

Whatever he lacked in resources, though, he compensated for with style, ambition, and an almost otherworldly amount of chutzpah. His love for the glamorous life was apparent by the time he was a young teen. Oldham was so enchanted by show biz and celebrity culture that just about every month or so, a friend said, "a new public personality would take pride of place in his young heart." A favorite Hollywood icon was Laurence Harvey, the Lithuanian-born actor who found international stardom in *Room at the Top* (in which he played an inveterate social climber) and *Expresso Bongo* (where he played a sleazy talent scout). Another favorite was Tony Curtis, who portrayed the gangsterish press agent Sidney Falco in *The Sweet Smell of Success.* None of these protagonists brought much good into the world, but Oldham wasn't interested in these films for their social messages. Instead, they fueled his ambition to become, as he put it, "a nasty little upstart tycoon shit."

Though of a very different temperament than Epstein, Oldham

was also theatrically handsome, and he shared Brian's love of fashion and *haute couture*. "He was the most concerned-about-clothes person I've ever met in my life to this day," claimed an old business partner. "He was meticulous." At age sixteen, after getting only three O-level passes, he strolled into Bazaar—the famous, youth-oriented boutique operated by Mary Quant—and sweet-talked his way into a job as an errand boy for £7 per week. His main responsibilities involved preparing tea, taking messages, and walking dogs, but sometimes he helped Quant dress the storefront windows, and she recalled "he had all the confidence in the world." For Oldham, the experience was invaluable. "I will always thank Mary [and her business partners] for teaching me about fame, fashion, money, and how to have fun getting it done," he said. Every evening after work, Andrew would venture over to Soho, where he held a second job waiting tables at a Ronnie Scott's Jazz Club. Though not musically gifted, he briefly tried to find an agent or a manager who thought he might be able to make it as a pop star. That didn't go anywhere, though Oldham was able to conjure some bright-hued aliases for himself: he wanted to be known as either Chancery Lane or Sandy Beach.

During this period, Oldham usually managed to constrain his dark side, but not always. His ex-wife Shelia Klein recalls the time when he'd enthusiastically arranged for her to visit a modeling agency. He helped her get styled by Vidal Sassoon, and had her professionally photographed, but then, on the morning of her appointment, his thinking made an abrupt U-turn. "He didn't want me to be a model anymore," Sheila remembered. "There was no discussion; he just locked me in the cupboard and wouldn't let me out. That was the end of my modeling career. Andrew definitely was different. His way of handling a situation was very effective."

After a brief sojourn to the South of France, Oldham returned to London and found work in public relations. As a result he was able to meet Phil Spector, the legendary pop producer who, even then, struck a foreboding presence. Spector made an overwhelming impression on young Andrew. The two of them "were a nightmare together," a friend recalled. "Andrew got hooked on Phil's not behaving very well." Riding together in darkly tinted limos and dining under the protection of bodyguards, Andrew plied Spector for advice about how to make it in the music industry.

Another very important person Oldham met was Brian Epstein. They crossed paths in January 1963 at the taping of the Beatles' second national television appearance, on ABC-TV's hugely popular *Thank Your Lucky Stars.* "Brian merely stood watching his boys, yet his belief and their talent permeated the room," Oldham recalled. In a conversation, Oldham persuaded Epstein to hire him as a London-based PR man for a monthly retainer of £25. Mostly, Oldham worked for two of Epstein's recently acquired acts, Gerry and the Pacemakers and Billy J. Kramer and the Dakotas, but sometimes he helped drum up publicity for the Beatles in music weeklies, teen magazines, and daily papers. On one glorious occasion, he even got to chaperone the Beatles to some radio shows and press interviews. Another time, he saw the Beatles play the Granada Theatre in Bedford, just as they were beginning their glide path to superstardom. "Onstage, you could not hear the Beatles for the roar of the crowd," Oldham rhapsodized. "The noise that night hit me emotionally, like a blow to the chest. . . . When I looked at Brian, he had the same lump in his throat and tear in his eye as I."

Andrew craved these sorts of heady experiences, but it was a routine lunch that changed his life. Peter Jones, of the pop periodical *Record Mirror*, mentioned that one of his colleagues had just written enthusiastically about the bourgeoning R&B scene and favorably mentioned a new band, "the Rollin' Stones," even though they hadn't yet made a record. "It looks like rhythm 'n' blues will make it big soon, so why not have a look at them?" Jones said. Oldham wasn't particularly enthused by the suggestion, but since he wanted to curry favor with Jones, he figured he should at least appear to be interested in his advice. The next Sunday, Oldham traveled to Richmond, where, he said, "I met the Rollin' Stones and said 'hello' to the rest of my life."

Oldham not only lacked managerial experience—he didn't even have a registered address, and it would be almost two years before he would be old enough to apply for an agent's license. The first person he phoned for help was Epstein, offering him 50 percent of the Rolling Stones management contract in return for some office space and enough upfront funding to finance a recording session. Citing his obligations to the Beatles and other Liverpool acts, Brian declined. Next, Andrew approached Eric Easton, an older, experienced, London agent who, after some hesitation, expressed interest in accepting a similar deal . . . if it could be arranged. Sean O'Mahony figured the Oldham-Easton partnership was an excellent one. "Andrew was the young go-getter with loads of good ideas for promoting groups and giving them an image," he said. "Eric was this rather conservative show business agent, a very straightforward businessperson, who had the necessary practical knowledge, knew how contracts worked, knew how to do bookings, knew that side inside out."

The following Sunday, Philip Norman writes, Oldham made "the most brilliant self-selling job the nineteen-year-old had yet pulled off, expertly mixing audacity with intuition. He came on to Brian, Mick, Keith, Stew, Bill, and Charlie as a London big shot who could give them anything they wanted and get anywhere they cared to go. At the same time, he was one of them, a rebel, an outsider who shared their quasi-Marxist ideals and evangelical zeal for bringing pure blues and R&B to a wider audience." The bit about Andrew being an R&B fan was a particularly hideous distortion; in fact, he was glomming on to a trend he'd only just learned about.

No doubt Oldham also stressed his connection to the Beatles. "He probably said, 'I am the Beatles' publicist'—how about that as a line?" Jagger mused. "Everything to do with the Beatles was sort of gold and glittery, and Andrew seemed to know what he was doing."

Nevertheless, Keith Richards maintains that Oldham "was looking for an alternative to the Beatles" from the very outset. Despite being from provincial Liverpool, the Beatles had already scored two big hits with "Love Me Do" and "Please Please Me." Never before had an act from so far north succeeded at that level. "I guess Andrew's mind would work this way," Keith reasoned. "If Liverpool can produce the Beatles, what can London produce? Liverpool was much further away from London than it is now. There were no streets, no highways. I mean, Liverpool is . . . as far as London is concerned, it's Nome, Alaska."

But in order to share in the type of success the Beatles were having, Oldham insisted that the Stones make some image and personnel adjustments. On the theory that six members was at least one too many for a successful group, Oldham made them kick out pianist Ian Stewart—who anyhow had too square a jaw for Andrew's liking. Keith Richards was bizarrely instructed to drop the *s* from his last name; Keith *Richard*, Andrew said, "looked more pop." Meanwhile, he added a *g* to the band's name, making them the *Rolling* Stones; otherwise, he said, no one would take them seriously. Twenty-six-year-old Bill Wyman was told to begin pretending he was twenty-one. But most significantly, Oldham persuaded the band to loosen up its performance. Though Jones still postured himself as the group's leader, Andrew recognized Jagger's electric appeal and insisted that he share in the limelight.

The idea to style the Stones as the *anti*-Beatles, though—to toughen up their image and encourage them to act as surly and defiant as they dared—came a bit later, and in fact that was the opposite of what Oldham originally had in mind. Instead, one of his first moves was to buy them a set of matching outfits. Wyman remembers a day when Oldham "marched us up to Carnaby Street to put us in suits, tabbed-down shirts and knitted ties." On other occasions, the band could be seen in tight black jeans, black turtlenecks, and Beatle boots. When the Stones debuted on national television, on *Thank*

Your Lucky Stars, they were conscripted into hound's-tooth jackets, high-buttoned shirts, and slim ties, looking every bit as dainty and amiable as the pop bands they despised. Wyman later remarked that in hindsight, it was "obvious" that "Andrew was attempting to make us look like the Beatles. From his association with them, he was well aware of the power of marketing, and he was initially slotting us as their natural successors rather than as counterparts."

The following month, though, when the Stones embarked on their first national tour (sharing a spectacular bill with Bo Diddley, Little Richard, and the Everly Brothers), they began wearing their outfits in a more slovenly style. One night, Charlie Watts unexpectedly doffed his waistcoat in a Fenland dressing room; eventually Keith's jacket grew so bespotted with chocolate pudding and whiskey stains that it was no longer wearable. Onstage, the whole group loosened up, and Jagger took to chewing gum as he sang. Offstage, a journalist observed, they appeared in "a jumbled assortment of jeans, silk cardigans, camel jackets and sloppy sweaters. None of the slick suits sported by Bill J. Kramer or Gerry and the Pacemakers." When the Stones appeared on a BBC program in October 1963, they frustrated their interviewer by greeting many of his questions with simple "yeah"s and "no"s. Rather than hurt their popularity, however, all of this seemed to boost their appeal. Their audiences were becoming more demonstrative and more raucous to the point where the Stones, just as soon as they finished their sets, were forced to flee their venues through the back door and quickly speed off to avoid getting mobbed. Without ever devising or articulating a formula for instigating a cultural revolt, the Rolling Stones began to stumble upon one.

Put another way, though widely held, the idea that Andrew Oldham conjured up a belligerent attitude for the Stones, *ab ovo*, is a myth. First, he tried to smarten them up. But Oldham was quick—very quick—to see the potential in this new approach. By the time the Beatles conquered America on *The Ed Sullivan Show*, on February 9,

1964, Oldham was actively promoting the Stones as "the band your parents loved to hate." "The Beatles were accepted and acceptable," he added, "they were the benchmark and had set the level of competition." By contrast, "The Stones came to be portrayed as dangerous, dirty and degenerate, and I encouraged my charges to be as nasty as they wished to be."

He "made sure we were as vile as possible," Mick acknowledged. "Andrew pitched it so we were very much the antithesis of the Beatles." Of course, the Stones proved masterful at projecting arrogant, sour attitudes. Surely, Jagger was deploying his best Cockney put-on when he told an interviewer, circa 1964: "If people don't like us, well that's too bad. We're not thinking of changing, thanks very much. We've been the way were are for much too long to think of kowtowing to fanciful folk who think we should start tarting ourselves up with mohair suits and short haircuts."

But Jagger was lying. It had only been a short while earlier that the Stones, eager for exposure, appeared on *Thank Your Lucky Stars* with acceptable hair and matching suits. If the Beatles had "sold out" by changing their image in order to improve their chances of becoming successful, so too did the Stones—only they went through *two* early transformations. First, they costumed themselves in matching suits and ties, just like any Liverpool pop group. Then within a few months, they began experimenting with a different approach of their own design—dressing sloppily, accentuating their sexuality, and behaving obnoxiously. That was an image that suited them perfectly. Though not quite "gentlemen" in the first place, they became rather convincing as thugs.

• • •

Even if they initially set out merely to become the best band in Liverpool, with their life options already severely circumscribed by the time they formed in 1960, the Beatles were quick to embrace one of rock's core myths: the idea that it promises an escape from the ordinary, workaday world into a parallel universe of wealth, prestige, and excitement. Lennon once revealed that as a child, his "most vivid dreams" involved either flying over Liverpool or finding hidden stashes of money. "I must have had ambition without realizing it," he mused, "a subconscious urge to get above people or out of a rut." But the odds didn't look good. Once when Lennon was a teenager, his headmaster forced him to produce a sheet of paper on which he was instructed to list some potential careers; Lennon wrote: "salmon fisherman." Though Paul seemed to have benefitted from his Liverpool Institute education, the rest of the Beatles were facing the likelihood of spending their lives in low-wage, low-prestige vocations. As Robert Christgau has suggested, the Beatles "loved rock and roll at least partly because rock and roll was a way to *make it*."

The Stones burned with ambition, too, but not because they were desperate. If white R&B had never caught on in England, and the Stones had never escaped London's dingiest clubs, it still would not have been impertinent for Brian Jones or Mick Jagger to hope that they might become stereotypically successful. Granted, it's hard to imagine Keith Richards doing anything besides playing rock guitar, but considering the British class system, as a teenager his prospects were always a bit better than those of the Beatles. Fortunately for the Stones, they didn't have to grind it out for years playing in slummy bars the way the Beatles did—otherwise they would never have made it. Jagger would have ditched the band to finish his education, and as a unit, the Stones were never friendly or trusting enough with each other to stay bonded for a prolonged, frustrating period. After the Beatles pried open a tremendous market for British bands, the Stones rose to fame comparatively quickly—as the *anti*-Beatles.

For the most part, the two bands were friendly toward each other. Especially early on, the Beatles were helpful to the Rolling Stones, and the Rolling Stones were grateful. But as the Stones began burning up the charts, the Beatles couldn't help but recognize that their act was (as

George put it), "more like [what] we'd done before we got out of our leather suits to try to get on record labels and television." And while it might have been ludicrous for the Beatles to be truly jealous of anyone, there's little doubt that if they thought they could have reached the toppermost of the poppermost without having to smile, bow, and wear suits, they'd have leapt at the opportunity.

Meanwhile, the Stones seemed to envy the Beatles' success more than their music. "Sure, they were very creative, but somehow they seemed to regard it all as a joke—and it was," Jagger later said. "The Beatles were so ridiculously popular, it was so stupid. They never used to play—they just used to go on making so much bread, it was crazy." Musically, Richards said, "We saw no connection between us and the Beatles. We were playing blues; they were writing pop songs dressed in suits." Furthermore, the fact that the Beatles emerged from Liverpool must have seemed stupefying to the Stones. "For the first time, London had been left out in the cold till the very last minute," a British writer remarked. But it was way more than that. When the Beatles were at the peak of their success, the poet Allen Ginsberg said, they briefly made Liverpool "the center of the consciousness of the human universe."

Eventually both groups would become settled enough in their success that they wouldn't worry so much about manipulating the media. In 1966, the Beatles even decided they'd had enough of their silly fan magazine, and so they stopped providing Sean O'Mahony with the access, interviews, and photographs he needed to keep *The Beatles Book* afloat. But O'Mahony would not be deterred so easily. In response to the Beatles' new attitude, he phoned his lawyer and called for a meeting. Epstein likewise showed up with his solicitor, plus two more advisors, and he matter-of-factly told O'Mahony it was time to wind down his publication of *The Beatles Book*. Asked for an explanation, he replied, "They feel you don't tell the truth. You're not reporting them as they are . . ."

"O'Mahony exploded with anger," said Epstein's biographer:

> *The truth? What do you mean? Do you mean for example when we were in Blackpool, John Lennon flinging open the window of the dressing room and shouting to the fans below: "Fuck off and buy more records?" Was that the level of revelation Epstein and the Beatles expected from their authorized mouthpiece? Should the Beatles be reported as they really were? Or were there no-go areas?*

A brief silence fell over the room, after which the two parties were able to proceed amicably enough to reach an agreement. O'Mahony continued publishing *The Beatles Book* until December 1969 (and then he revived it in 1976 and kept going until 2003). Though O'Mahony labored to keep the Beatles' images up-to-date, he went about his work delicately, always refraining from saying too much about the controversies in which the group became embroiled. To adopt a sharper or more discerning approach would, said O'Mahony, "be like shooting myself in the foot." Instead, he presented the Beatles as gentlemen.

CHAPTER TWO

"SHIT, THAT'S THE BEATLES!"

The Beatles played Liverpool's Cavern Club for the 292nd time, and for the last time, on August 3, 1963. They brought home £300 that night, and according to the Club's legendary compère, Bob Wooler, they put on a rip-roaring show, a bit reminiscent of the very first time they performed there, for only £5. Inside the venue, it was so sticky hot that the Cavern's electricity blew, and the show was interrupted as the club's owner rushed to repair a fuse. Still, the "fans loved it," he said. "It was such a marvelous scene."

It was also, however, a bittersweet occasion. The Beatles had obviously outgrown the cramped, dingy venue, and although Brian Epstein tried to reassure Wooler that someday his boys would be back, privately, he must have known that was unlikely.

By then the Beatles' debut album, *Please Please Me*, was resting comfortably atop England's hit parade (where it would remain for thirty weeks), and the group, now residing permanently in London, was growing accustomed to headlining national tour packages. In the nation's weekly pop periodicals, they received gushing praise; in teenybopper magazines, they appeared on color pin-up posters. And in an extraordinary effort to satisfy eager requests from every studio executive, disc jockey, newsman, photographer, and club owner who wanted something from them, under Epstein's direction, the four lads from Liverpool were working almost to the point of burnout. Even if the Beatles had found time in their frenzied schedule to play another homecoming show at the Cavern, Epstein probably would not have allowed it: henceforth, he declared, the group would play only in proper theaters with elevated stages. The new policy was necessary in order to prevent the Beatles from being overrun by a scrum of frenzied fans.

Perhaps inevitably, with their staggering success, the Beatles began spawning imitators (or, in early-'60s British parlance, "copyists"). About two months after they performed at the Cavern for the last time, pop fans could find on newsstands an issue of *Melody Maker* that contained an article headlined: "Boiling Beatles Blast Copy Cats." John Lennon, identified as "the group's spokesman," is quoted extensively throughout the piece, yet none of his remarks are challenged or contextualized, and in this way, the item has something of the flavor of a press release. But even if the Beatles' press officer, Tony Barrow, was primarily responsible for the item, he still would have needed Lennon's permission before putting it out, and Lennon was clearly rankled by bands that were aping the Beatles' style and sensibility. "Certain groups are doing exactly the same thing as us . . . pinching our arrangements," he complained. "And down to the last note, at that."

But it wasn't just that certain bands were trying to ride the Beatles' coattails by mimicking their outfits and nicking their arrangements. "To crown it all," Lennon carped, "other groups are climbing on this rhythm-and-blues bandwagon . . . by doing stuff we were playing two years ago"—that is, American R&B covers by the likes of Chuck Berry and Buddy Holly, which the Beatles used to pound out in grimy bars and run-of-the-mill dancehalls. The article continued:

> *And in a final blast, an angry Lennon said: "It happens in hair styles, as well. I see players in some groups even have the same length hair as us.*

> *"It's no good them saying they're students and they just happen to have long hair. We were students, as well, before we came to London and we didn't have these styles then, did we?"*
>
> *Lennon added: "I suppose people might say it's an honor to be copied, and I wouldn't have bothered to have hit back really. But when they have a dig at us, we're going to have a go. I've wanted to say this for a long time . . ."*

The notion that Merseyside acts like the Beatles were at odds with the groups coming out of London had been gaining traction. When a pop journalist asked Brian Jones about "the Liverpool-London controversy," however, Jones replied sharply: "It's all a load of rubbish. We are on very friendly terms with the Northern beat groups and there's a mutual admiration between us." Many years later, in his scrapbook-cum-memoir, *Stone Alone*, Bill Wyman said it was "a popular misconception . . . that we were at war with the Beatles." In reality, he maintained, the two groups were always bonded by "mutual respect." It was just "the newspapers" that always fueled the idea that the two groups were rivals. And in his celebrated memoir, *Life*, Keith Richards said "it was always a very friendly relationship" between the Beatles and the Stones.

The Beatles frequently echoed these sentiments. In August 1964, at an American press conference, Ringo called the Stones "very good friends of ours," and Paul added, "We hear some ridiculous rumors over here . . . like, 'The Beatles hate every other group on the face of the earth.' It's just not true." At another press event a few days later, John said about the Stones, "I know it sounds daft, us liking them, but we're good friends." And in 1968, he said flatly, "Our rivalry was always a myth."

Among music mavens, this has long been the conventional wisdom: While the press was busy making invidious comparisons between the Beatles and the Stones, the two groups remained above the fray, bonded by their mutual admiration, shared experiences, and obvious enjoyment of each other's company. The supposed "rivalry" between the Beatles and the Stones was a media creation, a faux controversy that arose from a press that was either base in its sensationalism or fanciful in its ignorance.

But if all of that is the case, who was it that Lennon was itching to "hit back" in October 1963? He never mentioned any names, but he clearly had a specific target in mind. He was thinking about a band that was now playing R&B of the type that the Beatles played in Hamburg; and he seemed particularly peeved at a newer, London-based group, made up at least partly of students, whose members refused to attribute their hairstyles to the Beatles' influence. Instead, they disingenuously maintained that they "just happen to have long hair."

Only one group fits the bill exactly. In the Rolling Stones' official biography, *Record Mirror* reporter Peter Jones (writing under the alias "Peter Goodman") describes a period in 1963 when "The Beatles were high in the charts" and "reporters were very interested to know if the Rolling Stones hairstyles had owed anything to the high-riding Liverpool group." But whenever Jagger was asked about the provenance of their shaggy hairdos, he turned defensive. With his "hands on his hips" and his "sweater awry as his shoulders gesticulated angrily," he replied: "*Art students have had this sort of haircut for years—even when the Beatles were using hair cream!*"

• • •

A Hollywood adage holds, "It can take a lifetime to become an overnight success." Of course, it didn't take the Beatles nearly that long; they managed to hit it big when they were still very young. Before they became household names, however, they paid their proverbial dues. Lennon and McCartney began their musical friendship on July 6, 1957, at a garden fete in Liverpool. Five more years would pass before the Beatles started recording with EMI. In between came all of the failed auditions and talent show competitions, the late-night sets in West German nightclubs, and the difficult personnel changes that endure so vividly in Beatles lore.

It was rather different for the Stones. In July 1962, the band's nucleus of Brian, Mick, and Keith shared a stage for the first time; almost a year to the day later, they appeared on British national television as Decca recording artists. Their first big break came in February 1963, when they secured a residency at the Crawdaddy Club at the Station Hotel (sometimes called the "Railway Hotel") in Richmond, Surrey, perhaps thirty minutes outside of central London by train.

The Crawdaddy's manager was Giorgio Gomelsky, a Soviet-born, Swiss-educated London transplant who in the 1950s had been a mainstay of the local jazz club scene. Then in the early 1960s, Gomelsky started promoting raw R&B, first in central London and then on the outskirts. "Brian Jones had been bending my ear constantly" about the possibility of landing gigs for the Stones, Gomelsky remembers. "He had that little speech impediment—kind of a lisp. It used be part of his charm. 'Come and lithen to us, Giorgio,' he'd plead with me. 'Oh, Giorgio, *pleathe* get us some gigs.' "

After catching a Stones performance at Sutton's Red Lion Pub, Gomelsky was suitably impressed—but he couldn't offer them work immediately, since he'd already committed to promoting the David Hunt Band, a promising but unreliable Soho-based group. "Listen," Gomelsky says he told the Stones, "I promised this guy a job, but the first time he goofs, you're in." Sure enough, the very next week, Hunt's band failed to show up for one of their regularly scheduled gigs, and Gomelsky turned their Sunday-night slot over to the Stones.

Bill Wyman says that when the Stones played their first Crawdaddy gig, they drew a crowd of about thirty. But Gomelsky recalls that snow fell heavily in London that night (a rare thing) and only three people showed up. He added that the diminished attendance might also have been accounted for, at least in minor part, by the transposition error in the flyers that he had illegally pasted all across town.

SUNDAY NIGHT, 7:30 PM.

RHYTHM AND BULSE

Gomelsky shrewdly understood that the Stones' real problem, however, was that they had yet to build up an audience for grassroots R&B in London. Fortunately, he had a plan. "He was the kind of guy where you could go round to his apartment, have some very strong coffee, smoke some Sobranies, and map out plots, because he was very plugged into the club scene," Keith Richards recalled. He advised the Stones that instead of hustling for gigs at every opportunity, they should focus on building their reputation with their regular Sunday-night performances. Once word got around, and with the right kind of promotion, he predicted that audiences would be flocking to see them.

Gomelsky says that Brian walked up to him that first night at the Crawdaddy and said: " 'Giorgio, there's six of us, and three of them. Do you think it's worthwhile? Should we play?' "

"I said, 'Brian, how many people do you think can fit in here? A hundred? Okay, well then play as if there were a hundred people in here.' And they did. And that was one of the reasons I rarely went to see the Stones in later times, because in some ways, that was like the best show they ever did. For three people."

Very quickly, Gomelsky's prediction proved accurate, and the Stones were playing to a packed house every Sunday night. To get inside, you had to queue in line, sometimes for hours. Once you got through the door, you found a smallish room that was pitch-dark, save for the tiny stage, on which the Stones performed beneath two small spotlights (one red, one blue). Drawing heavily from the nearby Kingston College of Art, early audiences consisted predominately of young men. As pop historian Alan Clayson explains, some among them "detected a certain Neanderthal *epater la bourgeoisie* in the group, and came to understand that this rugged type of pop music was 'uncommercial,' and thus an antidote to the contrived splendor of television pop idols." Others in the crowd didn't even necessarily identify as R&B fans. Groups of Mods started showing up, decked in tweed jackets, high-heeled boots, and choke-collar shirts, and so too came their supposed enemies, leather-clad Rockers. Before long, brawls between the two subcultures would lead to some sensational news stories in England, but not a single fight broke out while the Stones were playing at the Crawdaddy.

That may be partly attributed to the Stones' novelty. Initially, fans were riveted by their increasingly edgy performances, but they were unsure of how to respond, and many even seemed afraid to dance. Then one night, Gomelsky's young assistant, Hamish Grimes, leapt atop a table and started really whooping it up, waving his arms like windmills and yelling "yeah yeah!" Jagger spotted him from the stage, smiled widely, and he too said "yeah!" In an instant, Gomelsky says, "two hundred pair of arms were undulating like crazy! Man, that was something." For some time afterwards, the Stones made it their trademark to close their second 45-minute set with an extended, hypnotic Bo Diddley jam—either "Pretty Thing" or "Doin' the Crawdaddy"—that always whipped their fans into a tribal-like frenzy. "No one had seen anything like this in the sedate and reticent London of 1963," Gomelsky mused. "It was exciting and foreboding."

Had he been a little savvier and more business-oriented, Gomelsky might have secured a managerial contract with the Stones, but at the time he was so turned off by how vapid and crass the British pop scene had become that the idea scarcely crossed his mind. Instead, he planned to help rejuvenate "formula-ridden commercial popular music" with more authentic, uptempo electric blues, and eventually he hoped to set up "a kind of 'United Artists' of the London blues bands" that would "keep the show business sharks out of the scene." "My motivation in all this had been cultural rather than business-oriented," he explained. Besides, in addition to proselytizing for R&B, Gomelsky also dabbled in other bohemian-flavored pursuits, including Stanislavsky's Method acting and experimental film. And even as the Stones were burnishing their chops at the Crawdaddy, the energetic émigré had yet another project in mind: he wanted to direct a movie about the Beatles.

Outside of Liverpool, not many people could honestly boast that they were Beatles fans before the Beatles got famous. About two years earlier, however, while passing through Hamburg, Gomelsky had been lucky enough to catch the scruffy young Brits back when they were still playing bowdlerized R&B covers in seedy clubs. He remembered the Beatles as a "good, fluent band," and one night while they were on break, he'd chatted amiably with them. Now, perhaps six months before the birth of Beatlemania, Gomelsky hoped to direct an avant-garde film about the group, one that was intended "to bring about the still unperceived wit and knockabout charm of the Beatles offstage characters."

To that end, he met with Epstein at Teddington Studios on April 14, 1963, while the Beatles' manager was accompanying his group during the taping of their third appearance on ABC-TV's pop music show, *Thank Your Lucky Stars.* Epstein agreed to discuss the proposal further, but Peter Clayton, a *Jazz News* writer whom Gomelsky had enlisted to draw up a rough script, later surmised that he was probably wary of the idea from the get-go. Still relatively new to showbiz, he likely mistook Gomelsky's "explosive enthusiasm as just another attempt to stampede him into something."

Nor did the Beatles themselves ever seem terribly interested in the film. Clayton recalls one meeting at Gomelsky's flat when the group sat there eating omelets. "I suppose I should remember some of those tart witticisms which became such a feature of Beatles press conferences, but all I can recall are the omelets, each in the center of a big plate, like a stranded yellow fish," he said. At another meeting, Lennon picked quietly at a mandolin while everyone talked around him, and McCartney seemed quiet and guarded—"a closed book."

They perked up, however, when Gomelsky started raving about

the Stones. Neil Aspinall, the Beatles' road manager at the time, explained that the timing was propitious. The Beatles and their entourage were freshly arrived in London and therefore eager to hit the clubs, "to find out what was happening . . . since it was not yet our scene. We were the new boys in town." And it just so happened, Gomelsky enthused, that the Stones were playing that very night.

"Hey you guys, you've got to listen to this band on the way home tonight," he pleaded. "You've got to come and see this band when you finish recording the show, it's on the way back, you've just got to come."

"Yeah, okay, we'll come," someone said.

• • •

Over the next few years, the Beatles would have meticulously planned and well-documented summits with some of the most prestigious and successful performers of their era. Probably the most momentous such meeting was with Bob Dylan (at New York's Delmonico Hotel on August 28, 1964). As James Miller explains in *Flowers in the Dustbin*, Dylan "represented everything that Lennon still silently aspired to: artistic integrity, musical honesty, [and] the priceless cachet of being hip, not with screaming teenagers, but with serious adults—poets like Allen Ginsberg, artists like Andy Warhol, political leaders like Martin Luther King Jr." After sweeping past a roomful of people who had been waiting patiently to see the Beatles, and finding that John, Paul, George, and Ringo were just finishing up their room-service dinners, Dylan produced a lumpy bag of marijuana and started rolling up some joints. Though it has been said frequently that Dylan turned the Beatles on to pot for the first time, that may be just shy of the truth. According to Harrison, a Liverpool drummer had once treated the band to some low-grade schwag. But this was the first time the group had gotten themselves really and truly high. And it was under these combined influences, of Dylan and marijuana, that the Beatles began dramatically refashioning their attitudes, writing weightier and more experimental songs, and embracing personal styles that were truer to their bohemian origins.

By contrast, the Beatles had a dreadful time meeting with Elvis Presley a year later (at a rented Bel-Air mansion, on August 27, 1965). Whether sedated, stoned, or both, Elvis seemed strangely bored by the Beatles, and at one point he threatened to ditch the party and go to bed early. For their part, the Beatles seemed not to know how to behave in the company of their boyhood idol, and so mostly they just sat there gawking, except for Lennon, who committed numerous unpardonable solecisms. First, he broke into a bizarre Inspector Clouseau routine that he seemed reluctant to let go. Then, when he finally stopped speaking to Elvis in a cheeky French accent, he had the brass to chide him about his mid-career slump: his trite singles and lame movies. Later, Lennon explained that his impertinent behavior arose from his disappointment with what Elvis had become. "It was like meeting Engelbert Humperdinck," he sneered.

Seeing the Rolling Stones was altogether different. The Beatles were plainly curious about this new band that Giorgio had been exclaiming about, but they could not have been *that* excited. None of the Stones' music had yet been released. At the time, the Beatles were awed just to be living in London. "[W]e were provincial kids coming to the big city, so it was all magic to us," McCartney said.

By contrast, the Stones had been following the Beatles avidly. The richest firsthand account of the group's early behavior and attitudes comes from Jimmy Phelge, a flatmate to Brian, Mick, and Keith at Edith Grove (who claims to be the "Mr. Jimmy" that's referenced in the third verse of "You Can't Always Get What You Want"). In his 1998 memoir, *Nankering with the Stones*, Phelge reveals that the Stones heard the Beatles for the first time on a BBC radio program (probably *Saturday Club*, which featured the Beatles on January 26, 1963). Jones, in fact, had tuned in that day specifically in order to hear the Beatles, his curiosity having been piqued by the enthusiastic bits of press coverage they were garnering. But the moment he heard the first bars of "Love Me Do" blaring out of the radiogram, Phelge says that "Brian's face dropped," and he barked at Keith to come over from the next room.

"Love Me Do" was written in what the Beatles probably considered a bluesy idiom, but as musicologist Ian MacDonald points out, the song's most conspicuous element—Lennon's wailing harmonica riff—was played in a technically "overblown" style and was completely lacking in bent notes. As such, "it had little in common with any of the American style blues." Still, harmonicas were rarely used in British pop. Probably the Beatles got the idea to incorporate the harmonica from Bruce Channel, the Texas-born American crooner whose "Hey! Baby"—a number 2 hit in the UK in 1962—they used to cover. Regardless, it was enough to send the Stones into a tizzy. Phelge recounts the scene this way:

> *"Oh no," said Brian. "Listen to that. They're doing it!"*
>
> *"Hang on, let's hear the guitar," said Keith, listening intently. "Fuck it."*
>
> *"They've got harmonies too," said Brian. "It's just what we didn't want."*
>
> *I listened and thought the Beatles sounded OK, but so what? Just another group. "What's the problem?" I asked.*
>
> *"Can't you hear?" said Keith. "They're using a harmonica—they've beaten us to it."*
>
> *"They're into the same blues thing as us," said Brian. "We'll have to listen to see what they do later."*
>
> *I liked the song and I could hear the harmonies, but I did not think the music sounded anything like the Stones. Brian's point was that the Beatles were using the bluesy sound and that if they took off successfully, everyone else would copy it. The Stones would be just another group, it was important to be first. The Beatles did some more songs and later in the broadcast the Stones' spirits dropped further when they performed a Chuck Berry song.*

> *Mick heard this too and much debating was to take place later about whether the Beatles had professional arrangements or whether they were that good on their own account. The overall answer was a bit of each.*

"It was an attack from the North," Keith Richards said. "We thought we were the only guys in the world." Twenty-five years later, when he inducted the Beatles into the Rock and Roll Hall of Fame, Jagger likewise admitted that he was taken aback when he first heard about the Beatles. "They had long hair, scruffy clothes but—they had a record contract!" he said. "And they had a record in the charts, with a bluesy harmonica on it, called 'Love Me Do.' When I heard the combination of all these things, *I was almost sick.*" However strenuously the Stones would argue later on that their rivalry with the Beatles was invented on press row, it is plainly evident that when they heard the Beatles for the very first time, they felt deflated and threatened.

In subsequent months, though, the Stones learned to respect the Beatles begrudgingly, if only because of the resounding impact the Liverpool foursome was having on the British music scene. By the early spring of 1963, the entire landscape for beat and rock 'n' roll music was shifting under the Beatles' influence. In virtually every city and town, fresh-faced teens began assembling themselves into new groups, many of them bent on composing their own material. Mail-order companies that sold guitars and drum kits did booming business. Nightclubs and dance halls emerged to accommodate this sudden spike in interest. Suddenly, attention shifted to the North, where talent scouts could be found scampering to try to sign The Next Big Thing. Meanwhile, the local and national press was turning volte-face from its previous attitudes toward pop and rock; now they began treating it all seriously, rather than from on high. By April, the Beatles were atop the British music charts with "From Me to You"—another original song that featured Lennon playing the mouth organ.

It is little wonder, then, that Gomelsky had left the Beatles at their taping and rushed back to Richmond, where he found the Stones conversing over sandwiches before their first set.

"That's when I told them, 'Hey, something nice might happen today,' " Gomelsky said.

"What?"

"The Beatles might come to . . . "

Brian responded with an astonished whisper: " 'What? The Beatles? *You're joking! What, wha?*' This was all the encouragement they needed."

Gomelsky continues: "The club used to open at seven, the Stones used to go on first time at eight-fifteen to nine o'clock. Then a break, have to finish by ten-thirty, Sunday pubs close, and be out of the place by eleven. So first set they didn't come. Brian came and said, 'They didn't come, they didn't come.' I said, 'Brian, I told you they're probably finishing now they'll be here by nine-fifteen, nine-thirty.' He said 'all right.' He was so nervous."

Sure enough, shortly after the Stones launched their second set, Wyman says he was "staggered" to look up and see "four shadowy figures" standing shoulder-to-shoulder in the audience, all of them dressed in matching suede overcoats and leather caps. "Shit, that's the *Beatles!*" he exclaimed to himself. Richards tells the story similarly. "We were playing a pub, the Station Hotel, Richmond. . . . And we're whacking our show out and everybody's having a good time, you know. I suddenly turn around: there's these four guys in black leather overcoats standing there. *Oh, fuck me! Look who's here!*" Mick's reaction? "I didn't want to look at them," he recalled. "I was too embarrassed."

However goofy and good-natured the Beatles came across in their early television and radio appearances, in real life they often struck people differently. Writer Barry Miles observed that in this period the Beatles were bent on projecting "an intentionally intimidating image," and journalist Chris Hutchins, who was friendly with the group since their Hamburg days, agreed; he said their long leather jackets gave them the look of "gunfighters." About a month before the Beatles met the Stones at the Station Hotel, Andrew Oldham had watched in the wings while the Beatles recorded a television appearance in London. Away from the klieg lights and cameras, he said, they exuded a kind of "Fuck You, we're good and we know it" attitude. In early 1963, the teen-oriented *Boyfriend* magazine described the Beatles as "almost frightening-looking young men." (They looked friendly when they smiled, the journalist continued, but that was "not often." "The rest of the time they look wicked and dreadful and distinctly evil, in an eighteenth-century sort of way. You almost expect them to leap out of pictures and chant magic spells.") Even the preternaturally cool Mick Jagger would later admit that when he first laid eyes on the Beatles, they struck him as "four-headed monster."

Aspinall thought the Stones were just "okay" that night—not particularly better or worse than a typical Liverpool band playing at the Cavern Club. "They could do their stuff and that was all you needed to do. A lot of people couldn't." The Beatles, however, were much more effusive. "I remember standing in some sweaty room and watching them on the stage," Ringo recalled. "Keith and Brian—wow! I knew then that the Stones were great." Harrison was struck by the tremendous enthusiasm of the Stones fans. "It was a real rave," he reminisced. "The audience shouted and screamed and danced on tables. They were doing a dance no one had seen until then, but we all know now as the Shake."

Afterward, no one lingered around or chatted with fans for very long after the gig, since Jones had invited the Beatles and their crew over to the Stones' slummy Edith Grove apartment. When the Beatles arrived, Phelge remembers, they "carried themselves with the air of a professional outfit. . . . All the members of their entourage were smartly dressed in the same dark-colored overcoats as the band, giving the appearance of one big team." A few in the Beatles camp may have been disgusted by the putrid condition of the Stones' dimly lit flat—the piled high dishes, overflowing ashtrays, and accumulated rubbish—but Phelge says that after Paul surveyed the environment, "He did not seem unduly perturbed by anything—the look on his face said, 'I've been here before.' "

From interviews and firsthand accounts, we know just a few more things about what went on at Edith Grove that night. All evening long, records spun successively on the turntable, and members of both groups shared their musical likes and dislikes. Conversations proceeded energetically, with much crosstalk. "It was difficult to keep track of all that was being said," Phelge recalled. "Occasionally Mick or John would mention an artist or song and say, 'I like that. We used to do that.' . . . Everyone was trying to find out as much as possible in a short period of time." The Stones played the Beatles the five demo tracks they'd recently recorded at IBC Studios, and they were eager to show off their treasured collection of American imports.

"John was really nice," Mick said later. "I said, 'You play the harmonica don't you?'—he'd played harmonica on 'Love Me Do'—and he said, 'But I can't really play like you guys, I just blow and suck. We can't really play the blues.' " The Stones were caught off guard, however, by Lennon's curt dismissal of one of their heroes, the blues legend Jimmy Reed.

When Lennon fell into conversation with Brian Jones, the two men discovered they both had infant sons named Julian. (Lennon's son, in fact, was only six days old.) Lennon was also impressed with Brian Jones's deep musical knowledge, though he may also have felt a little insecure in Jones's company. Years later, Lennon seemed to admit as much when he recalled that Brian had asked him that night whether it was a harmonica or a harp that he played on "Love Me Do." Apparently not understanding the subtle distinction between the two types of harmonicas, Lennon said he replied "A harmonica with a button," meaning a *chromatic* harmonica, of the type that was used by jazz and big band acts of the 1940s and 1950s. (Lennon had shoplifted it from a music store in Arnhem, Holland, in 1960.) With an extra set of button-activated reeds, a chromatic harmonica provides access to all twelve notes of the Western musical system. By contrast, a diatonic harmonica—also called a "harp"—offers fewer notes but allows players to get a wailing bluesy sound by bending pitches. All the classical bluesmen used harps, and, of course, an aficionado like Jones would have regarded chromatic harmonicas as passé.

Another big topic was how to make money in the business. Until that point, no British pop act had ever been able to maintain their success over the long term, and everyone thought it was only a matter of time before the Beatles' pubescent fans began moving on in search of some other act to idolize. The Beatles even believed this themselves. At the time, they were chiefly concerned with parlaying their brief burst of popular success into the biggest possible financial windfall. The most the Stones could possibly have hoped for is that they, too, would have a brief run at the top—although they must have known that would require them to move in a more commercially oriented musical direction.

"Mick says [that meeting] is what made him want to get into rock 'n' roll," McCartney told his friend, Barry Miles, many years later.

> *He saw us come in and he thought, "Fuckin' hell! I want one of those coats! I want a long coat like that, but to do that, I'll have to earn money." This is what he said, and that was when he described us as a "four-headed monster." Which was true. It was one of our things to go around together because there was a great common bond between us.*

Jagger was also impressed to hear John and Paul boast of having already written one hundred songs together (in reality it was probably about half that many), and he was surprised to learn that Lennon and McCartney also had a share in their own music-publishing company, Northern Songs Ltd. If Mick sought out particular information about all this, however, he was probably disappointed. John and Paul knew they were getting rich—and quickly!—from royalties and publishers' rights. But at the time they were largely ignorant about music industry mechanics. Only later would they discover that they'd enmeshed themselves in several lousy deals.

The party carried on until very late, probably around 4:00 a.m. It has been said that just before the Beatles left, Brian Jones asked them to autograph a magazine photo, which he then proudly pasted onto the wall above the fireplace—just like any starstruck fan. But that is probably a myth. There is little doubt, however, that the Stones were favorably impressed. "They were very cool guys," Keith said.

Finally, though no one has ever mentioned it, it seems exceedingly likely—in fact, we can be almost certain—that at some point in the evening, Brian would have produced, for the Beatles to read, the very first press clipping that the Stones had garnered: a full-page rave that appeared in the *Richmond and Twickenham Times*. Written by a young reporter named Brian May, the piece was datelined April 13, 1963—just one day prior—but the Stones had just gotten hold of it that night, literally only a few hours before the Beatles showed up at the Crawdaddy.

"A musical magnet is drawing the jazz beatniks to Richmond," the write-up began. It went on to describe a thrilling "scene" that was coalescing around the Stones' brand of "deep earthy" R&B, a style of music that was said to give "all who hear it an irresistible urge to stand up and move."

Naturally, everyone was pleased by the effusive review, but no one took it to heart more than Brian Jones. He was flattered beyond measure. Even after the whole group had read it, Phelge recalled, "Brian read it again aloud to make sure we understood every word." For months afterward, Wyman said, Jones carried a matted copy of the clipping in his wallet, "showing everyone—proof to all the cynics that we were moving."

When he showed it to the Beatles, though, they would have noticed something else about the piece. A little deeper into the article,

May reported that the Stones "wear their hair Piltdown-style, brushed forward from the crown like the Beatles pop group." Sounding a bit sheepish, Jones was quoted this way: *"We looked like this before they became famous."*

• • •

Bumping along in a London taxi just four days later, on April 18, 1963, Brian, Mick, and Keith must have felt exuberant. Accompanied by Giorgio, they were heading to Kensington, where they would see the Beatles perform for the first time. Not only that, but they would be watching from the front row as the Beatles' special guests. As the Edith Grove rendezvous was winding down a few nights earlier, the Beatles had personally invited them.

That was a milestone date for the Beatles, too, but for an altogether different reason: it was the first time they would play the Royal Albert Hall, a theater of such impressive majesty that the Beatles could only have been awed at their developing good fortune.

Logistically, though, the show—a BBC program called *Swinging Sound, '63*—must have been a little aggravating for the Beatles, who appeared alongside over a dozen acts; as such, they had to share their rehearsal time with Del Shannon, the Springfields, and many others. According to a performance log, they were called out for rehearsals in the midmorning and early afternoon, but they didn't play until the evening, at which point they performed just two songs at 8:40 ("Please Please Me" and "Misery") and two more at 10:02 ("Twist and Shout" and "From Me to You"). As a result, they spent most of the afternoon goofing around in their communal dressing room, and bickering with the show's producers about how loudly they could play.

Whatever time the three Stones showed up is not clear, but it was probably on the early side, since the three bandmates who came to see the Beatles were also the three ones who weren't encumbered with day jobs. At some point, though, the Beatles must have welcomed them back stage. According to rock writer Stephen Davis, the Stones were "astonished to see the Beatles putting on stage makeup." If the anecdote is true (and it may not be), the Stones must have thought the procedure was effeminate. Davis says that McCartney said that the next time he saw the Stones perform, "Mick was made up like a tart."

When it finally came time for the Beatles to perform, the Stones were awestruck by how they were received. The evening's master of ceremonies later recalled that, try as he might, he couldn't even properly introduce the band that night: "In the end I just gestured into the stairwell, mouthed 'The Beatles' and walked off." A short article in *Radio Times*, the BBC's weekly newssheet, added that when the Beatles bounded onto the stage, the waterfall roar of the crowd "reached the threshold of pain."

One of the Stones, however, was particularly impressed. After the program's grand finale, during which all of the evening's performers crammed onto the stage for a three-minute instrumental version of "Mack the Knife," Brian and Giorgio helped the Beatles' two road managers, Neil Aspinall and Malcolm Evans, carry the group's gear out of the back of the theater.

"And there's a bunch of girls," Gomelsky remembers. "They start grabbing Brian Jones, 'Oh, can I have an autograph? Can I have an autograph?' And Brian was like, 'But I'm not a Beatle!' The girls hadn't been inside, so they didn't know. He had the long hair, looked like a pop star. I told him to sign anyway, and he did. As we're walking down the steps of the Albert Hall to go to my apartment not far from there, Brian looks at me and says, [he does the Jones lisp, with fervid intensity] 'Giorgio, Giorgio, *that'th* what I want! That'th what I want!' "

According to Wyman, Jones even continued in this vein long after the incident. " 'This is what we *like*,' he kept saying, 'being mobbed by people! This is what we *want*!' "

• • •

In envying the Beatles' success, the Rolling Stones were hardly alone. By the spring of 1963, it was widely assumed that Pete Best must have felt like the most hapless character on the whole British Isle (for getting kicked out of the Beatles right before they became famous). Another inconsolable figure, however, was record executive Dick Rowe. He was Decca's "A&R man"—the guy responsible for discovering and nurturing new talent at his label. At the time, Decca and its archrival, EMI, controlled nearly all of British music publishing. Not only had Rowe passed up an opportunity to sign the Beatles (after hearing just one audition tape and never bothering to see them perform live); his gaffe had also made it difficult for Decca to sign many other Mersey Beat artists. Now suddenly in high in demand, bands like Gerry and the Pacemakers, Billy J. Kramer and the Dakotas, and the Swinging Blue Jeans all wanted to go with EMI, the same label as the Beatles. According to a rumor, for years afterward, Decca executives held annual wakes during which they opened up their vaults, wiped the old Beatles audition tape clean of dust, and raised a ceremonial glass in mourning of their lost profits.

Desperate to redeem himself, Rowe had high hopes when he sat at the jury table of the Lancashire and Cheshire Beat Group Contest, which was held at Liverpool's Philharmonic Hall in the spring of 1963. It was a terrific opportunity to scout out new talent. What's more, George Harrison would be there, too; he was another of the judges.

"Nobody had *ever* played the Philharmonic—they wouldn't even let you *in*, let alone to do a rock concert," Harrison mused. But now, virtually every northern band was commanding respectful attention. "Groups were forming, right, left, and center to try to cash in on Liverpool's supposedly swinging scene," he said.

A local music writer concurred. "At the height of 'Pool mania," he said, "agents were getting off the train at Lime Street Station and signing up each other while, at the Cavern, it was difficult for a press photographer to get a shot which didn't include another photographer on the other side of the room."

Unfortunately, though, the showcase was a bust. The Liverpool scene had been tapped and drained. As the event plodded along, and a parade of lackluster performers rotated on and off the stage, Rowe says he turned to Harrison and wanly said, "I'd really had my backside kicked over turning your lot down."

But Harrison brushed the whole matter aside. "Well, I wouldn't worry too much about that. Why don't you sign the Rolling Stones?"

Rowe continues: " 'I said 'the Rolling *who*?'

" 'The Stones!'

"I said, 'I've never heard of them! What do they play? Where can I see them?'

" 'You'll find them at the Railway Hotel, in Richmond.'

"Well," Rowe says, "I left him *right there on the spot.*"

With minor variations, the story figures prominently in Beatles-Stones lore. By some accounts, Rowe didn't even bother to say goodbye before he exited the theater. "When George turned around, he found he was talking to himself. Rowe's chair was empty," says Philip Norman. Rowe had dashed out of the Philharmonic, boarded the first train to London, and then rushed to the Crawdaddy Club, where he would catch the Stones *that very night.*

Beatles biographer Bob Spitz tells the same story: "He took the next train to London, picked up his wife, and drove directly to see the band that captured George's attention." Stephen Davis, yet another bestselling biographer, puts just a tiny spin on the legend. Rather than taking a train, Rowe "*drove* all day to be at the Crawdaddy Club in time to catch the Rollin' Stones raucous rite of spring."

The only problem with this charming little tale is (as you may have guessed) it didn't happen. It rather strains credulity to suppose that Rowe would have so abruptly abandoned his jury responsibilities at a talent show (one that was sponsored by his employer, no less). Nor would he likely have left without so much as a "good-bye" to George Harrison. (Rowe is said to have been an exceedingly polite man.) Besides, the Lancashire and Cheshire Beat Group Contest was held on May 10, 1963—a Friday. The Stones played the Crawdaddy Club on Sunday nights. It would have been impossible to see the Stones on May 10 because on that date they were busily working at Olympic Studios, where Oldham had just plopped forty quid for a late-night, three-hour session so they could record their first single.

Rowe's ex-wife, Pat Smith, recalls a more plausible and ordinary sequence of events: "Upon his return [from Liverpool] Dick mentioned that George Harrison had said he should listen to a band called the Rolling Stones. There was no urgency."

Furthermore, since it was Rowe's policy never to speak directly with a band that interested him, but rather to always go through their manager, he would have first needed to get to a phone and canvass the main London agencies in order to figure out who represented the Stones. At that point, he would have been pleased to discover that one of the men the Stones had teamed up with was Eric Easton, a minor record industry acquaintance. Then, before the couple could venture to Richmond, they would have needed to arrange for a nanny to supervise their five-year-old daughter. In all likelihood, that was accomplished on May 12, 1963.

"When we arrived" at the Station Hotel, Smith continues, "the Rolling Stones were just setting up and it was clear we were expected by both the band and Andrew Oldham; we shook hands and had a nice conversation. I remember them as very respectful and nice young boys."

Another common misapprehension is that Rowe was so impressed by the Stones' earthy brand of R&B that he immediately rushed to sign them. Odd as it may sound, their music wasn't quite his main concern (and if anything, he worried that the band might be too rugged and unpolished to warrant a recording contract). Instead, he was most interested in the band's marketability—their looks, mannerisms, stagecraft, and ability to attract a devoted following. And the thing that piqued his interest above all else was the Stones' hip and enthusiastic audience, which consisted almost entirely of young men. "There wasn't a girl to be seen," he remembered. The tiny club was packed wall-to-wall with "crowds of boys, rising and falling on their feet." This was something new, and intriguing.

Oldham later said that he'd always thought that Decca was "the most logical place" for the Stones to wind up. "After all," he reasoned, "they'd turned the Beatles down, so maybe they'd panic and sign us." It is little wonder, then, that he and Easton both worked Rowe's tender spot, thickly laying on the idea that the Stones represented his shot at redemption. No British band could capture the attention of British teenagers for much longer than a year, they said. The Beatles were nearing their expiration date. The Merseyside wave was cresting. But the Stones! The Rolling Stones would be the *next* really big thing, the *next* Beatles. Decca simply mustn't make the same mistake twice.

Rowe wasn't the only one susceptible to that line of thinking. So too was Sir Edward Lewis, Decca's major shareholder. Lewis was a dour old man, with little passion for rock 'n' roll. But he had a great enthusiasm for moneymaking.

"I remember taking [the Stones' audition tape] to him," Rowe said, "and I wondered if it was *too* raw. But he was *so annoyed* that we had passed on the Beatles, that he was *determined* that the Stones were going to make it. He hadn't got the slightest idea what [the Stones] were about. And he said 'fantastic!' And I remember looking at him [and thinking to myself] 'fantastic?' "

On May 14, 1963—just a couple days after Dick Rowe first laid eyes on them—the Stones signed with Decca. And whereas the Beatles, lacking any real bargaining power, had found it necessary to accept EMI's chintzy royalty rate of just one penny per double-sided single sold (i.e., about 1 percent of the retail price), Rowe was proud to be able to offer the Stones a much better deal: 5 percent of the price of each record they sold.

The Stones' contract with Decca had another notable feature. Sometime earlier, pop producer Phil Spector had advised Oldham that if he ever managed a group, under no circumstances should he have them lay tracks in a studio that belonged to, or was paid for by, their record company. Instead, he should reach into his own pockets in order to finance independent studio sessions, and then lease the band's master tapes to their record company. These terms were virtually unheard of in England, but when Decca agreed to them, the Stones retained the copyright on their music. In this way, they also secured more artistic control over their work, and ultimately, they were able to garner much more money than they would have otherwise. "He had us totally beaten there," remarked Chris Stamp, the comanager of the Who. "[Other managers] didn't even know about that shit. When Andrew got that tape-lease deal . . . it was visionary."

It is unclear whether Decca executives acceded to this arrangement because they didn't fully understand its implications, or because of their determination not to be left in the lurch again, no matter the cost. Either way, it was the culmination of an incredible string of good fortune for the Stones. In little more than a month's time, they'd received their first glowing press report, befriended the Beatles, been discovered by a pair of talented agents, and signed a lucrative recording contract with one of Britain's two most prestigious record companies.

The Rolling Stones weren't yet stars, but they knew they had just been blessed with an extraordinary opportunity. About a year later, by which time the Stones truly were riding high, someone asked Brian Jones: "Who has been most helpful to you since you turned professional?"

Brian answered, "Our comanagers Eric Easton and Andrew Oldham, of course. But I'll never forget the early words of praise from the Beatles."

• • •

In a 2001 interview, Gomelsky reminisced about that night at the Royal Albert Hall way back in the spring of 1963, when a gaggle of teenage girls mistook Brian Jones for a pop star and then proceeded to tug at his clothes and beg him for autographs.

Jones told him: "Giorgio, Giorgio, *that's* what I want."

"And I said, 'Brian, you're going to have it. Don't worry about it. But when you get it you might not want it.' I was wrong—he never got enough of it . . ."

Some of the consequences of Jones's rising fame lust were predictable. First, he began backpedaling on some of his esoteric blues purism. Meanwhile, he started evincing a new willingness to compromise the band's "authenticity" (that was always the byword) in exchange for the possibility of greater commercial success. The trend was set in motion when the band released their first single in June 1963—a starchy cover of Chuck Berry's "Come On" that (even the Stones admitted) didn't really resemble what they were doing at the clubs. "In these hectic days of Liverpool chart domination it has become almost an event for any group outside Merseyside to break into the hit lists," observed *Hit Parade* magazine, "but that is just what the London-based Rolling Stones did" with their first single. (It peaked at number 21 on the UK charts.) A *Record Mirror* reviewer, however, damned the single with faint praise: "It's good, punchy, and commercial, but it's not the fanatical R&B that audiences wait hours to hear. Instead it's a bluesy very commercial group that should make the charts in a smallish sort of way." On a jury show, British pop singer Craig Douglas was more critical, proclaiming the song "Very, very ordinary. If there was a Liverpool accent it might get somewhere, but this is definitely no hit."

The diminishing comparison to the Beatles might have stung Jones a bit, but presumably the repeated descriptions of the song as "commercial" may have rankled more. After all, he had been crafting his whole identify out of his love for, and identification with, revved-up American blues. In the band's earliest days, Watts recalls, Brian "would sit for hours composing letters about R&B. The letters would go on forever—he used to write to *Melody Maker*" telling them that advertisements for Stones performances "must include the description 'R&B'; it couldn't be just a band. . . . It was a crusade to him a) to get us on the stage in a club where we could be paid half a crown and b) to be billed as an R&B band."

Yet now, Jones, once the most fiercely partisan of music fans, was laboring to justify his apostasy: "When we left the club scene," he explained to a reporter, "we also left the diehard R&B fanatics and we temporarily made a compromise to cope with the pop fans we came across in dance halls and on tours. It's all very nice, I suppose, to know you're appreciated, but it's also rather frightening."

Several of the varieties of denial that psychologists talk about can be found in just that short statement. Brian passively acknowledges that the Stones have shifted their approach, only he gets it wrong: they didn't "temporarily" compromise their artistic integrity in order to "cope with" the legions of pop fans that were flocking to see them in dance halls and on tour. When they released "Come On" in the spring of 1963, they had yet to play in any such venues; they were still confined to a few tiny clubs in London. In addition to reframing the situation, he shows willful blindness. The plain fact is, from the moment they signed with Decca, if not before, the Stones ceased being blues purists. True, they would continue reworking obscure R&B songs on some of their early albums, but the singles they released were meant to be broadly appealing. The whole band was on board with that approach, but Wyman said that Jones "was the most uneasy of all of us over the route to mass popularity we were driven along by Andrew Oldham."

Nor was Jones nearly as ambivalent about fame as his statement suggests. As the band's founder, he always believed it was desirable and necessary that *he* should also be its central figure, its biggest star. With Jagger in the group, that was always a ludicrous proposition, but it was something he never wavered from. "Brian was the only guy in the world who thought he could take on Mick as an onstage personality," Keith marveled. The contrast between the two was only heightened when Brian would spend hours practicing his stagecraft—literally rehearsing his moves in front of a mirror, and performing the identical feints, twists, and jives, night after night—whereas Mick's onstage vamping always seemed like a spontaneous expression of his personality.

Already insecure and paranoid, Jones also had the misfortune of being in a group whose members, on occasion, really did plot against one another. Mick and Keith, especially, seemed to revel in subjecting their bandmates to caustic jokes and sulfurous denunciations. "From the moment I joined," Wyman says, "I realized they had to have someone to poke fun at, not always in a humorous way, often spiteful and hurtful. They *had* to have a scapegoat or a guinea pig and in the early days it was me, followed by Brian." They teased him about his immoderately shampooed hair, his faint lisp, and his stubby arms and legs. They berated him for being an unreliable lush and a selfish egomaniac. Knowing full well that Brian was asthmatic, they often refused to even stub out their cigarettes in his presence, even while in a crowded van on tour.

Things got even harder for Jones around the fall of 1963, when Oldham started sharing a flat with Mick and Keith at 33 Mapesbury Road, in North West London. Jones took this as sign that the three were now in league together. He felt, and was made to feel, disconnected from the band's center of gravity. By about the middle of 1964, the whole band would occasionally treat Jones from on high, as if he were merely a session musician. Later that year, they began fitfully discussing whether to just get rid of him.

Then again, Brian orchestrated a lot of his own misery. Keith later explained the unhealthy dynamic this way:

> *You're on the road 350 days of the year and suddenly you've got this guy who is the one cog in the machine who doesn't seem to be*

considering how much the machine can help him. . . . If you've got to travel with somebody in a car for eight hours, do three gigs in the same night and then move on, you have to be a smooth team and support each other. But Brian either wouldn't turn up, or if he did he'd just make a lot of snide remarks, and he also developed some very annoying personal habits like his obsession with his hair. When you're alone with the guy so much, you start to mimic him. Then Brian would get pissed off that we were taking the piss out of him, and the whole thing became compounded.

It is difficult to exaggerate just how sullen and difficult Jones could be. Photographer Nicky Wright, who did the cover for *England's Newest Hit Makers*, shares a story:

Brian could be sweet—he was intelligent, would listen to your conversation carefully, and was very charming. But he could also seem totally psychotic and schizophrenic. We were coming back from Folkestone one night about nine o'clock, sometime in 1963, and had stopped to look for something to eat. We found a fish shop, but it was closed. We banged on the door and this chap came to the door and told us, "We've switched everything off, the fat's cooled down, we're closed." No-one argued until I shouted, "This is the Rolling Stones!" This little husband and wife were really sweet, and said come in and sit down while we see what we can do. So everybody's ordered their fish and chips, steak and chips, and it takes quite a long time while they heat up the fat or whatever. Finally they bring it to the table. Keith's happily eating away, so are the others, then Brian tries a forkful, and starts complaining: "I don't like this! It's soggy! I can't eat this!" He stands up, takes this bottle, and squirts ketchup over the table and knocks his food onto the floor. It was heartbreaking—there's this couple thinking, "Great, it's the Rolling Stones," then this happens.

On a few occasions he went so far as to undermine some of the band's live performances. Sometimes when the Stones performed their hugest hit, "Satisfaction," he would screw it up on purpose by playing, as a countermelody, the riff from "Popeye the Sailor Man." (He thought the two songs sounded alike.)

Even more self-sabotaging was Brian's constant jockeying for position in the band. When Oldham and Easton had approached the Stones about the possibility of a management deal, Brian privately told both of them that if they deemed it necessary, he was okay with the idea of sacking Mick Jagger (presumably to replace him with someone who sounded less black). Later, Brian unwisely tried pitting Mick and Keith against each another. On tour, he began finagling his way into slightly better hotels than the rest of the group, and somehow he persuaded Easton to pay him secretly £5 a week more than the others received. (Inevitably, the rest of the group found out. When they did, they were all appropriately furious.) He was also becoming increasingly fuddle-brained and erratic as he increased his intake of booze and started gobbling all sorts of drugs. He missed rehearsals, showed up late for gigs, and complained about all manner of ailments, whether real or imagined. Occasionally while on tour, he would get himself into predicaments that were embarrassing and debilitating even by the Stones' loose standards.

With all of this in mind, it is easy to assume that the Rolling Stones simply were not the type of outfit in which someone as petty minded and psychologically troubled as Brian Jones could be expected to thrive (at least not in the long term).

But did the Beatles' success also contribute, even in a small way, to Jones's downfall? Admittedly, the idea has not gotten much traction. You won't find that it has been pursued by the legions of journalists and biographers who have already said so much about the Stones. Nor is it a notion that is likely to strike a chord with your typical rock connoisseurs—the types of guys (usually they're guys) who normally find these sorts of imponderables so invigorating.

It is not, however, a novel idea. In fact, a couple of men who were particularly close to Brian in this period have put it across before. They put it across pretty emphatically.

"Brian embarrassed himself first, then he embarrassed us," Andrew Oldham concluded. "I believe it was seeing the Beatles at the Albert Hall that did it. He came out a two-headed monster. He wanted to be a pure artist, and he wanted out-and-out fame and he was never able to put them together and have a life."

Bill Wyman concurs: "Rubbing shoulders with the Beatles" at Edith Grove and the Royal Albert Hall "really whetted [Brian's] appetite. He suddenly seemed desperate for success—and quickly. It was obvious to all around him that he badly wanted to be a star, but a battle was going on inside him: he didn't want to compromise his musical integrity, or that of the band."

Make no mistake, Wyman clarified: Mick, Keith, and Andrew all likewise "idolized the Beatles and loved to be seen alongside them." But it was Brian who most craved their degree of fame. And just as soon as it seemed to be on the horizon, Mick, Keith, and Andrew all began shoving him to the margins.

In a sideways kind of way, the Beatles had something to do with that, too.

• • •

It was September 10, 1963, and the Rolling Stones were in a terrible mood. They were rehearsing at the Ken Colyer Jazz Club (also called Studio 51), but nothing was coming together. The band's debut single, "Come On," had registered on the UK charts, but only very faintly. They were now hard pressed to deliver a follow-up—something both commercial and distinctive—and yet they were flat out of good ideas. Initially, they'd hoped to release a 45 rpm with the Coasters' "Poison Ivy" on one side, and Benny Spellman's "Fortune Teller" on the other. But they didn't sound good (Dick Rowe called them "ghastly"). None of the other songs they were working on sounded good either.

In order to give the group some breathing room, as well as to cast off his troubled mood, Andrew Oldham decided he'd head out for a midafternoon stroll. He was not far along when he thought he overheard a couple of distinctive, adenoidal accents. Then he spotted two familiar figures popping out of a black taxi near right near him.

Dressed in matching wool suits, white oxfords, skinny ties, and Cuban-heeled boots, Lennon and McCartney looked for all the world as if they might have been en route to yet another of their marquee performances. In fact, they were just returning from a Variety Club luncheon at the Savoy Hotel, where soon-to-be British Prime Minister Harold Wilson had bestowed the Beatles with plaques that designated them "Top Vocal Group of the Year."

A photograph from the luncheon shows the Beatles smiling widely as they display their awards for the cameras, but they were never comfortable hobnobbing in such stuffy environments. Perhaps as a result, Lennon and McCartney had apparently gotten themselves well lubricated. Oldham recalled that while Paul seemed only "slightly tipsy," Lennon was "swaying visibly" as he counted out shillings to pay their driver. Not having seen any of the Beatles since he'd left Epstein's employ about nine months earlier, Oldham was a tad nervous about how he'd be received by John and Paul, but in fact they were happy to see him. They were not only cheerful but, once they discerned that he was in a troubled mood, solicitous. "The dialogue," Oldham said, "really did go like this:

" 'You're looking unhappy. What's the matter?'

" 'Oh, I'm fed up. The Stones can't find a song to record.'

" 'Oh—*we've* got a song we've almost written. The Stones can have that to record if yer like.' "

The three of them immediately headed over to the Stones' rehearsal space, where everyone greeted each other effusively. Lennon went on to explain that he and McCartney had been working up a Bo Diddley–ish number for Ringo to sing on their next album. Something they called "I Wanna Be Your Man."

"I remember teaching it to them," Lennon said. "We played it roughly [Paul, being left-handed, played Wyman's bass backward] and they said, 'Yeah, OK, that's our style.' "

Only problem was, it wasn't quite finished. "So Paul and I went off to the corner of the room and finished the song while they were still there, talking. . . . Right in front of their eyes we did it."

The Stones were impressed. "We liked the song," Richards said. "And the fact that John and Paul came down to a rehearsal of ours, and laid it on us, you know . . . It was just one of those *jams*! They got enthusiastic, and we got enthusiastic, and we said, 'All right, we'll cut it tomorrow.' "

Jagger would later flatter himself by expressing surprise "that John and Paul would be prepared to give us one of their best numbers." But Lennon said he judged the song a throwaway. "We weren't going to give them anything great, right?"

Oldham says the level of serendipity involved in all this left him with a hang-up he has never quite gotten over. "Instead of patting myself on the back and saying 'Only you, you lucky bugger, would have the luck to run into John and Paul and have them hand you a potential hit,' I get only mad internal chatter in my head about the what and why of it all. What if I hadn't left the Rolling Stones rehearsal at that particular moment? What if I had turned right? What if I'd turned left towards Covent Garden? What if I hadn't run into John and Paul?"

The Stones were just flabbergasted by the ease with which the two Beatles completed the song. And they watched them do it at the very time that they were growing anxious about their lack of suitable songs to cover. Until then, none of them had ever thought much about authoring their own material; they were just interpreters and performers. "A songwriter, as far as I was concerned, was as far removed from me as somebody who was a blacksmith or an engineer, a totally different job," Keith remarked. "I had the mentality of a guy who could only play guitar; other guys wrote songs." The Beatles, however, were changing the rules of the game; their first two LPs, *Please Please Me* and *With the Beatles*, each contained six cover songs and eight originals.

Oldham, especially, thought it was important that the Stones should follow suit. Richards remembers him saying: "Look at the other boys, *they're* writing their own songs." At first, the band was resistant; they said they were too busy, or too tired, or too distracted to try composing original material. Some, however, suspected a different sort of problem: perhaps they were too timid? "The Beatles had set this trend—you had to write your own material," recalled the Who's guitarist, Peter Townshend. "The Stones had not yet proven they could write . . . and I think there was a lot of panic that they might not be able to do it."

Richards always claimed, outlandishly, that Oldham finally became so fed up with Jagger and Richards's equivocating that he *literally* locked them in the kitchen of their Mapesbury Road flat and refused to let them leave until they'd written an entire song. "We spent the whole night in that goddamn kitchen," Richards said. "We've got some food, piss out the window or down the sink, it's no big deal. And I said, 'If we want to get out of here, Mick, we better come up with something.'" The result, he said, was a ballad, originally titled "As Time Goes By," and later renamed "As Tears Go By," on which Oldham eventually got a co-songwriting credit. Marianne Faithfull recorded it in 1964, and the Stones recorded it in 1965.

Jagger's memory is different. "Keith likes to tell the story about the kitchen, God bless him." In actuality, he explains, an exasperated Oldham might have jokingly said something along the lines of "I should lock you in a room until you've written a song!" But at no point were the two actually trapped anywhere. (And it would have been an odd kitchen if it locked from the outside.) The two also disagree about which was the first song they composed. Jagger says it was "It Should Be You," a monstrosity that the Stones recorded at Regent Sound in November 1963, but never officially released.

Either way, Jagger and Richards had taken their first tentative steps together as songwriters. Their initial efforts weren't worth much. "As Tears Go By" was a pretty and sensitive song, and it was perfect for an ingénue like Faithfull—the virginally beautiful daughter of an Austrian noblewoman, an ex-convent girl, and soon to be a Swinging London debutante, whom Oldham was grooming for mass success. ("I saw an angel with big tits and signed her," Oldham liked to say.) But at the time, it didn't really suit the Stones. The same held true for most of their early compositions, although a few of them were recorded by other artists (mostly Oldham protégés, like George Bean, Adrienne Posta, and the Mighty Avengers) and the American crooner Gene Pitney scored a Top 10 hit in the UK with a majorly rearranged version of a song of theirs called "That Girl Belongs to Yesterday" (originally titled "My Only Girl"). Had Jagger and Richards brought any of these cloying and sentimental songs to the rest of the group, however, they surmised they would have been laughed out of the room.

Of the twelve songs considered good enough to make it onto the Rolling Stones' 1964 debut album, only one of them, the Jagger-Richards composition "Tell Me," stands out, not because it's especially good, or bad, but because on a record that mostly consists of revamped R&B numbers, it is pleasant, popish, and not at all dissimilar from sound that the Beatles had hatched up in Liverpool. (Later they released it in the US as a single, where presumably it seemed a little less derivative, and it reached number 24 on the charts.) However uninspired, the song clearly indicated that the Glimmer Twins, as Mick and Keith would later call themselves, were gaining confidence.

Oldham has been rightly credited for helping Jagger and Richards realize their previously undiscovered talent for songwriting, but Lennon and McCartney played an important role as well. It wasn't just that they set a powerful example by writing their own material (though there is that). They also personally and vividly showed the Stones just how it was done, huddling up in a corner and writing the middle eight to "I Wanna Be Your Man" on a moment's notice. In this crucial period, the Beatles also gave the Stones precious words of encouragement. Jagger seems never to have forgotten this. In 1972, he sat down with the Australian pop music magazine *Go-Set*. "Even though people don't like giving them credit for it now, these days, because they're gone and they're passé almost," he said, "the Beatles told me we could write our own songs."

Why Oldham insisted that Jagger and Richards should start producing original material, without ever demanding the same from Brian Jones, has never been entirely clear. Obviously, Oldham's gambit paid off. Even if their earliest material wasn't quite right for the Stones, many of the smarmy ballads and pop songs that Jagger and Richards came up with were still good enough to donate to other artists, and several of them impacted the British music charts. In less than a year, Jagger and Richards had authored the Stones' first batch of hits, including "The Last Time," "Play with Fire," and (of course) "(I Can't Get No) Satisfaction," all of which appeared on the American version of their 1965 LP *Out of Our Heads* (an album that was nevertheless dominated by cover songs).

During this same period, however, it became increasingly obvious that Jones almost completely lacked the gift for songwriting. When it came to playing the riffs around which many Stones songs were built, he was always nimble and often brilliant. During rehearsals, his contributions could be valuable and creative. The raunchy slide guitar that he added to "I Wanna Be Your Man" is a case in point; dirtying the song up the way he did helped to make it almost indisputably superior to the Beatles' version, and it became the Stones' first bona fide hit, peaking at number 12 on the UK charts. Later, he'd add a sitar to "Paint It, Black" and marimbas to "Under My Thumb." No one else in the group had the ingenuity or the musicianship to attempt such things. But try as he might, when it came to authoring his own compositions, Brian was frustrated.

By some accounts, Jones was simply "incapable" of songwriting (Ian Stewart). Others remember him toiling away for hours on his own, often late into the night, only to come up with material that he was simply too fragile and insecure to present for the band's consideration. (To varying degrees, Keith Richards, Bill Wyman, Marianne Faithfull, Alexis Korner, and Jones's old girlfriend, Linda Lawrence, have expressed this point of view.) And on those rare occasions when Jones did bring songs to the Stones, Wyman says that they were invariably dismissed, not fairly or kindly, "but out of hand: '*You* can't write *songs*!' " Oftentimes, Lawrence recalls, Jones would come home "quite upset, almost crying" after a rough day of rehearsal.

All of this begs the question: When Oldham metaphorically locked Jagger and Richards in that kitchen and told them not to come out until they'd written a song, was he trying to foment a change in the Stones' equilibrium? If so, his plan succeeded brilliantly.

In his 2000 memoir, Oldham sounds almost Svengalilike when he describes moving in to Mick and Keith's cramped second-floor apartment in West Hampstead, London, in late 1963: "Now there was no distance to complain of, and three of the Rolling Stones' leading lights beamed as one." With Oldham's encouragement, Jagger and Richards soon began fitting songwriting sessions into their schedules wherever possible (usually after gigs). The three "leading lights" also typically stuck together whenever they hit the road: Mick, Keith, and Andrew would travel in one car, while Brian, Bill, and Charlie rode with Stu in his van. (Oldham and Jagger grew particularly close in this period.) Meanwhile, Charlie Watts was on his own, Wyman lived with his wife, and Jones was cohabitating with his pregnant girlfriend in a home he had inaptly christened—perhaps out of a desire to make it seem like a locus of activity—"Rolling Stone."

"Until that time Brian was pretty much the group's spokesman," remembered Glyn Johns, the engineer who first recorded the Stones. "Then Mick and Keith were encouraged to write and sell their songs, and the whole balance of power shifted to them. They and Andrew took over directing the band."

"Brian wasn't really a writer," Charlie Watts added, "so suddenly the band was going off in a direction he couldn't hold on to. Brian loved being what one would call a 'star.' "

It was the Beatles, of course, who gave Jones his first real taste of stardom, not as a remote fantasy (in the facile way that every young person who plays rock 'n' roll privately dreams of glorification) but in actuality. Hobnobbing with the Fab Four, carrying their gear out of the back of the Royal Albert Hall, and getting surrounded by a bunch of girls in the throes of teenage ecstasy—all of this gave Jones a sudden, visceral, and even a thrilling idea of what pop superstardom was all about. The fact that it was also a tragically limited understanding is somewhat beside the point; he didn't know otherwise. Having originally set out merely to revivify a blues aesthetic, primarily for an audience of London scenesters, now Jones suddenly possessed the same sort of vaulting ambition as the Beatles.

There was something about the precise nature of the Beatles' success, too, that seemed to hasten a transformation in the Stones: it was the fact that the Beatles wrote so much of their own material. Flush with confidence even to the point of being cocky, Lennon and McCartney planted the idea that the Stones didn't have to keep scrounging around looking for obscure American blues songs to cover. Instead, they could come up with material of their own (and make hefty amount of loot while doing so). It was the right direction for the Stones to begin moving, but Jones was left in the lurch. The creative stream that nourished Jagger and Richards's songwriting partnership in the mid-'60s just wasn't something that Jones was ever able to tap into.

Had Jones had an altogether different emotional makeup, he might have made peace with that fact. Had he been less needy, more agreeable, and more stable, he might have understood—the way Wyman and Watts seemed to understand—that the Stones was a band with multiple powerful and abrasive personalities whose talents nevertheless complemented each other's. From that point, he might have coyly reconciled himself to playing a more supportive role. But that was impossible. When the Stones alchemized into a Jagger-Richards-dominated band, his fate was sealed. He would have only a few years left on earth, and they would be unhappy ones.

Of course, no one knew that at the time. Outwardly, the prognosis for the Stones continued to look very good. On the afternoon of September 15, 1963, they even made a triumphant return to the Royal Albert Hall. This time, however, the Stones didn't show up as hangers-on or to help schlep anyone's gear out of the back door. They were performers! Along with eleven other acts, they were part of the Great Pop Prom, an annual benefit concert, hosted that year by the legendary DJ Alan "Fluff" Freeman and sponsored by the teen magazines *Valentine*, *Marilyn*, and *Roxy*. The Beatles, of course, headlined the bill, but the Stones—now Decca recording artists and just two weeks shy of launching their first national tour—were looking eagerly to whatever lay ahead. They were not yet "rivals" of the Beatles, in any plausible sense of the word, but they were certainly admiring and envious of them. And though the Beatles did not quite feel threatened by the Stones, Lennon would soon make it plain that he was frustrated with the way newer bands from London were nipping at the Beatles' coattails.

But none of this mattered a great deal. The two bands were getting along, working hard, and loving life. According to McCartney, at some point on the fifteenth, the Beatles and the Stones even found time to gather outside the Royal Albert Hall for a joint photo session. Alas, the photos that Paul recalls posing for have never surfaced; there does not seem to exist a single photograph of all the Beatles and all the Stones together. So Paul's memory may well be incorrect.

Then again, it is pretty specific memory. It was a sunny day, he said, and the Beatles and the Rolling Stones stood together atop the wide flight of stairs near Prince Consort Road. There we were, Paul said, "all in our smart new clothes with the rolled collars, and we looked at each other and we were thinking, 'This is it! London! The Albert Hall!' We felt like gods! We felt like fucking gods!"

CHAPTER THREE

A PARTICULAR FORM OF SNOBBERY

Would *you* let your daughter go out with a Rolling Stone? For a few years in the mid-'60s, that wasn't so much a question, but a slogan.

It didn't arise organically, however. Andrew Oldham recalls puckishly delivering the line to a *Melody Maker* journalist in early 1964; a bit later it reappeared, in a slightly different iteration, as a headline. That hardly could have come as a surprise. To a publication like *Melody Maker*, which had refashioned itself from a kind of trade magazine for dance hall bands and popular crooners, into something more favorable to the newly effervescent teen culture, the hype that Oldham was peddling was like catnip. A generational feud was brewing in England, he implied, and the Rolling Stones—long-haired, sullen, and libidinous—were on the side of rebellious youths. Oldham pushed this line of reasoning with such avidity that whenever things seemed to go badly for the Stones—if ever they were denied service at a hotel or restaurant, or treated roughly by the police, or jeered by the media—he reasoned that that was *good* news. "I've made sure the Stones won't be liked by too many older people," he boasted.

It helped that the Stones became closely identified with Swinging London—the trendy, youth-oriented cultural scene that emerged out of London's West End in the early 1960s. To older observers (and to some outsiders), the spirit presiding over Swinging London could hardly have been any more vulgar and narcissistic. In turn, the Stones and their cohorts—some of them models, photographers, fashion designers, and gallery owners—always made a point of underscoring that *they did not care* what the older generations thought. Their insolence was that calculated. Besides, having come of age amid a drab era of postwar austerity and sexual repression, they reasoned that England could use a good splash of Carnaby Street color.

That was precisely opposite the tack the Beatles wished to take. "Don't for heaven's sake say we're the new youth," Paul McCartney told a journalist who profiled them in the *Evening Standard* in 1963, "because that's a load of rubbish."

McCartney wasn't denying that youths idolized the Beatles. How could he? At the time, the group's popularity was strongest among young girls. With their good looks, nutty humor, and kindly dispositions, the Beatles knowingly and aggressively cultivated the teen market. But that is rather different from saying that they set out to tap into the volatile energies of those British youths who derided the old class system or who loathed the status quo. No, the Beatles were enjoying *mass* appeal. In England, it was not just teens that adored them, but also their parents, politicians, even the British Royal Family. Everyone touted them as a national treasure. Privately, the Beatles were a bit mystified by all the ballyhoo, but mostly they decided to roll with it.

The Beatles' musical versatility also helps to explain why they were more broadly appealing than the Stones. Having already spent years together, working the nightclub circuit and scrounging for bookings, they developed an enviable repertoire. By the time they ventured into Abbey Road Studios to record their first single, on the afternoon of September 4, 1962, they were well versed not only in souped-up rock 'n' roll, but also plangent ballads, covers of Motown girl groups, and even Broadway show tunes. And while the era's analog recording methods did not allow for much ingenuity in the studio, George

Martin was nevertheless able to provide the Beatles with the type of slick, polished sound that commercial-minded record executives slavered over.

By contrast, the Stones concentrated most of their energy on Chicago and Mississippi blues. True, they covered a couple of the same songs as the Beatles (Chuck Berry's "Carol" and Barrett Strong's "Money"), and they shared some of the Fab Four's enthusiasm for Motown. But mainly they were preoccupied with legends like Jimmy Reed, Muddy Waters, and Bo Diddley—artists that, outside of the art school crowds, weren't all that popular in England. One of the Stones' big achievements, in fact, is that they led a pack of artists including the Animals, John Mayall, and the Yardbirds, that helped to *make* the electric blues more popular. Even then, however, it remained a niche genre, not nearly as accessible as what the Beatles were performing. Meanwhile, Mick Jagger's mush-mouthed vocals, the primitive quality of the Stones' early recordings, and the bawdiness of some of their songs all lent credibility to Oldham's boasting about the Stones being "the band that parents love to hate."

Of course, there was never any good reason why teenagers across the world couldn't gush with equal enthusiasm over the Beatles *and* the Stones; obviously, many of them did just that. But to the degree that both bands took on totemic qualities in the early '60s, the Stones were always regarded as the more *authentic* group, and as a result, they won the fidelity of hipper and more pretentious youths. The Stones would never match the Beatles' phenomenal popular success, but especially in England, they drew a heftier measure of respect from Swinging London's tastemaking aristocracy—the frowzy, post-Beat bohemians who, even if they conceded the Beatles' creativity, nevertheless retained a bit of skepticism about their shiny pop songs and teenybopper fans.

"I thought of the Beatles as a boy band, a very manufactured group when they started out," celebrity photographer David Bailey recalled. By contrast, "the Stones seemed to grow organically. The Beatles' haircut was old-fashioned—it only seemed 'modern' to people who didn't realize it had been around a long time—and I personally didn't find lyrics like 'I want to hold your hand' very interesting." Virginia Ironside, a young pop music journalist from the *Daily Mail*, expressed a similar attitude: "Like a lot of my friends, I had reservations about the Beatles in those little suits and cute mop tops," she said. "They weren't really revolutionary enough. The Stones were much more interesting and much more honest." "Spanish" Tony Sanchez, who would become Keith Richards's drug supplier, remarked, "The Beatles were richer and sold more records [than the Stones]. But they had compromised their integrity with neat hair and command performances." Christine Ohlman, now a professional singer, said "Even in 1965 we Stones fans prided ourselves on being more on-the-edge. . . . We dug the Beatles—loved them—but there was no *danger* there."

One of the problems with this structuring opposition—the Stones as scruffy and authentic iconoclasts, the Beatles as heavily prefabricated—has already been suggested: both bands engaged in a bit of image mongering in this period. In some ways, the bohemian hauteur that the Stones cultivated was just as contrived as the happy-go-lucky image that the Beatles projected.

Another problem is that this dichotomy reeks of what critics nowadays might call "rockism"—an aesthetic that reflexively dismisses any music that seems as if it is calculated or contrived to generate mass enthusiasm, and therefore might be *too* popular. Coined in 1981, and popularized in the early 2000s, rockism holds that so long as it is put across sincerely, raw and unpolished rock 'n' roll almost always trumps slick and professional popular music. It favors unadorned, visceral rock; it privileges feelings over technique, and emotion over craft. Rockism means, according to music journalist Kelefa Sanneh, "idolizing the authentic legend (or underground hero) while mocking the latest pop star; lionizing punk while barely tolerating disco; loving the live show and hating the music video." It is a particular form of snobbery.

• • •

How did the Beatles ever manage to inspire such frenzy in the first place? People used to ask them all the time, and even they weren't entirely sure. When it comes to explaining Beatlemania—a phenomenon unlike anything the world has ever seen, before or since—it would seem that we've all been afflicted by a tremendous failure of collective discernment.

Hardly anyone disputes that the Beatles were talented, handsome, and charming. They also had the extraordinary luck to come along at precisely the right moment. Had any of the four been born just a few years earlier, the Beatles would not even have existed (since England didn't abandon its compulsory National Service program until 1960). Thankfully, instead of being shuffled off to various military bases for two years apiece, the four were able to find each other and devote several years to playing music together, burnishing their chops in front of small but adoring audiences. By the time they finally began hitting their creative stride, the first wave of post–World War Two baby boomers were reaching their teens. It was a time of unprecedented economic prosperity in the West, and for many listeners, the Beatles' joyous and optimistic music seemed as suited to the era as a soundtrack.

But this scarcely begins to explain the mass pathology that the Beatles inspired: teenage girls fainting, weeping, and peeing themselves *en masse*, even as battalions of policemen herded them behind fences and barricades. On more than a few occasions, distraught parents begged the Beatles to please just *touch* their disabled children, as if the group possessed shamanic healing powers. And always, of course: the screaming. It was more than a little disconcerting. Journalists compared the sounds made at Beatles' concerts to the nerve-shredding cries of pigs being brought to slaughter, or to the screech that New York City's subway trains make as they grind along the rails. When the group played Shea Stadium in 1965, the *New York Times* reported, the crowd's "immature lungs produced a sound so staggering, so massive, so shrill and sustained that it crossed the line from enthusiasm into hysteria and soon it was in the area of the classic Greek meaning of the word pandemonium—the region of the demons."

Nevertheless, it is clear enough that in addition to their great talent and fortuitous timing, the Beatles had some other unusual qualities that their younger fans found appealing. One is that, from the outset, they acted and behaved just as they saw themselves—as a tightly knit *group.* Previously, in both England and America, most successful pop and rock acts emphasized individuals: either those who performed solo, like Elvis Presley, or who fronted a well-known backing band, like, Buddy Holly and the Crickets or Bill Haley and the Comets. British pop, especially, seemed beholden to a formula where a lead singer with a flashy stage name, such as Billy Fury or Marty Wilde, performed in front of a generic backup group.

When the band we now know as the Beatles was first getting going, they easily could have put Lennon up front, and in fact they very briefly styled themselves as Johnny and the Moondogs. But they never seriously pursued that approach. Lennon later remarked that the day he first laid eyes on Paul—who at age fifteen already owned his guitar, on which he could perform a stellar rendition of Eddie Cochran's "Twenty Flight Rock"—he realized he'd stumbled into a dilemma. "I had a group [the Quarry Men]," Lennon said. "I was the singer and the leader; then I met Paul, and I had to make a decision: Was it better to have a guy who was better than the guy I had in? To let the group be stronger, or to let me be stronger?"

Lennon chose what was best for the group, and right away, he and McCartney struck up an energetic rapport. Oftentimes they would ditch school together in order to hang out at Paul's father's house, where the two taught each other what they knew about the guitar and took their first stab at cowriting songs. (Presumably, this is where they made their famous pact that everything they wrote would be credited "Lennon-McCartney," even though one or the other was usually the majority songwriter.) About a year later, in February 1958, Paul recruited George into the group. Though just shy of fifteen, Harrison looked to be only about twelve, and at first Lennon only barely tolerated him. "He used to follow me around like a bloody kid and I couldn't be bothered," Lennon said. "It took me years to come round to him, to start considering him as an equal or anything." Eventually, though, the three discovered they shared an extraordinary musical and personal chemistry.

In contrast, drummer Pete Best rarely seemed to click with the others; he was said to be too ordinary, too slow, soft-spoken, moody, a loner. When the rest of the band got hopped up on speed in West Germany, Best stuck with beer; when they started brushing their hair forward over their foreheads in the "exi" (short for "existential") style admired by Astrid Kirchherr, he kept his in a carefully sculpted quiff. The only reason the Beatles took him on in the first place, in August 1960, is because they desperately needed a drummer in order to take up an offer they'd received for a steady engagement in Hamburg; Best was the only one they auditioned. Two years later, when they fired him, they could hardly have been any more coldhearted about it: they told Epstein it was his responsibility to break the bad news, and then they never spoke to Pete Best again. Considering all the work he'd put into the band, the poor guy must have been mortified.

Then again, no one sanely doubts that it was the right decision. In addition to being the better drummer, Ringo had a goofy look, droll humor, and an amiable nature that suited the Beatles just perfectly. There was something intangible in his personality—Lennon called it "that spark [that] we all know but can't put our finger on"—without which the Beatles might never have cohered enough to be called "the Fab *Four*." Nevertheless, when the Beatles launched their recording career at EMI, producer George Martin came perilously close to insisting that they follow the custom and designate one of themselves the front man: either John or Paul. As he mulled over which of the two should become the leader, however, he also considered how well the Beatles got along together and how much he enjoyed their collective charisma. They "had that quality that makes you feel good when you are with them and diminished when they leave," he once said. Finally, he decided he wasn't prepared to force the issue if it might upset the group's lovely alchemy.

As a result, when most fans were introduced to the Beatles, they saw an indivisible group in which each member nevertheless had distinctive attributes: John was typecast as the clever, intellectual one; Paul, the romantic charmer; George, quiet and mysterious; and Ringo, the easygoing goof. They'd been tested by adversity, and together they reached a level of success that was so extraordinary and improbable that they soon began suffocating under its weight, at which point they began forging an even tighter bond: the special camaraderie that came from being the only ones on the planet who truly knew, firsthand, what it was like to be a Beatle. As a result, their inner circle became virtually impenetrable. "They became the closest friends I'd ever had," Ringo later said about the others. "We really looked out for each other and we had many laughs together. In the old days we'd have the hugest hotel suites, the whole floor of a hotel, and the four of us would end up in the bathroom, just to be with each other."

The Beatles were also distinctive in the ways they related to their female followers. In his book *Magic Circle: The Beatles in Dream and History*, scholar Devin McKinney shrewdly observes that when the Beatles first touched down at New York City's JFK airport, on February 7, 1964, the newsmen who covered the story all turned to military metaphors: the Beatles were "invading" and "conquering" America; they were "ruling" and "dominating" the music charts. "Had those reporters been women," McKinney speculates, the "defining words of Beatlemania would have been different." (Perhaps along the lines of "The British Seduction.") Meanwhile, the Beatles arrived Stateside just as a gargantuan teen market was emerging, and American society was becoming increasingly sexualized. For reasons that even psychologists could not agree upon, the Beatles seemed to exude a kind of sublimated sexual energy, coupled with a tender sensibility, which left young girls absolutely obsessed.

Although it has often been said that the Beatles settled upon their name as way of paying homage to Buddy Holly's backup band, the Crickets, there is at least a remote possibility that they were named after a group of young women. In the 1953 outlaw biker film, *The Wild One*, starring Marlon Brando, members of Johnny Strabler's motorcycle gang referred to their sexy girlfriends as "beetles." In a 1975 radio interview, Harrison suggested that this might have been the inspiration for "the Beatles," and he added that it may have been Sutcliffe, rather than Lennon, who dreamed up the idea. Stuart's sister, Pauline Sutcliffe, made the same claim in her 1994 memoir, *Backbeat.* Years later, Paul seemed to agree: "We were actually named after chicks, which I think is fabulous," he said. (Then again, George, Pauline, and Paul may well be mistaken. Others have suggested that it is impossible for the Beatles' name to derive from *The Wild One* because the film had not played in Liverpool while the Beatles were growing up.)

Regardless, the Beatles were androgynous in other ways. Beginning in April 1961 (around the time of their second trip to Hamburg), they started experimenting with the call-and-response vocals, skirling harmonies, and falsetto leaps that were characteristic of the American girl groups they admired, like the Shirelles (and later the Ronettes and the Shangri-Las). Few other male groups, on either side of the Atlantic, were as steeped in the girl group genre or as comfortable embracing its clichés. The Beatles covered nine girl group songs in their live performances, and five of these appeared on their first two LPs. All of the Beatles were briefly friendly with the New York City's premier girl group, the Ronettes (Lennon had a major crush on Ronnie Bennett), and in a 1963 *Melody Maker* report, George Martin described the Beatles as sounding like "a male Shirelles."

Usually when the Beatles sang songs by girl groups, they switched the relevant gender pronouns, but they didn't do so in every case. When they performed the Shirelles' song "Boys," which was a staple of the Beatles' live act from about 1961 to 1963 (it was their requisite "drummer number"), they sang the chorus just as it had been written, from a female's perspective: "I talk about boys now! (Yeah, yeah, boys!) What a bundle of joy!" In a 2005 *Rolling Stone* interview, McCartney recalled that the song was a "fan favorite" (Pete Best had sung it before Ringo), though he added, "if you think about it, here's us doing a song that was really a girls' song. . . . Or it was [as the Beatles played it] a gay song. But we never listened. It's just a great song. . . . I love the innocence of those days."

More than other performers, the Beatles also had a habit of seeming to sweetly and directly address their girl fans through their use of personal pronouns ("P.S. *I* Love *You*," "With love, from *me*, to *you*," "*I* Want to Hold *Your* Hand," and so forth). In fact, the Beatles' second US album, *Meet the Beatles!*, was packaged by Capitol Records so as to contain *only* songs about relationships. Once, when an American reporter asked Lennon about the Beatles' heavy reliance of first-person pronouns, he drew a sarcastic reply: "Should it be 'I Want to Hold *Its* Hand?'" Lennon said. "Or, 'She Love *Them*?'" But that was merely his way of obscuring the fact that he and McCartney were consciously writing formulaic songs that they hoped their young female listeners would personally identify with. It was a "little trick," McCartney admitted. "We try to do that, you know, to make it personal."

The Beatles also flavored some of their popular early songs with a dash of innuendo. A rough draft of the song that became "I Saw Her Standing There" went: "She was just seventeen / Never been a beauty queen." McCartney recalls that Lennon laughed incredulously when he first heard it, and then he supplied the roguish "and you know what I mean." And certainly it's difficult, nowadays, to listen to "Please Please Me" as anything other than an exasperated plea for oral sex. But few of the group's contemporary listeners had much to say about any possible sexual insinuations in the Beatles' work. They projected sexual charisma, to be sure, but it was a charisma that was tamed and domesticated for their youngest female fans. More than anything else, teenagers seemed to swoon over the tenderness and vulnerability that the Beatles expressed in their songs.

Were the Beatles, in the early '60s, as romantic and chivalrous toward women as they appeared on their records? Hardly. John's marriage to Cynthia completely lacked the gauzy optimism we associate with modern-day matrimony. Theirs was a shotgun wedding, held at the local register office, that only five people attended (Epstein, McCartney, Harrison, and two of Cyn's relatives). After it was over, they decamped to a nearby restaurant, where they all had a lunch of fried chicken and water. According to John's aunt Mimi, the night before the ceremony, he paid a visit to his boyhood home, where he flitted from room to room and reminisced about his childhood, before finally plopping down at the kitchen table, and weeping. "I don't want to get married," he kept saying. Several years later, when a reporter asked him for his thoughts about "the Pill"—a major topic of conversation because of its impact on sexuality, motherhood, and popular culture—he replied, "I wish they'd had it a few years ago."

Although Lennon acted honorably when he married his pregnant girlfriend, he never seems to have considered embarking upon a life of constricting monogamy. Nor did any of the other Beatles, who for the most part had steady girlfriends. In fact, the entire group regularly engaged in behavior that no famous person could dream of keeping under wraps in today's media environment. Peter Jones, a journalist who covered them for the *Record Mirror*, recalled being in a "difficult position" because he was expected to "gloss over" the Beatles' tawdry indiscretions. "It was decreed that the Beatles should be portrayed as incredibly lovable, amiable fellows, and if one of them, without mentioning any names, wanted to have a short orgy with three girls in the bathroom, then I didn't see it."

And though he could scarcely believe his eyes, Larry Kane, an American journalist, likewise stayed mum about the night at an Atlantic City hotel suite when about twenty prostitutes were trotted out before the Beatles and their entourage. "Take your pick," a local promoter told all the men in the room. Another time, at a Dallas nightclub, Kane looked on as McCartney asked photographer Art Schreiber to fetch him a particular cocktail waitress, just as if he were in a whorehouse. In New York, he listened to Ringo complain about being "sore" from his previous night's exertions. Ronnie Bennett was likewise aghast when, during the same tour, Lennon led her into a hotel room where people sat ringside around a bed while a woman had acrobatic sex with one of the Beatles' friends. When the Beatles toured Australia, one of their personal MSS guards said, "The only thing they seemed to be interested in was [sic] the very young girls that we were regularly instructed to let past the security screen around their hotel rooms."

It is doubtful that most of the Stones saw quite as much activity so early in their career. A bit later on, the types of young and adoring women who sexually serviced the Beatles would become known as groupies, but since that term had not yet been invented, the Beatles unkindly referred to them as "slags." In Liverpool they had picked up a more charming vernacular expression, however, to describe the hurried and furtive sexual encounters they sometimes indulged in (quickie blowjobs and whatnot): these they called "knee-tremblers." Philandering is not an unusual vice in the pop world, but one would be hard pressed to name many other musicians or celebrities in the '60s for whom the gap between the private reality and public façade was so humongous.

The Beatles strove to maintain their carefully polished image because their goal, which they frequently acknowledged and rarely qualified, was to get as rich as possible. The day they landed at New York City's Kennedy Airport for the first time, someone from the press corps asked them if they would sing something. "We need money first," Lennon quipped. Henceforth, Lennon's sound bites about the group's material ambitions became a mainstay of their press conferences. What will the Beatles do when all the mania about them subsides? someone asked. "Count the money," he said. What do you intend to do with all of your money? "Spend it!" How much money have you made? "A lot!" Are you setting any examples for American youths? "Only how to make money quickly." What has the Beatles' success meant to you, personally? "More money than I had before." Would the Beatles ever consider performing behind the Iron Curtain? "If they've got enough rubles." Is that really why you got into this [the journalist asks incredulously]: to get rich? Paul and John together: "Yes!"

After the antibourgeois social movements of the late '60s got under way, the Beatles became more cautious about discussing their finances. But it would be wrong to suggest that there was ever anything campy, subversive, or affected in the way they talked about money during their mid-'60s publicity junkets, as if they were only joking, or lampooning the West's acquisitive tendencies. They spoke the same way in private, too.

"Somebody said to me, 'But the Beatles were antimaterialistic,' " McCartney later remarked. "That's a huge myth. John and I literally used to sit down and say, 'Now, let's write a swimming pool.' " In a 1965 interview with *Playboy*, McCartney summarized his feelings thusly: "We'd be idiots to say that it isn't a constant inspiration to be making a lot of money."

Nor is it surprising that the Beatles should have been so giddy about all of the loot they were raking in. After all, they had been born into modest circumstances, and they came of age in a rigidly segmented and class-conscious society. And yet while they were still very young, the four Liverpool scruffs suddenly began accumulating fortunes rivaling those of politicians, captains of industry, and heirs and heiresses—the very types of people who, in any other circumstance, would surely have snubbed them. Meanwhile, just about everyone kept reminding the Beatles that they were but a fad. (An extraordinary fad, to be sure, but one that would soon wither and die.) As a result, the Beatles resolved to work feverishly, attempting to earn as much as possible before their narrow window of opportunity was completely shut. And that meant churning out pleasant and appealing pop songs that appealed to their market, which—though it was large and varied—mainly consisted of teenage girls.

That was the sticking point with so many hip Londoners in the early '60s. Whereas they admired the Stones for dealing frankly with sex, lust, angst, consumerism, depression, and suburbia, the Beatles had reined in their bohemianism. They respected propriety because to do otherwise would run counter to their goal at the time, which was to cash in on their unique ability to elicit a hormonal response from young teenage girls. No one in this era referred to Stones fans as rockists, but that was roughly their perspective. They felt that in seeking to appeal primarily to little girls, the Beatles had set the bar awfully low.

Even back then, however, careful observers might have discerned that the Beatles had more far-reaching ambitions than they were being given credit for. First, there was the moody, black-and-white Robert Freeman photo they used on the cover of their second album, *With the Beatles*, which was inspired by the artsy shots that Astrid Kirchherr and Jürgen Vollmer took of them in Hamburg. Clad in black turtlenecks and staring impassively into the camera, the Beatles looked like common beatniks, the types of subterranean youths who clustered together for poetry readings and jazz nights at Greenwich Village coffeehouses. EMI absolutely loathed the photo—why weren't the Beatles grinning?!—and Epstein begged them to agree to something more in keeping with their happy-go-lucky image. They would not.

Then on November 4, 1963, the Beatles played a four-song set at the Royal Variety Show, which was nationally televised. The Queen Mother, Princess Margaret, and Lord Snowdon were all in attendance. As the Beatles prepared to launch into their final number, "Twist and Shout," Lennon famously asked for the audience's help: "Will the people in the cheaper seats, clap your hands? And the rest of you, if you'd just rattle your jewelry." Had Lennon gone ahead with the line he'd privately threatened to deliver ("rattle your *fucking* jewelry"), he would have derailed the Beatles' career. As it happened, he brought down the house. It was a cheeky reminder that the Beatles always knew there was something incongruous about the way they were embraced by the establishment.

Eight months later, in July 1964, the Beatles released *A Hard Day's Night*. The soundtrack to Richard Lester's loony comedy film hinted at the Beatles' quickly evolving creativity. It was their first album to contain only original material, and more than anything they'd done so far, it demonstrated the Beatles' oft-remarked ability to make popular music that on the one hand seemed safe and familiar, and on the other hand, was daring and inventive. (It would take more than forty years, and a mathematician, to even definitively figure out how they played the opening chord—*"Chaaaaaang!"*—on the title track.) Meanwhile, their film, with its pseudo-documentary style, subtle satire, allusive references, and intelligent repartee, was almost universally regarded as being several cuts above the types of banal, pop exploitation pics that preceded it. Even professional movie critics, who expected *A Hard Day's Night* to be terrible, wound up loving it. "This is going to surprise you—it may knock you right off your chair—but the film . . . is a whale of a comedy," said the *New York Times*. The *New York Journal-American* compared it to the Marx Brothers' comedies of the 1930s. A *Village Voice* writer called it "the *Citizen Kane* of jukebox musicals."

Around the same time, John Lennon published his first book, *In His Own Write*, a slim, elegantly designed hardcover collection of surreal short stories, line drawings, and nonsense verse. Lennon had been dashing off that kind of stuff going all the way back to high school, mostly for his own amusement, and he downplayed the idea that his book would reward careful critical analysis. Nevertheless, it promptly drew comparisons to the works of Lewis Carroll, Edward Lear, James Thurber, Mark Twain, and James Joyce. Reviewing *In His Own Write* for *Book World*, Tom Wolfe called Lennon "a genius of the lower crust." Another writer, in the highbrow *Times Literary Supplement*, recommended Lennon's collection to "anyone who fears the impoverishment of the English language and the English imagination."

All of this ought to have rendered ludicrous the rockist notion that the Beatles, because they desired the approval of teenyboppers, were therefore not to be taken so seriously. Then again, some of the group's condescending critics might also have just paid more consideration to what the Beatles were actually saying—literally.

It was at a book launch party, celebrating the release of *In His Own Write*, that George Melly, the venerable jazz singer and music writer, buttonholed Lennon and started a conversation about the Beatles' musical influences. One expects Lennon would have liked Melly. After all, they were both brazen and somewhat rakish characters, and they both hailed from Liverpool. Also, though Melly did not attend art school, he shared some of its enthusiasms, and he was donnishly smart about surrealism. Lennon might have been unnerved by Melly's bisexuality, but he would have admired his hard-drinking insouciance.

Nevertheless, that particular meeting did not go well. "During the course of the party," Melly remembered, "I suggested that despite his fame and money, [Lennon] was surely prepared to own up that not only did he owe a considerable debt to such Negro blues singers as Muddy Waters, but that objectively they were greater artists."

Was that a bold statement? At that time, the Beatles had released three impressive albums and six singles—about two hours of music in total. And yet Lennon bristled at the notion that the Beatles weren't any better than the American blues singers currently in vogue. In fact, it seems he had by then become seriously annoyed at the way so many young Brits were sacralizing the blues.

"He turned on me with sublime arrogance," Melly remembered. "He'd admit no such thing. Not only was he richer but better too. More original and better." Better than Muddy Waters, Howlin' Wolf, Willie Dixon, John Lee Hooker, Jimmy Reed—the whole damn lot of them. "We almost came to rather drunken blows."

• • •

It can be bracing to recall that the first group that threatened to dislodge the Beatles from the top of the hit parade wasn't the Rolling Stones, but rather, another London-based group. Styled in tweed jackets, high-heeled boots, and choke-collared shirts, the Dave Clark Five didn't look or sound all that different from many of the Northern beat groups. Nevertheless, some claimed that they represented a new, commercial vanguard—the "Tottenham Sound"—which was poised to finally steal the spotlight from the flourishing scene that Brian Epstein was presiding over in Liverpool. In January 1964, the Dave Clark Five's hit "Glad All Over" knocked "I Want to Hold Your Hand" from the number 1 position on the UK charts, leading the *Daily Express* to proclaim in a headline, "Tottenham Sound Has Crushed the Beatles." Considering that "I Want to Hold Your Hand" had already occupied the top spot for two whole months, and could already be found in an estimated 25 percent of phonograph-owning households in England, it was a bit of hyperbole—but it still fueled speculation that the Beatles were on the way out.

"Cartoonists had a field day," reported Michael Braun. "Cruelest of all was an Elmwood cartoon in the *Daily Mail*: standing outside a theater where the Dave Clark Five are performing, a group of young girls are pointing at another girl of about sixteen. 'She must be really old,' they are saying; 'she remembers the Beatles.' "

Publicly, the Beatles never appeared the least bit bothered, but privately, they were concerned. "We couldn't help it," Lennon later admitted. "Everyone was telling us, 'Dave Clark is coming, you've had it now.' It worried us, but just for a minute, the way we'd worried in Liverpool that Gerry [and the Pacemakers] would beat us in the *Mersey Beat* poll."

Later in 1964, however, they started fielding questions about a different group. In 1964, the Beatles cut off a journalist who began to ask, "Are you concerned about a poll in Britain which indicated that a group called the Rolling Stones—"

"There's *many* polls," Ringo snapped. "They just won one of them."

An exchange with a female reporter at a Jacksonville, Florida, press conference went this way:

REPORTER: Are you worried about rumors going around that the Rolling Stones are now more important than the Beatles?

RINGO: Is it *worrying* us?

JOHN: [turning toward Paul, taking the piss] "Is it worrying us," she said! No.

GEORGE: Not at all.

PAUL: It doesn't worry us, 'cuz you get . . .

JOHN: [interrupting] We manage our grief.

PAUL: [giggles] You get these rumors every so often, you know. I mean . . .

GEORGE: [dings his teacup with a spoon] Dave Clark!

PAUL: Dave Clark was [supposed to be] bigger than us a couple months ago.

JOHN: Blind fool.

GEORGE: Every two months we hear of 'em taking over.

Still, the Stones had by then garnered a large amount of media attention, in which they were reliably portrayed as noisy upstarts who faithfully reflected the concerns of disgruntled teenagers. An early and paradigmatic article of this type, headlined "Rebels with a Beat," appeared in the February 18, 1964, issue of *Melody Maker.* Ray Coleman began his profile of the Stones by describing an exchange he'd had with a forty-two-year-old London cabbie who had picked him up in Mayfair.

"Was that the Rolling Stones you just left?" the driver asked him.

"Yes. What do you think of them?"

"A bunch of right 'erberts!" he replied. ("Herbert" being mildly abusive slang for scruffy, working-class youths.) "'Ere, aren't they the boys they say are trying to knock the Beatles off the top?"

Coleman remembered thinking at that moment that if he'd been a talent agent or a record executive, "[He] would probably have signed that taxi driver immediately as [his] trends advisor. The Rolling Stones might have had other ideas, like punching him on the nose. Because they deeply resent any suggestion that they are attempting to overtake the Beatles. Yet if the Beatles are to be knocked off from their perch in the future, by a British group, the popular notion is that the Rolling Stones could easily be their successors."

The reason, Coleman continued, had a great deal to do with their image, which he said was "perfect." He described the Stones as "five disheveled rebels who have already made a firm imprint on the hit parade, who have gained a huge following among young people, who never wear stage uniforms, and who JUST DON'T CARE."

"There are even rumblings inside show business of a swing against the Beatles in favor of the Rolling Stones," Coleman added. As evidence he cited a letter that an "alert writer" had sent to *Melody Maker*. "She asserted that young pop fans instinctively turn against an idol whom their parents endorse, like the Beatles. Fans actually enjoy hearing their elders spurning their worship of their heroes. That way, there is an outlet for their emotional involvement."

When Coleman sat down with the Stones, and asked them if they were jealous of the Beatles' success, Jagger reflexively answered "Yes!" while the rest of the group said "No!" A bit later in the interview, though, Wyman boasted that in some circles, the Stones were being touted as London's answer to the Beatles. That prompted an interjection from Jagger: "Whatever you do, don't write that article saying we're knocking the Beatles," he said. "They're good mates of ours. We like 'em and they've done much good for the whole scene, see?"

Coleman was also behind the "Boiling Beatles Blast Copycats" story mentioned in chapter 2, as well as the infamous "Would You Let Your Sister Go with a Rolling Stone?" headline. He did not, however, fancy himself as the type of lowbrow hack who was always trying to stoke controversies. Privately, he had middlebrow tastes (jazz, chess), and by the time he joined *Melody Maker* in 1960, at around age twenty-three, he had already worked in the newspaper trade for eight years, having started out as a copy boy for the *Leicester Evening Mail*. At *Melody Maker* he hoped that by taking a serious approach to his trade, he could help vitalize the public discussion about pop music.

Nevertheless, he soon began lamenting that the show business beat at *Melody Maker* was too much about the "biz" side of things. He was compiling tour date listings and cranking out celebrity puff pieces, rather than writing sharp and penetrating profiles. Eventually he grew so bothered by the paper's fatuity that he tried to defect to the more highly regarded *Daily Telegraph*, but he was unsuccessful. At his interview, an executive asked him where he currently worked.

"*Melody Maker*," Coleman answered.

"And where did you work before that?"

"The *Manchester Evening News*."

His interviewer fixed him with a quizzical look. There was a pregnant pause. Finally, he said, "Tell me, Mr. Coleman: Why did you leave journalism?"

The exchange motivated Coleman to work even harder at trying to improve *Melody Maker*. Eventually he became the paper's editor-in-chief and then a respected celebrity biographer. In his writings on the Beatles and the Stones circa 1963 and 1964, however, he was in a transitional phase. His "Rebels with a Beat" profile showed his penchant for putting across shrewd insights while at the same time indulging in a bit of promotional hagiography. The Beatles were fond of Coleman, because he was one of the few writers they encountered who always expressed interest in their music, as well as their celebrity; but they may not have been thrilled to see the Stones—whom they had in some ways befriended, and whom they'd given a song—characterized as their new rivals.

Regardless, the template that Coleman helped to construct was picked up again and again. Many of the same journalists who had complacently described the Beatles as boyish and good-humored were now lazily portraying the Stones as filthy and obnoxious. "They look like boys who any self-respecting mum would lock in the bathroom!" a *Daily Express* journalist remarked, just ten days after Coleman's piece came out. "But the Rolling Stones—five tough young London-based music-makers with doorstep mouths, pallid cheeks and unkempt hair—are not worried what mums think! For now the

Beatles have registered with all age groups, [but] the Rolling Stones have taken over as the voice of the teens." An Australian journalist, Lillian Roxon, remarked that while the Beatles "looked as if they had been personally scrubbed down by Brian Epstein himself, the Rolling Stones looked as if they had been sent to bed every night for a week with the same clothes on and no supper. The Beatles' songs had been rinsed and hung out to dry. The Stones had never seen soap and water. And where the adorable little wind-up Beatle mop-tops wanted nothing more than to hold a hand, the hateful rasping Stones were bent on rape, pillage and plunder."

A bit paradoxically, some of the Stones' popularity owed to the obscurity of the music they championed. Unlike "ordinary" teens, who could be counted on to unthinkingly embrace whomever the show-business Establishment decreed should be the flavor of the month, the Stones' supporters fancied themselves as curious and more discerning types. In this way, they somewhat prefigured modern-day hipsters—those urban twentysomethings who prize, above just about everything else, their supposedly superior cultural knowledge. When the niche constituency for R&B started growing in England in the early 1960s, Jagger even wrote an unguarded (some would say "uncool") letter to *Melody Maker* solely for the purpose of stressing that he had been in the vanguard of the whole scene. "I used to write letters to Pye Records [a British label] pleading with them to release Chuck Berry and Bo Diddley records long before this beat thing got commercial," he said.

> *I don't know if the people at Pye remember my name, but they ought to. They sent me back catalogues and they were very sympathetic. To the critics, then, who think we're a beat group who came up overnight knowing nothing about it, we invite them to examine our record collection. It contains things by Jimmy Reed, Elmore James, (John Lee) Hooker and a stack of private tapes by Little Walter. That's a good start.*

Nevertheless, he had a point; it was not easy, in early-'60s England, to come across authentic Delta blues or amped up Chicago-style R&B. You had to make an effort. Oftentimes, that involved getting those types of LPs directly from the labels, such as Chess, in Chicago, or Specialty, in Los Angeles. American records were usually pricier than British ones, and of course you had to pay for shipping, too. Mick Jagger started ordering imported blues LPs as a teenager. "He'd send money orders," remembers Marshall Chess, whose father and uncle cofounded Chess Records in 1950. "I worked in the shipping room. I remember sending boxes of records to England. Filling out the customs forms. That first wave of blues lovers wanted those Chess albums. . . . It was rare. It wasn't an everyday thing, to get an order from England."

The Stones' name, of course, was a tribute to Muddy Waters's 1950 song "Rollin' Stone," and their earliest fans would have gotten the reference immediately. As the group's popularity swelled, however, the majority of youths who heard about them would not have experienced such a pleasurable frisson of recognition. Initially, Stones fans were predominately city dwellers, and they fancied themselves as a savvy and discerning lot. They were the types of youths who, in addition to liking R&B, may also have been conversant in jazz. They might have taken some of their style cues from the Beats—Kerouac, Ginsberg, and Burroughs. A few of their more literary minded enthusiasts might have gone so far as to line their bookshelves with Rimbaud, Dostoyevsky, and William Blake. They'd have bonded over, and felt protective about, their beleaguered "outsider" status, and they would have snickered at pop's lumpen love of the Beatles. One Stones fan from the Netherlands recalled that at his local disco, the Pink Elephant, "Beatles fans were not allowed. The sign on the door said 'Stones Fans Only.' "

Naturally, when parents declared that they were horrified by the Stones, or tried to make life difficult for them, they only bolstered the group's status as rebellious icons. Later on, of course, the Stones would become the most gargantuan touring band of all time, and with a retinue of lawyers and personal assistants, they practically immunized themselves from petty hassles. But it was very different in the early '60s. At some hotels, nighttime porters even prevented the Stones from bringing female guests into their rooms. Other times, they were banned altogether from hotels, refused rides by taxi drivers, denied service in restaurants, or heckled by local yokels. "We'd even go into a shop to buy a pack of cigarettes and they would refuse to sell us any," Wyman recollected. "We don't serve the likes of you in this establishment," they'd sneer. "Kindly leave." Once, when the maître d' at the Grand Hotel in Bristol turned them away, it provoked yet another tabloid headline: "The Rolling Stones Gather No Lunch."

Uptight authorities even picked on Stones *fans*. In May 1964, the *Daily Mirror* reported that a Coventry headmaster had suspended eleven students for "imitating the Stones' hairstyle." They were told to stay away from the school until they "cut their hair neatly, like the Beatles." American music critic Anthony DeCurtis recalls that in October of that year, the day after the Stones appeared on the *Ed Sullivan Show*, "[E]very single one of my teachers gave a lecture about the Rolling Stones and how repulsive they were. They'd pat you on the head for liking the Beatles. They got a kick out of them. They didn't get a kick out of the Rolling Stones."

Similarly, some parents forbade the Stones. One fan recalled feeling lucky growing up, because although her parents would have preferred it if the Beatles had been her favorite band, they at least allowed her to keep Stones LPs in their home. By contrast, most of her young girlfriends "had to sneak the records and hide them from their parents," she said. "This, of course, just added to the fun. I can remember listening to *England's Newest Hit Makers* with my friend Linda, the record player muted under a stack of pillows in her bedroom. That was how much her mother hated the Stones."

On July 4, 1964, the Stones made a notorious appearance on *Juke Box Jury*, the BBC's nationally televised music panel show. The footage has since been lost, but a surviving photo captures the group's mood. Instead of chatting amiably about the records they heard, the Stones were impolite and abrasive. "Nobody was particularly witty or anything," Keith Richards said later. "We just trashed every song they played." According to a *Daily Sketch* reviewer, the Stones "indicated their pleasure or displeasure by catarrhal grunts that an ear, trained in the illiterate school of young people, could sometimes distinguish as 'Well, yeah, er, I, er, mean, like, well it's, ha-ha, awful then. Naw, definitely not, in'nit?' " Even *New Musical Express*, a music paper that was normally favorable to the Stones, called their appearance on *Juke Box Jury* "an utter disgrace." In lieu of an apology, the Stones later maintained that they had not set out to cause a furor, but rather that the show's producers had asked them to comment upon a boring batch of records.

Ten days later, the Stones headlined a gig at the Empress Ballroom in Blackpool that ended in a major riot. The trouble began when a youth started spitting at Brian Jones from the front of the stage. (According to an eyewitness, he'd taken exception to Brian's "effete posturing.") Keith responded first by standing on the kid's hands, and then by kicking him in the face. Instantaneously, the whole hall erupted. The Stones beat a hasty retreat, and before police could restore order, fans had thrown shoes, bottles, and coins, ripped up their seats, torn down curtains, smashed a bunch of crystal chandeliers, and leveled a Steinway grand piano. Fifty people required hospital treatment for their injuries, and the town council banned the Stones from ever appearing there again.

A late-night incident at a gas station in Stratford wound up providing the Stones with even worse (read: better) publicity. It was March 18, 1965, and the Stones were in an upbeat mood; they'd just been voted the most popular recording artists in France, and they were on their way back from their last stop on a short and successful tour with the Hollies—fourteen shows in fourteen consecutive nights. At around 11:30 p.m., they stopped off to stretch their legs and let Bill Wyman use the restroom. But the attendant, a button-downed forty-one-year-old man named Charles Keeley, curtly told them that there wasn't one. Wyman knew that there was, and so he persisted in asking to use it, only to be denied again. Then the other Stones joined into the fray, badgering the attendant to just let Wyman use the bathroom. Neither side would budge, and the conversation quickly grew heated.

"Get off my forecourt! Get off my forecourt!" Keeley supposedly shouted.

"Get off my foreskin!" Jones responded.

Three of the Stones—Jagger, Jones, and Wyman—then proceeded to unzip their trousers and relieve themselves against a nearby wall.

The incident would have been forgotten if an offended eyewitness had not taken down their license plate number. But he did, and so this led to The Great Urination Bust of 1965. Three months later, Wyman, Jagger, and Jones were made to appear before the East Ham Magistrates' Court in London. According to sworn testimony, as Jagger was urinating that night, he yelled, "We'll piss anywhere, man!" Then the others, as if on cue, supposedly began chanting the phrase: "We'll piss anywhere! We'll piss anywhere!" One of them even allegedly did a weird dance as well. As they peeled out of the service station, several of them allegedly stuck their hands out of the windows of their chauffeured Daimler touring car and showed the attendant "a well-known gesture."

Noting that Mr. Keeley had referred to the Stones as "long-haired monsters," the defense attorney asked him if he was pressing charges simply out of spite.

"The conception of 'long-haired monsters' did not influence my decision to complain," Keeley testified, "although it might have started the ball rolling. It made me determined not to let them go to the staff toilet."

The three Stones were fined £5 each for "insulting behavior" and ordered to pay court costs. The magistrates' chairman concluded, "Whether it is the Rolling Stones, the Beatles or anyone else, we will not tolerate conduct of this character. Because you have reached the exalted heights in your profession, it does not mean you have the right to act like this. On the contrary, you should set a standard of behavior, which should be a moral pattern for your large number of supporters. You have been found guilty of behavior not becoming young gentlemen."

The trial got heavy coverage in London's tabloid press, and as rock writer Marc Spitz points out, it added substantially to their growing legend. "The notion that the Stones should act in a way that would firmly establish them as volatile Cains to the Beatles' true-blue Abels was already planted in the band members' heads, and so here was the water-passing, watershed moment. The Beatles pissed where pissing was designated. The Stones did what they liked."

Occasionally, the Stones professed to be aggrieved at the treatment they received by adults. Sometimes they claimed they were unfairly persecuted for their long locks. Other times, they protested that the reports about their bad hygiene and slovenly appearance were inaccurate. "Simply because we chose to do something different and wear our hair long they had to make up these ridiculous stories about our hygiene," Brian Jones complained. "I happen to be particularly fastidious when it comes to washing and wearing clean clothes, so the kind of rubbish which reporters wrote about our not washing is both untrue and unnecessary." But they must have known that this was a mug's game. No amount of remonstration was going to deter anyone who wanted to believe that the Stones had fleas leaping off their heads.

That's why the Stones more commonly answered their critics with practiced arrogance: "I don't particularly care either way whether parents hate us or not," Jagger told an interviewer. "We know a lot of people don't like us 'coz they say we're scruffy and don't wash," he said another time. "So what? They don't have to come and look at us, do they?" "My hair is not a gimmick," Jones added. "To be honest, I think it looks good. I think I look right with long hair. So I'll tell you this much: my hair's staying as it is. If you don't like it: hard luck."

Fans, of course, loved it. Along with their hair, the motley assemblage of colorful clothes that the Stones draped over their skinny frames was an essential part of their appeal. A teenager's letter to the editor in 1964 amplified the point:

> *Suggestions that the Stones should go and have short back and sides are not just wrong but beside the point. You might as well suggest Jackie Kennedy should not dress elegantly, or that Fidel Castro should not have his beard. . . . The Stones are popular because they wear sweatshirts and cord trousers that we can buy too. Long hair is a sign of protest against the crop-headed discipline of the army during wartime. Bright, casual clothes for men are fashionable as a reaction against wartime grey and drab demob suits.*

"I'm fed up with people saying they hate the Rolling Stones because of their hair," wrote another fan. "England should be very proud of them. People are always moaning that Liverpool is beating the South in talent. Now we have a group to be proud of and half the people moan about them."

Nonconformist teens were likewise drawn to the Stones' live performances, which crackled with an air of danger, and in that important respect were completely unlike what any of the Merseyside acts were doing. "Keith and I will talk about the music hall thing, the vaudeville influence that lay behind all these groups like the Beatles," Jagger said later on. He was referring to their post-Hamburg professionalism—their hackneyed stage banter, choreographed bowing, and contrived cheerfulness. Jagger continued: "The North of England was so much further behind London culturally at the time—that wasn't really a bad thing, they just were. So all those young groups had been brought up knowing about the music hall, going to it with their parents, so when a band like the Hollies actually got up on stage, they'd behave like vaudeville entertainers. They were not cool."

By contrast, the Stones strutted onto the stage with angry intensity. Cordons of police officers shielded them from their fans, just like they did for the Beatles, but they had to contend with unrulier audiences, who often rushed to the front of the theater, surging and swaying in a great mass ("like palm trees in a hurricane," Jones once said). "We'd walk into some of these places and it was like the battle of Crimea going on," Richards said. "People gasping, tits hanging out, chicks choking, nurses, ambulances." It was just what the Stones wanted. Jagger learned to bait the crowds, vamping and goose-stepping like a rabies-infected soldier. Jones went for the same effect, advancing to the very rim of the stage, leaning over, and leering at one girl or another. If she seemed to be with her boyfriend, then all the better: he'd smack his tambourine right in the guy's face and flash a wicked grin. Fans hurled gifts and souvenirs at the Stones from every direction. Sometimes, their performances lasted only a few minutes before pissed-off cops forced them to quit. Once the curtains fell, security bums rushed the band out of the venue and into their getaway vehicles. To let them linger any longer was to risk catastrophe.

The Stones also provoked a more complicated sexual response than any other act, and much of it owed to Mick Jagger's visual appeal as an androgyne. Jagger's long hair, wispy frame, and wide Caravaggio mouth gave him a feminine quality to begin with, and his preening and teasing mannerisms—the ways he shimmied, gestured, pranced, and wiggled—put it over the top. (It wasn't for nothing that he'd later be called "the king bitch of rock.") Phil May, the lead singer of the Pretty Things, always thought that this one of the reasons that Stones' audiences always had a heavier male quotient than other acts. "The way he performed, he had a sexual appeal for the girls and a homosexual attraction for the boys," he said. "And I'm not talking about homosexual boys—Mick aroused heterosexual guys as well." May's view, which echoes a popular theory that Alfred Kinsey first put across in the 1940s, holds that sexual attraction exists on a gay-straight continuum. "The fact is that everybody has some homosexuality in his makeup," May surmised, and somehow Jagger was uniquely capable of triggering latent or suppressed desires in some of his male fans. "I'm sure if you had asked any of them that question, they'd have denied it. But there was a duality, especially in the Stones, no denying it."

Either way, until the Stones came along, teenage girls were the most avid fans of popular music groups. "They had pictures of Gerry and the Pacemakers on their walls, Paul McCartney, but the guys didn't do that," May continued. What's more, when guys did attend rock shows, it was usually just as a courtesy to their dates. Oftentimes, they'd stand amongst themselves in the back of the room, snickering and gawking. The Stones, however, provoked a totally different response; boys would be muscling girls out of the way in order to get choice spots in front of the stage. "The chicks were pushed further and further back because they were physically overwhelmed. As a result, the first twenty-five rows would be guys." That had never happened before.

Of course, sexual attitudes were already unloosening in the British Isles well before the Beatles and the Stones came along in the early '60s. Teenage promiscuity was becoming a public worry, censorship was on the wane, and the stodginess of the older generations was being cleverly satirized in the legendary *Private Eye* magazine, and in the popular comedy stage revue *Beyond the Fringe*, performed by Peter Cook, Dudley Moore, Alan Bennett, and Jonathan Miller. Nevertheless, the Stones were completely alone in deciding that a song like Slim Harpo's "King Bee" was fit for teenage consumption. ("I can make honey, baby, let me come inside.") When the Stones covered Willie Dixon's "Little Red Rooster"—ostensibly a song about a chicken—Jagger sang it with such lascivious intent that American radio stations refused to play it. And of course the Stones' monster 1965 hit, "(I Can't Get No) Satisfaction," which reached number one in England and America, was about as sexually frank as anything that had ever been played on commercial radio: In the third verse, the narrator complains because the girl he wants to fuck is on her period ("baby better come back, maybe next week.")*

* Some listeners hear Jagger sing, "baby better come back, *later* next week."

Meanwhile, many youths began championing a new ethos of candidness and authenticity in personal relations. No doubt this was largely a response to the glad-handing insincerity that was so rampant in the conformist-minded '50s. Few baby boomers were as sensitive to the cultural reserve of the Lonely Crowd than punk poetess Patti Smith, who saw the Stones for the first time from her living room, when they performed on *The Ed Sullivan Show* in 1964. Her father, a Jehovah's Witness assembly-line worker, was watching as well, "glued to the screen, [and] cussing his brains out" during the band's entire three-song set. He'd probably have been even more upset if he'd known that at that that very moment, his daughter was experiencing a sexual and generational awakening. Years later, she'd write about it in a weird, modernist-flavored prose poem. "I was trapped in a field of hot dots," she said:

> *the guitar player had pimples. the blonde kneeling down had circles ringing his eyes. one had greasy hair. the other didn't care. and the singer was showing his second layer of skin and more than a little milk. I felt thru his pants with optic x-ray. this was some hard meat. this was bitch. five white boys sexy as any spade. their nerve was wired and their third leg was rising. in six minutes five lusty images gave me my first glob of gooie in my virgin panties.*

Mick Jagger would later be rather cruel to Patti Smith. In a 1977 interview with the British magazine *Sounds*, he called her "crap," "awful," "full of rubbish," "full of words and crap," "a poseur of the worst kind," "a useless guitar player," "a bad singer," "not attractive," and "not really together musically," before finally concluding (incongruously) "she's all right." Flash back to 1965, however, and she was precisely the type of fan the Rolling Stones were connecting with. She certainly wasn't a teenybopper. At the time, she worked in a New Jersey toy factory, and she longed to go to art school even though she couldn't afford it. She was creative, aware, and literate, a thrift-store scavenger and a shoplifter of esoteric books. Personality wise, she would have been at stark odds with the types of young teens who, Stones fans claimed, were fecklessly glomming onto the Beatles.

At the same time that the Stones courted fans like Patti Smith, they were busily insinuating themselves into the extravagant lifestyles of the English upper class. Jagger was by far the most socially anxious of the whole bunch. When he started dating Chrissie Shrimpton in the fall of 1963 (he was twenty years old and she was eighteen), it was probably at least partly because he saw her as a ladder up to where he wanted to be. Chrissie was the well-heeled younger sister of Jean Shrimpton ("the Shrimp"), arguably the world's first supermodel. Known everywhere as the sexy face of new London, Jean was engaged to England's hippest photographer, David Bailey. (Later she'd be linked to the nation's trendiest actor, Terence Stamp.) Chrissie wasn't quite the doe-eyed knockout that her older sister was, but she was certainly very pretty, and she was confident beyond her years. Legend holds that she introduced herself to Jagger by boldly approaching him after a gig asking, "Will you kiss me?"

They were a power couple, and initially, Chrissie had the upper hand; she was more worldly and better connected. Nicky Haslam, a British socialite and interior designer, remembers that when Chrissie first started bringing Mick around, she sheepishly joked to her fancy friends, "he's my cleaner—I put an ad in the paper and he turned up."

Soon enough, though, she was raving about her new boyfriend to everyone in fashionable London. "He's great," Bailey remembers her saying. "He's going to be bigger than the Beatles."

The only problem was, the two rarely seemed to get along very well. Almost everyone in the Stones' orbit back then remembers how frequently and furiously Mick and Chrissie used to argue with each other. In his memoir, *Stoned*, Andrew Oldham recalls when he went to see the Stones for the very first time in April 1963—before he even knew exactly who Jagger was, or what he looked like—he saw Mick and Chrissie having a blazing dispute in an alleyway outside the Crawdaddy Club. Marianne Faithfull has a similar recollection in her memoir about the night *she* met Jagger, in March 1964, at a record release party for Adrienne Posta. Chrissie "was crying and shouting at him, and in the heat of the argument her false eyelashes were peeling off," she said. Maldwyn Thomas, a friend of the couple, remembers "famous, plate-throwing, Hollywood-style rows." Sometimes, Chrissie would attack Mick in a pugilistic fury, lock him out of the house, or find someplace to disappear to for a few days, so that he had no way of reaching her. "Mick would cry a lot," Shrimpton said many years later. "We both would cry a lot."

Oldham figures that many of their problems arose as the relationship's balance of power shifted as a result of Mick's "growing charisma . . . and his obvious enjoyment of it." Chrissie arrived at the same conclusion. "We'd be walking down the street," she said, "and suddenly he'd see some Stones fans. My hand would suddenly be dropped, and he'd be walking ahead on his own.

Eventually, Jagger would vent his frustrations in his music. "Under My Thumb," "Stupid Girl," "19th Nervous Breakdown"—each of those scathing and abusive songs are thought to have been written about Chrissie Shrimpton. Jagger's most vicious put-down was probably "Out of Time," which the Stones recorded while he was simultaneously winding things down with Chrissie while avidly courting his next inamorata, Marianne Faithfull. ("You're obsolete my baby, my poor discarded baby . . . you're out of time.")

Then again, Chrissie had done a lot for young Mick. She introduced him to London's fashionable intelligentsia, and she took him to trendy boutiques, like Bus Stop and Biba. She was also the first person to get him entry into forbidding clubs like the Ad Lib, the Cromwellian, and the Scotch of St. James, where Mick mingled with pop culture royalty. "Mick liked to imagine their romance to be the stuff of newspaper gossip columns," a biographer observed. "So he would refer to it, in tour interviews with provincial journalists, sitting on the cold back stairs of some northern Gaumont of ABC, sniffing with the faint flu that plagued all the Stones and tilting a Pepsi bottle against his lips.

'... there's all those lies being written about me and Chrissie Shrimpton.'" After the Stones became popular in the US, Chrissie even started writing a column for *Mod*, called "From London with Luv," in which she kept American girls informed about all of their fabulous activities.

"Mick and I went down to visit George and Pattie Harrison last week," ran a typical entry.

> *They were just about ready to go out to a Saturday night movie when we arrived and so they asked us to go with them. The film happened to be at John Lennon's private home cinema. What a great way to see a movie. We saw a film called Citizen Kane [by] Orson Welles surrounded by Bourneville chocolate and cups of coffee! . . . Recently I had my 21st birthday. . . . Mick gave me a huge rocking horse on big rockers which I named Petunia. Also a birdcage with a Victorian brass bird in it. The bird sings. That is, it does if you put money into it.*

But of course when Mick and Chrissie first met, Jagger wasn't famous at all. At that point, he didn't even know that it was customary to leave a tip at a posh restaurant! Bailey recalled taking Jagger to an extravagant dinner at a place called the Casserole, on King's Road. "I told him to leave a tip and he said, 'Leave a tip? What the fuck for?' I said it was normal practice and suggested he leave a ten-shilling note, one of those old brown banknotes. Mick put the ten-bob note on the plate, but as we were putting our coats on, I noticed his hand slip out and pop the ten shillings back in his pocket."

Bailey tells another anecdote: "Later I introduced Mick to Andy Warhol, who I already knew. The first time I took Mick to meet Warhol was at Baby Jane Holzer's." Holzer was a flamboyant and well-connected young model who had recently married a wealthy real estate heir; together they shared a colossal property on Park Avenue. "Mick sat down and stuck his feet on her favorite lattice Chinese table," Bailey continues. "I thought, 'Fuck, she's not going to be pleased,' because I wouldn't have done something like that, but Mick could get away with it, because *the Stones were the cool group*."

The Stones were the cool group because they valorized youth in ways that the Beatles did not. That's one of the reasons they wore their reverence for bawdy American blues like a badge: it drew a distance between themselves and polite adult society. Blues music was gritty, earthy, and true to real life; it dealt with hardship and exploitation, of course, but also with themes that have always been on the minds of bohemian youths, like disillusionment, traveling, and sex. That sort of material was anathema to the commercial pop music that the older generations sanctioned.

Meanwhile, the Stones found that by simply exaggerating their already ingrained haughtiness, they could provoke a considerable amount of consternation among their elders. It was self-intensifying: the more parents obsessed over the Stones—the more adults griped and complained about their hair, their clothes, their hygiene, and their bad manners—the more they fueled the group's popularity among disaffected teens. And so the Stones had an incentive to just go on behaving badly. "We were encouraged, especially by Andrew, to be a little more outrageous than we even felt," Keith Richards later confessed. "Since then it's become a well-known scam."

In contrast, the Beatles had won acclaim from the highest stratum of British society. Beatlemania was a "multigenerational psychosis," said one smart observer. A lighthearted *Daily Mirror* editorial following their triumphant performance at the Royal Variety Show (the one where Lennon said "rattle your jewelry") had made that resoundingly clear. "You'd have to be a real square not to love the noisy, happy, handsome Beatles," the national tabloid said. It was even "refreshing" to see the Beatles generating such enthusiasm from a "middle-aged" audience. The *Daily Mirror* continued:

> *Fact is that Beatle People are everywhere: From Wapping to Windsor. Aged Seven to Seventy. And it's plain to see why these*

> *four energetic, cheeky lads from Liverpool go down so big. They're young, new. They're high-spirited, cheerful. . . . They wear their hair like a mop—but it's WASHED, it's super-clean. So is their fresh young act. Youngsters like the Beatles . . . are doing a good turn for show business—and the rest of us—with their new sounds, new looks. GOOD LUCK, BEATLES!*

• • •

At the end of 1963, the London *Evening Standard* issued a special supplement, "The Year of the Beatles." "An examination of the heart of the nation at this moment would reveal the word BEATLES engraved upon it," the paper said.

These were the types of accolades that made certain disaffected teens skeptical of the Beatles. The first wave of Stones fans thought of themselves as cultural savants. At the same time they admired the supposedly "authentic" and "iconoclastic" Rolling Stones, they formulated a set of aesthetic criteria that held that *only* acts like the Stones—only those who could be considered daring, stylish, and edgy—were really worthy of their fandom. There was something wrong, they thought, about the way the Beatles succumbed to the Establishment's pampering. That made them "sell-outs." No one put it quite that way, of course, but that was the idea: the Beatles couldn't be taken too seriously, because they catered to the naïve romantic fantasies of early adolescent girls.

It was always a flimsy complaint. Sure, the Beatles did everything they could to advance their careers and please their fans, but then again, they never pretended to be doing otherwise. "Selling out," in fact, is where many show business professionals thought that the Beatles were headed. When everyone got a bit older, and all the frenzy died down, it was very widely assumed that the Beatles would be forced to leave their teen idol reputations behind, at which point the most they could hope for would be to occupy a more traditional role in showbiz, as schmaltzy, low-key, all-around entertainers. Perhaps, like Elvis, they would begin starring in a succession of vapid, formulaic movies? Or host a variety program on television or radio, featuring skits and light comedy? Maybe Lennon and McCartney would reinvent themselves as Denmark Street songsmiths (England's equivalent of Tin Pan Alley)? Unless they retired, these seemed to be their options. There simply wasn't any precedent for pop stars doing anything else.

The Beatles had heard all this, of course. Murray "the K" Kaufman, New York City's eccentric, fast-talking deejay—the one who had done so much to promote the Beatles when they first came to America—remembers sitting around with the group in February 1965, in Nassau, while they were on a break from making their motion picture *Help!* Probably they were all stoned out of their gourds. At one point, Paul played some of the Beatles' own recent records.

Murray remembers the dialogue going like this:

> PAUL: I bet that about ten years from now, when someone mentions the Beatles, some young kid will say, "Go on now. Here's your Beatles [pointing both his thumbs down]. Don't go palming off those old groups from the olden times." So, you see, we're just temporary, Murray, babe. Just temporary.
>
> GEORGE: [smiling] Yeah, that's right.
>
> JOHN: Oh well.
>
> RINGO: Who's got a cigarette?

In other words, they did not seem too concerned. Instead of petering out, the Beatles decided to outmaneuver everyone: They grew more, rather than less, ambitious. They started recording material that challenged their audiences with unfamiliar and disorienting words, sounds, attitudes, and images. In the process, they helped to transform pop into art. They pointed to a new future for popular music, and they had a galvanizing effect upon virtually all of their contemporaries. Including, of course, the Rolling Stones.

CHAPTER FOUR

YANKOPHILIA

The number of people who can remember what it was like when the Beatles made their first few visits to the United States is dwindling every year. Find an American who *can* recall their first encounters with the Beatles, however, and they're likely to rhapsodize about how fun and exciting it always was. Along with some other sainted and iconic figures from the '60s—Martin Luther King, Jr., and Muhammad Ali both come to mind—the Beatles have become almost immune from baby boomer criticism. It bears remembering, though, that the Beatles were responsible for an awful lot of unpleasant commotion back in their day. Consider what it took just to host them at a New York City hotel.

In February 1964, when they showed up at the Plaza on their first visit to the United States, it took one hundred city cops, a squad of mounted policemen, and a fleet of hired private detectives just to ensure everyone's safety. Throngs of teenagers congregated outside, singing, shouting, and waving placards. Fan mail poured in by the heavy bag load. The hotel lobby, normally sedate and luxurious, looked like a battle camp headquarters. To get in and out of the building, the Beatles had to wind their way through the kitchen and use the service elevator, and after they left for good, the Plaza's management issued an apology for allowing them to stay there. Their rooms had been booked months earlier, they explained, before anyone in the United States had even heard of the Fab Four.

The following August, the Beatles stayed at the Delmonico. Their exact location was supposed to be kept secret, but when they arrived in the wee hours of the morning, hundreds of fans already stood waiting for them on Park Avenue and Fifty-Ninth Street. Soon after daybreak, thousands more teenagers joined them. Penned behind police barricades, they listened to radio updates about the Beatles, tried to slip past security, and screamed insanely whenever anyone inside the hotel so much as passed by a window. Finally, the chief of police asked the Beatles to stay well inside their hotel rooms and keep the lights down. Nevertheless, some Beatlemaniacs stayed outside hollering until 4:00 in the morning.

A year later, they made their third visit to New York, spending four nights at the Warwick Hotel, where they had rented the entire thirty-third floor. If anything, the situation there was even worse. "The mop-haired singers were the cause of considerable exasperation among more than 100 policemen, who spent the day trying to hold in check about 1,500 adolescent adorers," said the *New York Times*. Police erected barriers on the nearby streets, and to get within about a half mile of the hotel, you had to either prove that you were a guest there or explain that you had business visiting a nearby building. The Beatles were dazzled by Manhattan, and they ached to see more of it, but they could not leave their rooms the entire time they were there, except for two important engagements.

They were in town, first, to record their third (and final) appearance on *The Ed Sullivan Show*. They headed over to CBS Studio 50 at about 11:00 a.m., and they spent the whole day there, rehearsing just six songs. They made their final taping at 8:30, and except for when Lennon seemed to stumble briefly over one of the lyrics in "Help," their performance was masterful.

The following day, the Beatles headed to Shea Stadium, in Flushing, Queens, for their historic performance there. At the time, it was by far the largest concert in history: 55,600 people attended. "We spent weeks drawing up plans, as if they were battle plans, trying to ensure the Beatles' safety," said promoter Sid Bernstein. First, a limousine whisked the Beatles away from their hotel. Since city officials had completely shut down the major streets along their route, their limo barreled through every intersection and stoplight in its path. Upon reaching the Pan Am building, about a mile away, they ascended to the rooftop and boarded a waiting Boeing Vertol 107-II—a large, dual-propeller helicopter. The chopper's pilot treated the Beatles to a brief aerial tour of the city (which the Beatles did not particularly want) and then veered toward Shea. When the chopper lulled briefly over the parking lot, a disc jockey seized the stadium's PA system: "You hear that up there? Listen . . . *it's the Beatles!* They're *here!*" So many flashbulbs went off simultaneously that the Beatles' chopper appeared bathed in the incandescent wash.

The Beatles landed at a nearby heliport and then clambered into a Wells Fargo armored van that sped them the final distance into the stadium. When Ed Sullivan called them to the stage, the roar at Shea had never been louder. Thousands of teenagers screamed, swooned, fainted, sobbed, and watched in rapturous agony as the Beatles trotted onto the field, smiling and waving. It remains one of the most breathtaking scenes in pop music history.

Taking all of this in from the opposing team's dugout were four special guests: Mick Jagger and Keith Richards, along with the Stones' manager, Andrew Oldham, and journalist Chris Hutchins, who covered the show for *NME*. All of them were amazed by the frenzy the Beatles created.

"It's frightening," Jagger said.

"It's deafening," Richards replied.

"Without a doubt," Hutchins wrote, "it was the greatest, most awe-inspiring night any of us had ever witnessed."

Earlier that day, however, Jagger had stressed that he did not desire the Beatles' unprecedented popular success for himself. "I don't envy those Beatles," he remarked. He made the statement while lounging around in the Hudson River basin on a luxury yacht named *Princess*, which belonged to Allen Klein, the American music executive who was soon to become the Stones' manager. "Look how much freedom we have, and they're locked up in their hotel bedrooms without being able to take a car ride, let alone do something like this."

It was true: the Beatles felt trapped, besieged, stressed out, and exhausted. They were also often quite terrified by the bedlam that went on around them. They worried about creating a scandal, a riot, an accident, or being assassinated. And when they weren't anxious, they were frequently bored. Sure, a show like Shea could be thrilling—it *was* thrilling!—and yet shortly after it was over, the Beatles were sequestered yet again in their hotel rooms. The whole next day had been left "open" on their schedule (a rare thing), but they could barely afford to crack a window. And so they just sat around, smoking weed and watching television. True, they must have enjoyed the company of some of their visitors, including the Ronettes and Bob Dylan. But Mary Wilson, of the Supremes, remembers that when she showed up along with group mates Diana Ross and Flo Ballard, the Beatles were so surly and unpleasant that they all wanted to leave just as soon as they had arrived.

The rivalry between the Beatles and the Stones, however, was not just about who had the more appealing lifestyle or the greater freedom of movement. It was also increasingly about talent, craft, and influence. And as the Beatles became more creatively ambitious in the mid-1960s, they started functioning a bit like generational pied pipers, inspiring the jealous admiration of their peers as well as legions of imitators.

It's almost enough to make one wonder whether Jagger might have envied the Beatles after all. That was the impression that a journalist on assignment for the American pop magazine *Hullabaloo* arrived at in the summer of 1966. The writer doesn't identify himself by name, but on the eve of the Stones' fifth American tour he got a chance to spend three days with the group. At first, they received him coolly. But on the second day, he at least shared a quick car ride with Jagger as the Stones traveled from their hotel to a press event that they held on a yacht, the SS *Sea Panther*, which was moored up at West Seventy-Ninth Street. En route, they passed an unusual poster advertisement: it was for a car rental company that boasted it was *second* best in the land. Only one other rent-a-car service was ranked higher. Jagger noticed the sign, then turned, unbidden, and said "That's us . . . We have to be better because we're only number two."

It seemed odd, this candid and somewhat forlorn admission. It wasn't really Jagger's personality to say such a thing. So the journalist said he peered back at Mick, looking for a sign that he was joking. But apparently he was not. He seemed "deadly serious."

• • •

Just because British teens regarded the Beatles and the Stones as natural rivals, it was never foreordained—or even likely—that Americans would do the same. Until the Beatles came onto the scene, British popular culture had not made much of an impact in the US. Also, the two nations had such different media environments. The British had long loved their tacky tabloid newspapers, and popular newssheets like the *Daily Mirror* and the *Daily Sketch*, which expressed fanatical reverence for the Beatles, were usually harshly critical of the Stones. Meanwhile, England had a robust music press, which was likewise lacking in the US. Weekly papers such as *Melody Maker* and *NME* teemed with hyperbolic headlines proclaiming who was up one week, who was down the next, and who beat whom in the latest readers' poll.

Those sorts of updates could be thrilling to fans, but they also yielded the distorting impression that a rough parity existed between the two groups. In fact, the Beatles always outsold the Stones by a huge margin. In 2005, Mick Jagger recalled an episode, probably in 1964, "when we were all hanging out at one of the clubs. George was giving me a big spiel about how many records the Beatles had sold more than us. Which wasn't in dispute! He was so anxious to make the point."

Many American reporters, however, may not have known any better. Most of them were well educated, professionally trained, and (they liked to think) "sophisticated." They practiced a bland and cautious style of journalism, and in some context that standpoint served them well, but it left them almost entirely unequipped to cover the latest youth culture fads. As a result, they tended to parrot what they heard from England: the Beatles and the Stones were "rival bands." In May 1964, a London-based public relations firm spoon-fed the storyline to US reporters. "Stones Set to Invade," their press release read. "In the tracks of the Beatles, a second wave of sheepdog-looking, angry-acting, guitar-playing Britons is on the way. . . . Of the Rolling Stones, one detractor has said: 'They are dirtier, streakier and more disheveled than the Beatles, and in some places, they are more popular than the Beatles.' "

It is little wonder, then, that questions about the Beatles nearly dominated the Stones' first American press conferences. Asked if he would consider joining a "Stamp Out the Beatles" club, Keith Richards said "no." But when he was asked, "Are you a Beatle fan," he equivocated. "I'm not a fan," he said. "I appreciate some of their stuff. I like them; I think they're good." When Charlie Watts was asked the same question, he likewise failed to give a direct answer: "I met Ringo when he came back from here, very tired. Er, yeah, you know, I think they're very talented fellas. Lennon and McCartney, yeah. I am a Beatles fan, if you can call it that."

The most persistent line of questioning about the Beatles, however, was directed at Jagger.

REPORTER: How do you compare your group with the Beatles?

MICK [smoking, smiling, and mugging for the camera]: I don't know, how do *you* compare it the Beatles? I don't compare it at all. You know, there's no point.

REPORTER: Well, let's get right down to brass tacks. Do you think you're better than they are?

MICK: At what? You know, it's not the same group, so we just do what we want and they do what they want, and there's no point in going on *comparing* us. You can prefer us to them or them to us. This is diplomatic, you see!

REPORTER: Very diplomatic, and I don't want to belabor it, but do you feel that *you* do what *you* want to do better than *they* do what *they* want to do?

MICK: Uh . . .

MYSTERIOUS OFF-CAMERA VOICE: Yes.

MICK: Probably, I don't know! I don't know what they want to do, you see? Very diplomatic!

Despite having practically invited questions about the Beatles, the Stones soon began to chafe at them. It's not hard to see why. When the Stones hopped the Atlantic in June 1964, they had been preceded by only a few of their contemporaries: the Beatles, of course, as well as Gerry and the Pacemakers, the Searchers, and (just barely) the Dave Clark Five. All of those acts were rapturously received by teens, and the Stones didn't disguise the fact that they hoped for the same treatment. "Obviously, we hope we are a success, at least as much as the other British groups that have gone to the US," Jones told *The Rolling Stones Book* on the eve of their tour.

At first things looked promising. Thanks to a bit of advance publicity from London Records, about five hundred enthusiastic fans turned out to greet the Stones at the airport. Afterwards, the Stones did a press conference, posed for photos and (though they were on a tight budget) ostentatiously rode away in a great convoy of limousines—one car for each member. Later that night, they appeared on *Murray the K's Swinging Soiree*, hosted by Murray Kaufman, the "happening" WINS-AM disc jockey that the Stones had recently met in London through the Beatles. Kaufman says that shortly after they were introduced, the Stones asked if he would promote them in America as ardently and successfully as he had Beatles.

Problem was, at the time of their arrival, there was only so much Murray the K *could* do for the Stones. Despite their popularity in England, the sallow-cheeked quintet didn't yet have a hit song in the US. ("Not Fade Away" was only at number 88 on a popular chart.) The Stones had only just released their debut album (subtitled in America: *England's Newest Hit Makers*). It featured a moody, beatnik-inspired cover photo (not all that different from the one the Beatles had just used on their second album), and it was a very good first record. Nothing else on the market resembled what the Stones were doing. But Capitol Records had spent $40,000 promoting the Beatles before they came to America, and the Stones did not get anywhere near that support. It's not as if the Stones had a fleet of antic deejays saying, "It's 6:30 a.m. Rolling Stones time! They've just left London. They're flying over the Atlantic Ocean. It's currently 49 Rolling Stones degrees," and so on.

Nevertheless, the Stones figured that if Murray the K was good enough for the Beatles, he was good enough for them as well. The Stones smiled wanly as he went through his loony routine: "Whadja think of the Beatles, guys—are you pals or rivals?" "How long since you had a haircut? Just kiddin', Murray luuuuvvves you." "I can assure my listeners they are clean, the Stones are clean. They do wash—don't you, guys?"

("Oh, just play the fuckin' record and announce the concert date so we can piss off," Oldham remembers thinking.)

The next night, the Stones got another inkling of what they were in for in America when they made their first television appearance, on the locally broadcast *Les Crane Show*. It was a Wednesday and the program didn't air until 1:00 a.m., when most of the Stones' target audience was no doubt asleep. Furthermore, Crane did not "get" the Stones, not even remotely. He was pugnacious and (worse) phony. Instead of asking the Stones about their music, he pestered them with inane questions about their reputation and appearance. Oldham silently fumed. "What a dolt! Didn't he know that this kind of banter was reserved for Mop Tops and Herman's Hermits?" Oldham also remembered being surprised as it began dawning on him that the Stones all felt rather vulnerable in the US. Perhaps their collective hide was not as thick as they had thought.

The next morning they awoke early to catch a transcontinental flight in order to perform on ABC's *Hollywood Palace*, a televised variety program that struck them as awfully square. Unlike its competitor, *The Ed Sullivan Show*, this program relied on various guest hosts, and when the Stones were on the master of ceremonies was the legendary Rat Packer Dean Martin. He wasn't exactly a fuddy-duddy, but you only had to notice Brylcreemed hair, tuxedo, and Vegas-style shtick to know that he wasn't likely to "get" the Stones either. The Stones were further deflated when they learned that the other acts that night included a group of singing bouffanted Mormons called the King Sisters, plus some performing elephants and a trampoline artist. To this day it's not clear whether Dino was tipsy when he hosted the show, or just pretending to be half in the bag, but some of the jibes to which he subjected the Stones were not friendly.

"And nowwww," he said, with mock apprehension, "something for the youngsters: five singin' boys from England who've sold a lot of al-bee-ums, er, albums! They're called the Rolling Stones. I've been rolled while I was stoned myself, so . . . I don't know what they're singing about, but here they are *at*."

The Stones performed "I Just Want to Make Love to You," the randy Willie Dixon cover from their first album. To most white Americans back then (and certainly to the network's censors) the idea of "making love" had a different connotation than it does now. When Frank Sinatra sang "Mind If I Make Love to You?" to Grace Kelly in the 1956 film *High Society*, he was gallantly asking for permission to try to *woo* a woman, not necessarily to take her to bed. The Rolling Stones, it is safe to say, had a different idea. They played the song with gusto, but ABC wound up airing only about a minute of it. Then as soon as they were finished, Dino started heckling them.

"The Rolling Stones, aren't they great?" he said, with a big sarcastic roll of the eyes.

"You know something about these singing groups today?" he continued. "You're under the impression they have long hair. *Nah!* Not true at all! It's an optical illusion. They just have low foreheads and high eyebrows.

"They're going to leave right after the show for London. They're challenging the Beatles to a hair-pulling contest."

Then when Martin introduced the trampolinist, he said this: "That's the father of the Rolling Stones; he's been trying to kill himself ever since."

Back home, the Stones didn't mind if they upset narrow-minded prudes or dowdy old authorities. At least that meant they were being taken seriously. But they did not expect to be mocked and jeered during their American network television debut, to actually be laughed at, as if they were "some dumb circus act" (as Richards put it).

It also turned out that their tour had not been well planned. Co-manager Eric Easton was responsible for arranging the Stones' appearances, and the North American bookings agency he relied upon, GAC (General Artists Corporation), had done a terrible disservice to the Stones. In many cases, they arranged for the band to play at large auditoriums alongside a bunch of other acts that were obviously geared toward families, not plugged-in teens. The Stones were humiliated to be a part of these stupid variety bills. Making matters even worse, they now realized they had far too many days off in their schedule, and they found themselves in a foreboding mood. When they all fell into some petty squabbling and mickey taking, that only made things worse.

Their attitude briefly improved after their first public performance, at San Bernardino's Swing Auditorium. Several thousand youths from across the Inland Empire turned out to catch their first glimpse of the Stones, and somehow they knew the words to all the songs. The Stones beamed at the realization that they had a minor cult following around LA, and when some of the girls tried to climb on the stage, or when they threw stuff at the band—jelly babies, autograph books, mash notes, or whatever—they made it feel a bit like home. At the same time, many of differences between Southern California and London were pleasing to the Stones; they loved the sunny weather, the palm trees, the big muscle cars, and the whole beach mystique.

The next day, however, the Stones got a different kind of culture shock when they arrived in Texas. They had just had their first glimpse of America's most enticing cities, New York and Los Angeles, but now they'd been sent to San Antonio. Oldham called it a "sawdust fiasco." They were there to play at an outdoor fair where the main attraction was a rodeo, and they literally shared a bill with a bunch of performing monkeys. The Stones did two sets, one in the afternoon and another in the evening, and they were probably two of the most unsettling gigs in their entire career next to Altamont. Some in the audience sniggered and scoffed; others weren't sure whether to take the Stones seriously or regard them as a comedy act. A few of the tough, beer-swilling cowboys in the audience fixed the Stones with flinty stares and made them feel afraid. It was a different order of hostility than they were accustomed to. "In America then, if you had long hair, you were a faggot as well as a freak," Richards said. "They would shout across the street, 'Hey, fairies.' "

Next up for the Stones was 2120 South Michigan Avenue—the home to Chess Records, in Chicago. Richards would later tell a story about how he walked into the building, came down a corridor, and encountered a slightly paunchy, middle-aged black man wearing speckled overalls and standing on a foot ladder: it was his all-time hero, McKinley "Muddy Waters" Morganfield. "I get to meet The Man—he's my fucking god—and he's out of work," Richards marveled. "That throws you a curve, 'ere's the king of the blues painting a wall."

It was Richards's way of admitting that his own good fortune was thick with irony. In the '50s and '60s, derivative white rock 'n' rollers had such better professional opportunities than African American originators. It was a horribly unfair situation, and it was decent of Richards to acknowledge it. But the business about Muddy painting the interior of Chess Records never happened. If it had, the Stones surely would have mentioned it at the time. Richards seems not to have made the claim, however, until 1989: six years after Muddy had passed away. Besides, no one who worked at Chess could imagine such a scenario. Muddy Waters grew to have such a regal bearing that many people who knew him for years can't recall ever seeing him in anything other than a custom-made suit, a silk shirt, and cufflinks.

Still, it was thrilling to spend two days working in the legendary studio where Muddy Waters recorded "I'm Your Hoochie Coochie Man," and Howlin' Wolf made "Moanin' at Midnight"—the edifice of rock 'n' roll. In addition to reveling in the atmosphere, the Stones were wowed by the studio's technicians, who were so much more adept than their British counterparts. During their first session, Willie Dixon turned up and tried to hustle some of his songs. Buddy Guy came around, too, curious to know what a bunch of skinny young Brits were doing in such a tough neighborhood. The next day Muddy came by (this was the origin of the painting myth). So too did Chuck Berry, who—though he was not a friendly man—nevertheless peeked his head into the studio to say, "Swing on, gentlemen!"

And why shouldn't he have been encouraging? The Stones impressed these blues and R&B pioneers. They dug the band's vibrant, earthy sound, and if they were feeling magnanimous, they might also have been gratified to see these five white kids from England expressing such fanatical reverence for what was once marginalized as "race music." Besides, people like Chuck Berry and Willie Dixon stood to make a good bit of money from the Stones.

The various highs on their US sojourn, however, were balanced out by low moments. An interview with a Chicago radio personality,

Jack Eigen, proved reminiscent of the Dean Martin debacle. Irritated by the host's pesky questions, the Stones were less than loquacious, and after they left the studio, Eigen took revenge by implying that they all had lice. A hastily organized show in Minneapolis produced a crowd of only about four hundred. Before another show, Keith says he stared down the barrel of a revolver for the first time: a macho cop had pulled it out after he'd refused to tip out the contents of his plastic cup while in a public area. Another night they played the Detroit Olympia ("The Old Red Barn"), the beloved home of the Red Wings hockey team. That would have been a huge thrill if the stadium had been full, but only about a thousand people showed up—less than 10 percent of its capacity.

No wonder the Stones were so relieved to get back to New York City. Their final two shows, on June 20, 1964, had a different flavor than most of the others. First, they were held at Carnegie Hall, arguably the world's most prestigious music venue. That was no coincidence: the Beatles made headlines when they played there too, on their first American tour. Now just four months later, the controversial Stones were bringing their raucous act to same illustrious stage. Also, those last two shows on tour were barnburners. Fans surged up front and jammed themselves in front of the stage; others stood on their seats, screaming. Taken by surprise, the police first called for reinforcements, and then they made the Stones cut their second set short for fear of a riot. "I've never seen anything quite like this," said Brian. "It's marvelous, but it scares me a bit at the same time."

It was an upbeat ending to a schizophrenic tour. On the one hand, the five Yankophiles all came back with some good stories. While in Texas, Bill reveled in the low-down allure of some authentic juke joints he found, while Charlie and road manager Ian Stewart bought pistols and roamed the countryside looking for rattlesnakes to shoot. Keith got a gun, too, and when he got back to England he told an amazed journalist, "You can buy them as easily as you can buy candy floss." In Detroit, Mick and Brian hung out with boxing manager Jackie Kallen, tooling around Belle Isle in her '64 Mustang convertible and taking turns driving "on the wrong side of the road." They loved soaking in the California sunshine, and they all returned with stacks of new records. That first American tour also saved them from complacency. They had to work to win over their American audiences, and later they agreed that it made them an even sharper band.

And yet when it was all said and done, they were unhappy about how they had fared in America. It didn't help that back home, London tabloids had gleefully kept everyone abreast concerning the indignities the Stones faced. A dispatch filed for the *Daily Mirror* said "Britain's Rolling Stones got 'the bird' when they appeared at a show in San Antonio, Texas, last night." The report went on to explain that although local acts drew cheers and applause, and even the trained monkeys were brought back to the stage for an encore, the Stones "were booed." Sometimes, other men taunted the Stones with wolf-whistles. A girl was quoted asking if they also wore lipstick and carried purses, like transvestites.

Some thought that after their big success at Carnegie, the Stones should have extended their stay in New York. Oldham claimed that was impossible; they had to fly back to Heathrow in order to honor a contract they had made the previous year, when they were only semi-famous, to appear at Magdalen College, Oxford, for a mere £100. And they did do that gig (sullenly). But the more prosaic truth was that they were flat broke. "Oldham could not afford to keep them, or himself, in New York a minute longer."

Even journalist Peter Jones, now the band's official scribe, didn't bother trying to put much of a positive gloss on the tour when he wrote about it for the *Rolling Stones Book*. Instead, he wondered whether the Stones were a good fit for America. It had taken "guts" for the band to crisscross the US before they even had a hit record there, he pointed out, yet the results were mixed. They had done well in New York and Southern California, but elsewhere they elicited derisive, sniggering laughter. About all they could do was use the experience to try to shore up their identity as hip Londoners. The Stones were "not interested in the funny faces, red noses and all the guff that goes with the ordinary variety," Jones said. "But one thing will always be true. The Stones are *our* boys, *our* group. Essentially British—and thoroughly loved by hundreds of thousands who accept them for what they are."

• • •

It would only be about a year before "(I Can't Get No) Satisfaction" would become an international juggernaut, at which point the Stones began enjoying the success that at first eluded them in America. Ironically, during the same period that the Stones were fast rising, the Beatles began experiencing the downside to being so popular.

Recent findings in social psychology can help us understand how a group of young men with such stupendous good fortune as the Beatles could nevertheless be miserable a lot of the time. Part of the problem was that, like most humans, they weren't very good at predicting what would make them happy in the first place. Surely they were euphoric when their career started taking off. (Joan Baez tells a charming story about meeting the Beatles relatively early in their career. "They had discovered that the Coke machine in their sitting room in the hotel was *free*. They were thrilled!") Naturally, every time they reached a new milestone—when they first heard themselves on the radio, when they had the first number one hit, when they played *Sunday Night at the Palladium*, and so on—they beamed with justified pride.

It was not long, however, before Beatlemania became the omnipresent, all-consuming force in their lives. They lived it every day, and so it started to seem almost normal, at which point they went back to experiencing the world within the same baseline levels of satisfaction and dissatisfaction they had always been accustomed to. It's a well-known phenomenon.

Additionally, the Beatles were now burdened with such tremendous pressure. Everyone wanted or expected something from them—

an interview, an autograph, a photo, a chance to be seen with them or to bend their ear. Music industry bigwigs were always clamoring for a new record, a new film, another tour—and their schedule hardly ever let up. From about June 1962 until August 1966, they only had one extended vacation. "Everybody saw the *effect* of the Beatles, but nobody really ever worried about us as individuals, or thought, 'I wonder how the boys are coping with it all?' " George Harrison later lamented. "It was a very one-sided love affair. The people gave their money and they gave their screams, but the Beatles gave their nervous systems, which is a much more difficult thing to give."

The touring hassles the Beatles faced are well known. Their most agonizing stretch came in the summer of 1966. In July, while in Manila, the Beatles politely declined an invitation to a ritzy reception that the president's wife, Imelda Marcos, had arranged to be held in their honor at the presidential palace. Had they better understood the political culture there, they would not have made such a foolish mistake. Marcos took revenge first by withdrawing security protection for the group, and then by having her gun-toting security goons intimidate and rough up the Beatles. Officials confiscated the Beatles' earnings from their two concerts there (attended by 80,000), and when the group finally got out of Manila, they felt as if they were fleeing for the lives.

Later that month, Lennon's infamous remark that the Beatles were "more popular than Jesus" provoked the wrath of religious zealots in the American South. When the quotation first appeared in a London newspaper in March 1966, Englanders scarcely seemed to notice. But when it was reprinted in the American teen magazine *Datebook*, it led to a frenzy of recriminations. Radio stations sponsored the mass burning of Beatles records, the Ku Klux Klan organized anti-Beatles protests, and death threats poured in to the Beatles' London headquarters. The group was nearly forced to cancel its tour at the tune of $1 million. At a show in Memphis, someone chucked a lit firecracker onto the stage, which the Beatles momentarily mistook for a gunshot.

Others threw debris and rotten fruit that splattered on the stage at their feet.

Another cause of worry, less often mentioned, was the threat that bad weather posed when they were scheduled to perform outdoors. After the Memphis disaster, the Beatles were meant to play in Cincinnati, but a heavy downpour earlier in the day had made it risky; the stage was still so soaking wet that the Beatles could have been electrocuted. Yet they feared that if they did not play, a riot might break out. They ended up postponing the gig until early the next afternoon. Then just as soon as they were done, they packed up their gear and flew 350 miles to St. Louis, where they encountered still more rain. This time, the group soldiered on and played beneath a flimsy tarpaulin. "After the gig, I remember us getting into a big, empty, steel-lined wagon, like a removal van," McCartney said. "There was no furniture in there—nothing. We were sliding around trying to hold onto something, and at that moment everyone said 'Oh, this bloody touring lark—I've had it up to here, man.'

"I finally agreed. I'd been trying to say, 'Ah, touring's good and it keeps us sharp. We need touring, and musicians need to play. Keep music live.' I had held on to that attitude when there were doubts, but finally I agreed with them."

When the Beatles played San Francisco's Candlestick Park on August 29, 1966, no one knew for sure that that would be their last-ever regular concert. But the Beatles surmised as much. McCartney asked press officer Tony Barrow to record the show for posterity, and in between songs, the Beatles took pictures of themselves with time-set cameras that they'd placed on their amplifiers. Flying out of town to Los Angeles, en route to London, Harrison told the others, "That's it. I'm no longer a Beatle."

In the ensuing years, whenever they were asked why they gave up touring, the Beatles usually gave the same answer: it was too stressful. The implication has always been that if going on the road had not become such an excruciating, moiling farce, they would have liked to continue. To get an idea of how seriously they took their craft, you need only to see a short clip from the *Beatles at Shea Stadium*, which shows Paul and George backstage before the big show, warming up their fingers with fretboard exercises, just like any professional musician would. But to what end? They knew going in that the audience's high-decibel screaming was going to overwhelm their every note.

At the same time that touring was becoming nearly unbearable, the Beatles were increasingly finding satisfaction in Abbey Road Studios. For roughly the first three years of the Beatles' recording career, producer George Martin said he felt a bit like a teacher with his pupils. The Beatles did whatever he asked of them, not because he was particularly officious, but because that's just how things were done back then. Besides, the Beatles didn't know anything about recording. Meanwhile, Martin did not attempt to make a big creative imprint upon their work. "They were four musicians—three guitarists and a drummer—and my role was to make sure they made a concise, commercial statement," he explained. "I would make sure that the song ran for approximately two and a half minutes, that it was in the right key for their voices, and that it was tidy, with the right proportion and form." He did a terrific job, but many other salaried producers probably could have gotten a comparable result.

The relationship between the Beatles and Martin began changing, however, in the mid-1960s. Several of the tracks on *Help!* exemplified the group's new audacity, and Paul McCartney's most famous song, "Yesterday," was clearly a bellwether. Paul said that one morning when he was just twenty-two years old, he awoke with the melody playing in his head. Still foggy from his previous night's sleep, he sat down and worked out the chords on a nearby piano. It sounded lovely, perhaps even flawless, but for a long time he was reticent to do anything with it for fear that he'd subconsciously lifted it from somewhere else. Then when he finally decided otherwise and recorded it, in June 1965, he had a new concern: it didn't sound like a Beatles song. There was nothing for the rest of the group to do. As Paul strummed it on his guitar, however, it also seemed a bit spare.

Martin suggested they add a string quartet. That wasn't quite a novel idea (a few other pop songs had featured strings), but it was still a daring one. At first, McCartney was leery of the suggestion, for fear that it might turn out schlocky, but Martin insisted that it could be scored in a restrained and tasteful manner. To further put young Paul at ease, Martin allowed him to oversee the whole arranging process. "[Paul] would say, 'Can we have cello doing this bit?' And I'd say 'Sure, why not?' or 'No, that's out of their range.' . . . So it was kind of a collaborative experience." Paul was also in the studio when the overdub was recorded and mixed into mono. Later on the rest of the group heard it, and they all agreed it sounded fabulous.

As the Beatles began experimenting with newer and more sophisticated aesthetics, Martin's role was, on the one hand, greatly enhanced. His arranging work, technical knowhow, and salutary advice deeply impacted some of the Beatles' finest songs. In another sense, however, Martin's role was diminished by the group's evolving artistry. Soon they began telling him what *they* wanted their songs to sound like—as when Paul recorded "Yesterday"—and he would oblige. Fortunately, the new dynamic didn't pose many problems. "As I could see their talent growing, I could recognize that an idea coming from them was better than an idea coming from me," Martin generously allowed. "In a sense, I made a sort of tactical withdrawal, recognizing that theirs was the greater talent."

A few months later, the Beatles regrouped at Abbey Road to record *Rubber Soul*, their so-called transitional album. Critics said it was thematically richer and more sonically adventurous than anything the Beatles had yet attempted, and John and Paul agreed. "You don't know us if you don't know *Rubber Soul*," Lennon told a young interviewer shortly after the album was released. "All our ideas are different now." Paul echoed his partner: "If someone saw a picture of you taken two years ago and [they] said that was you, you'd say it was a load of rubbish and show them a new picture. That's how we feel about the early stuff [compared to] *Rubber Soul*. . . . People have always wanted us to stay the same, but we can't stay in a rut. No one else expects to hit a peak at 23 and never develop, so why should we? *Rubber Soul* for me is the beginning of my adult life."

The title of the album was a punny and playful corruption of a term that they had heard from a skeptical African American musician who disparaged the Rolling Stones by saying they played "plastic soul"—by which he meant, he thought the Stones were just okay. Interesting, perhaps, but limited: a cheap knockoff of the real thing. Now the Beatles may have been trying to show how it was possible to appreciate Memphis soul, and incorporate elements of it into their work, without ever being called spurious.

In fact, the riff that propelled the very first song on the record, "Drive My Car," was probably inspired by Otis Redding's hit "Respect." But the song also showed a glimpse of the Beatles' new lyrical sophistication. Previously, John and Paul had almost always referred to women from a male narrator's perspective. What's more, their focus was on how *she* made *him* feel (and it was never that complicated: she made him feel happy or sad). In "Drive My Car," the agency belongs to a woman. Right off the bat, she announces that she wants to become famous, "a star of the screen." More immediately, though, she wants to get laid. (Presumably, she's not offering someone a job as chauffeur.) She is also a modern woman, a bohemian, unlikely to be seduced by the clichés that were mainstays of the earliest Beatles songs. We know that because she stresses that her sexual invitation stands independent of the possibility of real romance ("and *maybe* I'll love you," she says). No doubt many misheard that crucial lyric, and the reason they discerned Paul to be singing "and *baby* I'll love you" is because they were so steeped in the platitudinous idealizations of boy-girl relationships that dominated the mid-'60s pop universe. Now the

Beatles were moving in the opposite direction. "Drive My Car" isn't terribly poetic or profound, but it is subversive.

The next song on the record, "Norwegian Wood (This Bird Has Flown)," offers more tantalizing possibilities for interpretation. Lennon was the song's primary author, and he later admitted it was about an affair he'd had, done in an intentionally elliptical (he said "gobbledegook") style in order to spare his wife's feelings. The story in the song begins with the narrator coming over to a woman's flat. He "sits on her rug," bides his time, drinks her wine, and soaks in the décor: the cozy wood-paneled walls. He expects that soon they'll make love, but then comes a surprise: she brushes him off. When the narrator realizes they won't be having sex (she says she has to work in the morning), he disappointedly crawls off to sleep in the bathtub. When he awakes, she's gone. What happens next is not entirely clear, but in one plausible reading, he takes his revenge by setting her apartment on fire.

In another interpretation that Beatles fans have bruited about, however, the song describes a successful late-night hook-up. In this view, the outcome was never really in doubt, because the narrator was an obvious prize. ("I once had a girl, or should I say, she once had me?") Lennon was famous for his impish wordplay, and the phrase "Norwegian wood" sounds a lot like "knowing she would," as in, "Isn't it good, knowing she would [put out]?" In the last verse, when the guy says "I lit a fire," he might have been referring to a cigarette (smoked with smug satisfaction, James Bond style?) or a joint (Lennon once called *Rubber Soul* "the pot album"). Some believe the song disguised an encounter that Lennon had had with Maureen Cleave, the journalist; more likely it was about Sonny Freeman, a German-born model who was married to the Beatles' favorite photographer. In any case, fans were left to wonder: what is it about, *really*? It's a question the Beatles would continue to put to their listeners throughout the rest of the decade.

Mature and autobiographical themes abound on *Rubber Soul.* Lennon also channels desperate romantic obsession ("Girl"), writes touchingly about his past ("In My Life"), and turns his gaze inward (on "Nowhere Man," which reflected his stoned isolation in his Weybridge mansion). The group presages the counterculture's celebration of "love" as a universal principle ("The Word"), while McCartney parodies French cabaret music ("Michelle") and chronicles his relationship troubles with Jane Asher ("I'm Looking Through You" and "You Won't See Me"). The Beatles also demonstrated their growing eclecticism on *Rubber Soul.* "Norwegian Wood" was the first pop song to make use of a sitar, the 800-year-old plucked string instrument that George Harrison had lately become intrigued with. The guitars at the end of "Girl" sound like Greek bouzoukis. On "In My Life," George Martin contributed a baroque piano solo that he played on a keyboard at half-speed, then sped-up on playback, in order to create a quivery harpsichord effect.

The Beatles were not alone, of course, in pushing back the lyrical frontiers of pop music or experimenting with exotic sounds. The entire group admired and perhaps were even a bit intimidated by Bob Dylan, whose influence on Lennon was obvious. They had heard the Indian flavorings in hits by the Yardbirds ("Heart Full of Soul") and the Kinks ("See My Friends"), and Harrison in particular was intrigued by the Byrds' big jangle pop sound ("The Bells of Rhymney"). They saw the Animals capture the pathos of teenage life in a fuller way than most pop artists had attempted ("We Gotta Get Out of This Place"), and they observed the Beach Boys moving away from formulaic surf ditties in order to explore slightly subtler soundscapes ("California Girls"). Nevertheless, when the Beatles ceased trying to be "cute"—that is, when they started conceiving of their albums as vehicles for mature artistic expression, and stopped worrying about how to turn on teenage girls—they had a galvanizing influence on the entire pop scene, and particularly upon the Rolling Stones.

Remember, Mick Jagger and Keith Richards had already concluded that the first proper song they wrote together, "As Tears Go By," *was not fit for the Stones*. They seemed awfully certain about it, too. Richards said that if they had brought that melancholy acoustic ballad to the rest of the band's attention, they'd have been "laughed out of the goddamn room." It would have been "Get out and don't come back." They only wrote it at Oldham's insistence, and according to legend, he had been quite particular about what he wanted. He wanted "a song with brick walls around it, high windows and no sex." It was perfect for Marianne Faithfull, the beautiful ingénue. But it was *not* a Stones number.

Lo and behold, four months after the Beatles released "Yesterday," the Stones came out with "As Tears Go By." Both songs consisted of only a vocalist, a quietly strummed guitar, and a string arrangement. And just as the Beatles had released "Yesterday" as a single in the US (but not in England), the Stones released "As Tears Go By" as a single in the US (but not in England). It was in fact the Stones' "Christmas Disc" in America, and thanks to the heavy rotation it received on easy-listening stations it rose all the way to number six on the *Billboard* pop chart. So why didn't the Stones put it out as an A-side in the UK? "Because we'd have had to go through all that dreadful business here about trying to copy the Beatles' 'Yesterday,'" Jagger moaned to a British journalist.

A few months after the Beatles released *Rubber Soul*, the Stones headed to Hollywood to record most of the songs for their next record, which they planned to call *Could YOU Walk On The Water?* but was released as *Aftermath*. Previously the Stones were known for getting in and out of the studio quickly. Now Oldham wanted everyone to know they were working with Beatle-like intensity. He phoned all the way to London to boast about it to a *Disc* magazine journalist. The Stones had "completely isolated" themselves in the studio, he said. One marathon session had lasted for seventeen straight hours, from 11:00 a.m. until 4:00 a.m. Then the next day they were back at it, doing overdubs. Oldham added that the Stones had hired Phil Spector's brilliant protégé, Jack Nitzsche, to assist with the recording, and he went on to spin a hilarious yarn about how the Stones were using a revolutionary new instrument, a Nitzschephone. "This is actually a child's toy piano, which is projected through two separate amplifiers," Oldham stated. "Jack is able to make it sound like any instrument you like; on some tracks it even sounds like a trombone."

That last outrageous bit of mountebankery was no doubt inspired by the Beatles' growing reputation for studio sophistication, which was reverberating across the English pop landscape. Suddenly everyone was talking about "production values," which the Stones had not heretofore considered. Their goal in the studio had always been to project, as much as possible, the same rough mood and funky sound that they got while playing in the clubs. Now, however, the Stones realized that if they were to stay *au courant*, they would need to showcase some of the originality and subtlety that the rest of the pop world was exemplifying. And some were wondering whether they had it in them.

"Everything in the Rolling Stones' garden is very nice at present," a *Melody Maker* writer observed in January 1966. "But despite their height of appeal, they haven't got the staying power of the Beatles. Because of changes in taste in popular music, the Stones cannot hope for lasting popularity. The very nature of their music precludes drastic change. . . . It is difficult to see or discover which direction they are travelling in. Where do they go from here?"

Aftermath helped to answer that question. Anyone who had doubted the Stones' adaptive potential was left feeling kind of foolish. Front-loaded with some of their best tracks to date, *Aftermath* was the first Stones album to be completely comprised of original material, and when it came out in the spring of 1966, it was impossible not to notice the similarities to *Rubber Soul.* The Beatles had just released their most "mature," adventurous and lyrically sophisticated work to date, and now the now Stones were vying to critically reposition themselves in a similar way.

The moods of the two albums, however, were at odds. Whereas

Rubber Soul is sentimental and mirthful, *Aftermath* is dark and disturbing. Jagger had already shown a capacity for slurring trenchant and socially observant lyrics, but now the Stones were going even further in skewering genteel culture, venting their frustrations, and cultivating their rude, macho swagger. The first song on the British version of the album, "Mother's Little Helper," took up a topic that had not been addressed in pop music before: middle-class drug dependency. "Life's just much too hard" for the delicate, nervous woman in the song, and so she bakes cakes out of a box, cooks frozen TV dinners, and takes her little yellow pills (Valium) four at a time. She gets them from her doctor, though, so it's socially sanctioned. She's obviously in distress, but Jagger addresses her plight without a scintilla of sympathy. When Jagger sings "What a draaag it is getting old," it comes off like a taunt.

On the US version of *Aftermath*, the opening track is "Paint It, Black," which officially made the Stones the world's second pop group, after the Beatles, to use a sitar. Reviewing the album in the *Record-Mirror*, Peter Jones said, "Brian played the sitar like he played rhythm guitar. It probably made George Harrison cringe, but it worked brilliantly." Here again, the Stones veered into unlikely thematic territory. Whereas a great many pop songs had focused on melancholy and lovelorn characters, this might have been the first one in which the narrator is obviously clinically depressed and possibly suicidal. ("It's not easy facing up when your whole world is black," he says. "I want to see the sun blotted out from the sky.") Beyond that, the song lends itself to various interpretations. Some associated it with the wretched feeling that sometimes accompanies an LSD comedown; others linked it to the Vietnam War; still others wondered about the inexplicable comma in the title (was it a racial thing?) and the "red door" in the song (was it the entryway to a brothel?). More likely the song reflects the outlook of a guy whose lover has just unexpectedly died. Asked about its meaning in 1966, Jagger replied with exasperation. "It means paint it black," he said. " 'I Can't Get No Satisfaction' means I can't get no satisfaction. The rest of the song is just expanding on that."

Elsewhere on the record, it becomes almost impossible to distinguish between the singer (Jagger) and the narrator. In "Stupid Girl," Jagger lashes out against his girlfriend, a vain and cynical sourpuss. "She's the sickest thing in this world!" he sings. She grates on his nerves to no end and, to top it off, she isn't even sexually competent (considering "the way she grabs and holds"). "Under My Thumb" is in the same vein. It's a revenge fantasy, a kind of inverted funhouse mirror sequel to Lennon's "Girl." Now Jagger is gleefully in charge of the girl who once had him down. Now she's a "squirmin' dog" who "does just what she's told." Now it's down to him, "the way she talks when she's spoken to." These are undeniably catchy and appealing songs, and yet forty years later, their misogynistic stench still lingers.

Remarkably, the Stones were not immediately stigmatized for the chauvinism on *Aftermath*. (That would come a bit later.) Instead, the record was hailed as an artistic breakthrough, on par with what the Beatles had just done. The *Rolling Stones Book* boasted that *Aftermath* was "doing a *Rubber Soul*," in reference to the fact that contemporary artists were quick to cover a lot of the songs on both records (always a feather in a songwriter's cap). Just as Lennon and McCartney had crowed about how *Rubber Soul* showed their band moving in a new direction, Jagger called *Aftermath* "a big landmark" and "a real marker" because "it was the first time we wrote the whole record." A *Disc* reviewer opined, "the time has come to elevate the Jagger-Richard[s] songwriting team to the ranks of John and Paul."

None of this seemed to strain the social relationships between the two groups, however. "There must have been a bit of competition because that's only natural, but it was always very friendly," McCartney said later. In fact, the two groups always kept each other abreast of what they were doing in order to ensure that, as much as possible, their record sales would not be diminished by direct competition. It was "very cannily worked out," Richards said, "because in those days singles were coming out every six, eight weeks. And we'd try to time it so that we didn't clash. I remember John Lennon calling me up and saying, 'Well, we've not finished mixing yet.' 'We've got one ready to go.' 'OK, you go first.' "

The two groups seemed to hang out together the most in two separate eras. The first was in early 1963, shortly after they met, when the Beatles were still getting acquainted with London and the Stones were just kicking off their professional career. The second period began after the Beatles stopped touring in 1966, and extended until late 1967, when Swinging London was in its twilight phase. "That was a great period," Lennon said. "We were like the kings of the jungle then, and we were very close to the Stones." They would tool around behind tinted windows and linger in the expensive darkness at clubs like the Ad Lib, the Scotch of St. James, and Bag o' Nails. "We were at the peak of our careers," McCartney said. "We were young, we were looking pretty good and we had all this power and the fame and everything so it was difficult to resist playing with it."

The Beatles and the Stones also sometimes tried to defuse tabloid news stories about their supposed rivalry. One night in 1965, for instance, Chrissie Shrimpton got into an altercation with some young teens who were staking out Ringo Starr's home in Bryanston Mews East, which happened to be just around the corner from Mick's flat. "Chrissie was knocking the Beatles and I won't let anyone get away with that," one fifteen-year-old girl alleged. Jagger admitted that he wound up kicking the stupid girl squarely in her bottom (although he was wearing plimsolls, he said, so she "didn't get hurt much"). He denied, however, that the kerfuffle had anything to do with the Beatles. "She was laying into my girl and using filthy language," he said. "They were not Beatles' fans. Some papers are still trying to whip up a Stones-versus-Beatles war which does not exist."

The groups also stayed mum to the press about a blazing row that took place between their managers, Epstein and Oldham, at a *NME* annual poll winners' concert at the Empire Pool (now Wembley Arena) in the spring of 1966. *NME* called it "The Line-Up of the Century" because it featured the Beatles and the Stones in the same show, along with the Who, the Yardbirds, the Small Faces, Roy Orbison, and a bunch of tertiary acts, all playing short sets before a lucky audience of about ten thousand.

Everyone expected the Beatles to close the show, but that raised a concern. If the Beatles were the very last act on the roster, a throng of fans might be tempted to rush toward that backstage exit as they were finishing up, in which case the group would be trapped in the arena. It was a scenario they definitely wanted to avoid. Derek Johnson, a longstanding *NME* editor, remembers that about a week before the concert, a stinky-looking bum came tottering into his office; it was Lennon, dressed down in disguise, and eager to talk about the upcoming show. The two men apparently struck an unusual agreement: the Beatles would *not* be the poll winners' concert headliners.

Around the same time, however, *NME*'s founder Maurice Kinn received an unexpected phone call from Andrew Oldham. The Stones had earlier declined an invitation to play, but now Oldham said they were up for it. They didn't even desire to be paid. Oldham had just one important stipulation on behalf of his group, however: the Stones would not go on immediately before the Beatles. That wouldn't look right. They didn't want to cement their status as England's second biggest group, or appear before their fans as if they were the Fab Four's warm-up act. Mr. Kinn happily agreed to the arrangement, and he put his commitment down in writing. (At the time, he may not have been aware of the agreement that Lennon made with Johnson.)

The concert was held on May 1, and when the Stones strode onto the stage, the place just went wild. They played "The Last Time," "Play with Fire," and "Satisfaction." The audience's screams "thundered on" throughout the short set, said one concert reviewer, growing "louder and louder until suddenly it was over."

According to the schedule, after the Stones were done performing, *NME* was to hand out everyone's awards, and then the Beatles would play four songs. When the Stones were about halfway through their set, however, the Beatles had turned up at the bottom of the stage, carrying their guitars. Lennon announced that they were going on next.

"I said to Lennon, 'John, you're much too early,'" Kinn remembered. "'The Stones have got another ten minutes, then it's the awards. Go away, you're not on for another thirty minutes.'" But Lennon insisted the Beatles would play next. "I said they couldn't and John shouted, 'Didn't you hear me the first time? We're going on now or we're not going on at all.'"

Epstein and Kinn huddled up and frantically laid out their dilemmas to one another. Epstein proclaimed that he was powerless: Lennon was insisting the Beatles go on immediately after the Stones, and that was that. The Beatles would play next, or they would not play at all. Kinn answered that in addition to being honor-bound to Oldham, he was legally required not to let the Beatles stride onto the stage right immediately after the Stones.

"I took my life into my hands," Kinn recalled, "and said to Brian:

> *"'Let me tell you the position. The Beatles are not going on next. I'm going to tell [compère] Jimmy Saville to tell the audience the Beatles are here but they refuse to appear. There will be a riot, this place will be smashed up, and not only will you, Brian, be responsible for the thousands of pounds worth of damage, but you'll be sued by* NME *for the irreparable harm you've done to the reputation of my paper.' Epstein gave me a bawling out: 'We'll never appear here again as long as we live. You can't do this to us.' I said, 'I don't care if it's the King and Jesus Christ together. I can't change it. I gave it in writing to Andrew. That's it.'"*

According to Kinn, after Epstein explained the situation to Lennon, "John absolutely exploded! He gave me abuse like you've never heard before in all your life. You could hear him all over the backstage area. He said, 'We'll never play for you again.'"

And they did not. The Beatles played just four songs—"I Feel

Fine," "Nowhere Man," "If I Needed Someone," and "I'm Down"—and that turned out to be the Beatles' last regularly scheduled performance in the UK. (Their fee was a token £70.) Remarkably, the whole contretemps was kept hush-hush for so long. The tabloids might have loved the story, but it did not become known until many years later.

Still, the two groups couldn't always stop the press from fueling the rivalry narrative. One day in April 1966 when the Beatles were hard at work, they had their friend and road manager Mal Evans run out and fetch them a copy of the freshly pressed *Aftermath*. That same day, a photographer snapped a photo of John and George in the studio. They were both wearing headphones and sunglasses and holding up Stones records. George hid his face behind the Stones' single "19th Nervous Breakdown," whereas John posed holding *Aftermath* in front of his chest and smiling inscrutably. Probably they meant this as a simple and supportive gesture, as if to say, "These are our friends, check 'em out." But when the photo was published in *16* magazine, the accompanying caption had a sarcastic ring. It reads: "Wait a minute Paulie—George and I are coming up with a couple of really original ideas."

The Beatles did not write the caption, of course. Nevertheless, if the Stones saw it, they might have wondered if they were being mocked for their unoriginality compared to the Beatles.

Just to recap: A little more than two years earlier, the Beatles had put a moody black-and-white photo of themselves on the cover of their second album—a photo that veered sharply from the cartoonish conventions of pop photography. A short while later, the Stones used a similar looking photo of themselves on the sleeve of their debut L.P. Then a few months after the Beatles released "Yesterday," Paul's poignant ballad about lost love that features a string quartet, along came the Stones with "As Tears Go By," a soulful ballad on which Jagger is likewise accompanied by strings. Later that year, the Beatles released *Rubber Soul*, a stylistically diverse album of original material designed to showcase their growing artistic maturity. The following spring, the

The Beatles in Hamburg: Pete Best, George, John, Paul, and Stu Sutcliff. Scholars agree that the Beatles' experience in Hamburg was formative.

Astrid Kirchherr/Ginzburg Fine Arts

At the Cavern Club in Liverpool, Pete Best on drums.

Michael Ochs Archive/Getty Images

Beatles' manager Brian Epstein.

John Rodgers/Getty Images

Giorgio Gomelsky gave the Stones their first big break—a residency at the Crawdaddy Club—and he introduced them to the Beatles.

Jeremy Fletcher/Getty Images

Andrew Loog Oldham, manager of the Rolling Stones. He said he wanted to be known as "a nasty little upstart tycoon shit."

Richard Chowen/Getty Images

Early photo of the Stones. Bill Wyman later said it was "obvious" that Andrew Loog Oldham "was attempting to make us look like the Beatles. From his association with them, he was well aware of the power of marketing, and he was initially slotting us as their natural successors rather than as counterparts." Only later did Oldham begin styling the Stones as the "anti-Beatles."

Michael Ochs/Getty Images

She likes the Beatles. *Max Scheler/Getty Images*

She likes the Stones. *Mirrorpix*

The Beatles elicited complicated responses from their fans. This photo was taken during their appearance at the ABC cinema in Wigan, October 13, 1964. *Mirrorpix*

Mick and Chrissie Shrimpton at the wedding of David Bailey and Catherine Deneuve, August 1965. Chrissie introduced Mick to some important figures in the Swinging London scene. *Mirrorpix*

Daily Mirror

Tuesday, September 8, 1964

Wilson's first Election shot

'TIME FOR DECISION'

Unions get a call to arms—and a strike pledge

LABOUR'S election campaign was opened by Mr. Harold Wilson here today in a speech of great realism and frankness to the Trades Union Congress.

The Labour Leader warned that only by getting the economic machine into top gear could they achieve their hopes of a greater Britain and better housing, pensions, education, health and welfare.

Mr. Harold Wilson drives home a point in his speech to the TUC

The Aga Khan—an apology

IN our issue of Friday, August 28, we published information purporting to have been given by the Aga Khan and to describe the situation which arose when the yacht "Amaloun" with Princess Margaret and her husband on board ran aground off the coast of Sardinia.

The Aga Khan has informed us that he at no time spoke to our reporter, nor did he authorise any statement to be made to our reporter on his behalf.

Telephone

Replies

Opportunity

Ovation

LOAF MAY GO UP A PENNY

Costs

THE STONES BEAT BEATLES IN FAN POLL

Awards

The *Daily Mirror*, September 8, 1964. When the Stones beat the Beatles in a fan poll, it was front-page news. *Mirrorpix*

Keith Richards and Brian Jones in conversation with Paul McCartney at the premier party for the Beatles film *A Hard Day's Night.* *Mirrorpix*

John and Paul frolic in the ocean at Miami Beach while on tour in 1964.
Popperfoto/Getty Images

The Rolling Stones (sans Keith Richards) in New York City during their first visit to the United States. *Stan Mays/Mirrorpix*

Hysterical fans frequently interrupted the Rolling Stones' performances in the mid-'60s. This photo was taken at Newcastle City Hall on October 7, 1965. *NCJ/Mirrorpix*

The Beatles first appearance at Shea Stadium. At the time, it was by far the largest pop concert in history: 55,600 people attended. *New York Daily News/Getty Images*

ohn and George holding up the Stones' re-
ords *Aftermath* and "Nineteenth Nervous
reakdown." When this photo ran in *16* maga-
ne, the caption read: "Wait a minute Paulie—
eorge and I are coming up with a couple of
eally original ideas." *Sean O'Mahony*

Paul scrutinizes the Rolling Stones' album *Aftermath*. *Sean O'Mahony*

Workers on the production line in the EMI factory in Hayes, Middlesex. Fans argued about which group was better, but the Beatles always outsold the Rolling Stones by a wide margin. *Keystone/Getty Images*

The Beatles and their manager arriving in London, July 8, 1966. *Bettmann/CORBIS.*

Producer George Martin and Paul McCartney at Abbey Road Studios recording *Sgt. Pepper's*. "As I could see their talent growing, I could recognize that an idea coming from them was better than an idea coming from me," Martin said. *Sean O'Mahony*

New York City police try to restrain teens near the Warwick Hotel, where the Beatles were staying, August 12, 1966. "I don't envy thos Beatles," Mick Jagger said at the time. "Look how much freedom we have, and they're locked up in their hotel." *Bettmann/CORBIS*

Rare photo of David Snyderman (aka David Jove) and Keith Richards at West Wittering Beach, February 12, 1967. They were both on LSD when this picture was taken. A few hours later, the police would raid Richards's home, and Snyderman/Jove would be accused of being a police plant. *Michael Cooper/Raj Prem Collection*

Mick and Keith leave court after being charged with drug possession after the bust at Redlands. *Bettmann/CORBIS*

May 11, 1967. Brian Jones, haggard and frightened, arrives at court to answer a drugs charge. *Getty Images*

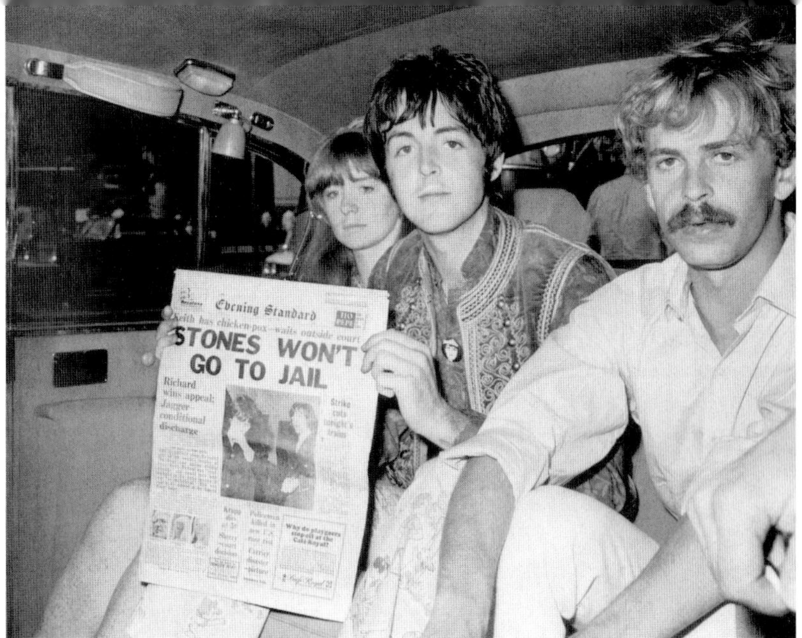

Jane Asher, Paul, and Beatles' assistant "Magic Alex" Mardas arriving in London, July 1967. After a public outcry, Mick and Keith had their drug convictions overturned. *Getty Images*

Mick and Paul prepare to board a train from London to Bangor, Wales, in order to attend a seminar on spiritual enlightenment led by the Maharishi Mahesh Yogi. *Bettmann/CORBIS*

Mick and Marianne Faithful in a carriage, traveling with the Beatles to North Wales, August 25, 1967. *Mirrorpix*

Ringo, George, and John speak briefly with reporters shortly after learning that their manager, Brian Epstein, had died. "Meditation gives you comfort enough to withstand something like this," George said. *Mirrorpix*

Mick at a 1968 antiwar rally outside the US Embassy in Grosvenor Square, London. About fifty people were injured when demonstrators clashed with the police. Mick left the rally after being recognized by too many fans. Afterward, he wrote the lyrics to "Street Fighting Man."

Michael Cooper/Raj Prem Collection

Mick on stage at Madison Square Garden, November 28, 1969. The Omega symbol on the front of Mick's shirt was the symbol of Resistance, an American antidraft group. *Micheal Ochs/Getty Images*

John and Paul at a press conference to announce Apple Corps. "We're in the happy position of not really needing any more money," Paul said, "and so for the first time the bosses aren't in it for the profit." *Elliott Landy/ Getty Images*

The Apple Boutique, 94 Baker Street. According to Paul, the Beatles envisioned this retail store as "a beautiful place where beautiful people can buy beautiful things," but it quickly went out of business. *Redfersn/Getty Images*

On the set of *The Rolling Stones Rock and Roll Circus*. From left to right: John, Yoko, Keith, Mick, Brian, and Bill Wyman. *Mirrorpix*

The Dirty Mac: Eric Clapton, John, Mitch Mitchell (of the Jimi Hendrix Experience), and Keith. They performed two songs for *The Rolling Stones Rock and Roll Circus*. The show was filmed in December 1968, but it wasn't released until 1996.

Getty Images

John and Yoko in a recording studio. The rest of the Beatles hated it when John insisted on bringing Yoko to Abbey Road. Here, they are likely listening to a playback of their debut album together, *Unfinished Music No. 1: Two Virgins.*

Time & Life Pictures/Getty Images

Allen Klein, manager of the Beatles and the Rolling Stones. "Klein is essential in the Great Novel as the Demon King," quipped Derek Taylor, the Beatles' publicist. "Just as you think everything's going to b alright, here he is. I helped bring him to Apple but did give the Beatles certain solemn warnings."

Getty Images

Stones did much the same thing with *Aftermath*. To Lennon, all of this amounted to a clear case of artistic larceny. "Everything we do, the Stones do four months later," he supposedly said.

Of course, the Stones weren't simply mimicking the Beatles. They were in fact highly inventive, and their successful take on American rhythm and blues influenced other bands down the UK scene, like the Pretty Things, the Troggs, and the Downliners Sect, as well as worldwide imitators like the Chocolate Watchband (from San Jose, California) and Los Mockers (from Montevideo, Uruguay). Even after the Stones backpedaled on their blues purism and started fashioning records that were appealing to the pop masses, they still had a rawer and more blues-inflected sound than the Beatles did. Moreover, they often put the unusual instruments they were now fooling around with—sitars, dulcimers, harpsichords, marimbas, bells, and so forth—to better and more innovative use than the Beatles normally did. Finally, the Stones' original compositions in the mid-'60s seemed to grow out of their personal experiences and reflect their increasingly jaded outlook. The same thing could be said about the Beatles, but perhaps not to the same degree. Nevertheless, there is no gainsaying that as the Beatles began opening up some thrilling new musical possibilities in the mid-'60s, the Stones were drawn to what they were doing.

Put another way, there was a time when the Beatles were a creative muse to the Rolling Stones. Even today, if you read the main Stones memoirs—Bill Wyman's *Stone Alone*, Keith Richards's *Life*, and Andrew Oldham's *Stoned* and *2Stoned*—it's impossible to miss how preoccupied they always were with the Beatles, and how often they measured their own success against the Beatles' accomplishments. It must have been difficult at times.

In March 1966, *NME* journalist Keith Altham published a short puff piece on Brian Jones. Reading it today, however—knowing that the Rolling Stones finally fired Brian in June 1969, and that he had to be scooped from the bottom of his swimming pool less than a month later, at age twenty-seven, with inflamed lungs, an enlarged heart and a diseased liver—it's a little sad. It describes how Jones had just returned to England from the US, four days later than the rest of his bandmates, "due to the fact that clubs in New York are open 24 hours a day and he had been in one for four days with an insane Welsh harpist called 'Hari Hari' waiting for it to close!" (That's probably not too far from what actually happened.) When he got to his home in Earls Court, he discovered he'd misplaced his keys, so he just smashed his way in through a ground-floor window and then summoned his friends for a party. He didn't even know what day it was. Nevertheless, they all got rip-roaring drunk while Brian crowed about the Stones' recent success. Later they sent out for beef curries and veal scallops.

"America is a great scene for us at present," he said. "We've never been so powerful there . . . We overtook the Beatles 'Nowhere Man' in the charts with '19th Nervous Breakdown' and although I've no delusions about being bigger than the Beatles . . . it's something an achievement."

Altham wrote, "The possibility of the Rolling Stones becoming a bigger attraction than that Beatles in America is intriguing, and I asked Brian how he saw the shape of things to come."

Brian "smiled" (perhaps tightly). "You must understand that the Beatles are a phenomenon," he said. "You can't be as big as the Beatles until you've done something like Shea Stadium—and I doubt whether even they could do that so successful again."

CHAPTER FIVE

POLITICS AND IMAGECRAFT

The last time Mick Jagger had appeared in court, everyone commented on how dashing he looked in his mod fashion garb. Sporting a King's Road double-breasted blazer, olive colored trousers, a ruffled shirt, and a striped tie, he seemed like an embodiment of resplendent, insouciant youth. Now, however, as he stood before Lord Chief Justice Hubert Parker, of Waddington, at the Royal Courts of Justice, in London, for his appeal hearing, he wore an ordinary, slim-fitting suit. His conservative attire befitted his somber attitude. If not for his longish hair, he would have looked utterly conventional, like a young businessman or a lawyer. It was July 31, 1967.

Mick had good reason to be nervous. A month earlier, a Chichester judge had sentenced him to three months in prison for possession of just four amphetamine tablets without a prescription. Keith Richards got an even more severe sentence: an entire year in prison simply for allowing some friends to smoke weed on his property. The group's manager, Andrew Oldham, had always said, "For the Rolling Stones, bad news is good news," but now this maxim was being severely strained. Jagger had been forced to spend two nights in Lewes Prison and another night in Brixton before he was released on £7,000 bail, and he desperately wanted to avoid being sent back.

Fortunately for the Stones, the hearing went well. Keith's conviction was overturned on the grounds that the judge had "erred" in his instructions to the jury, and Mick's sentence was reduced to a one-year conditional discharge. "That means," Lord Parker told him, "if you keep out of any trouble for the next twelve months, what has happened will not be on your record as a conviction. If you *do* commit another offense, you will not only be punished for that offense, but brought back and punished for this one."

The judge also tacked on a stern warning: "You are, whether you like it or not, the idol of a large number of the youth in this country. Being in that position, you have very grave responsibilities. If you do come to be punished, it is only natural that those responsibilities should carry higher penalties."

Mick did not actually agree with that last bit of extemporizing from the judge, but no matter; he was thrilled to be unburdened from the prospect of jail. He also had an exciting day ahead. After a brief celebration with his lawyer, and a quick press conference in Soho, he clambered into a small helicopter with Marianne Faithfull and John Birt, a researcher for Granada Television's *World in Action*, a hard-hitting public affairs program. Later Birt would be named director general of the BBC, but in 1967 he was just twenty-two years old and relatively new to broadcasting. Nevertheless, he had come up with an extraordinary idea: *World in Action* should host a "meeting of the generations" in which Mick Jagger, representing the "new youth," would engage in a sober exchange of views with representatives from "the Establishment"—a newspaper editor, a lord, a bishop, and a Jesuit. Somewhat to everyone's surprise, Mick agreed. And so they were whisked away to a beautiful country estate, which would provide a photogenic backdrop for the summit, all three of them squished together on a small bench behind the pilot. "We swooped exhilaratingly over a verdant countryside on a glorious, cloudless, summer's day," Birt recalled. "Faithfull—relieved her man was not in jail—snogged him ferociously, unselfconsciously grinding her bum against me as she did. A shy man, I looked the other way."

Given the widening chasm between England's youth and their parents, Mick's television appearance aroused much fanfare. The program's opening shot shows the chopper landing on a spot of grass and then Mick bounding out. He'd cast off his courtroom attire and, presumably, his gloomy mood as well. Now he was wearing a thigh-length floral shirt with an embroidered collar and striding confidently across the lawn in order to meet his patrician interlocutors, who sat waiting for him in an English garden. The whole setup seemed very odd. One British TV critic said it came off "like a lost scene from Lewis Carroll."

William Rees-Mogg, the newly appointed editor of *The Times*, served as the show's moderator. "You are often taken as a symbol of rebellion, and mothers deplore the influence of the Rolling Stones," he said to Mick, not unkindly. "Do you think that the society that you live in is one you ought to rebel against, or do you think you're rebelling against it?"

"Yes, definitely rebelling against it," Mick answered. Yet he cast himself as a reluctant spokesman. "I haven't until very recently been into this kind of discussion at all, because I haven't really felt it has been my place through my knowledge—which I don't think is enough—to start pontificating on these kinds of subjects," he said. Now, however, he aimed to rise to the occasion. The dry laconicism with which he sometimes answered provincial journalists was nowhere to be found. He was forthcoming with his answers, and he used his proper London accent, as opposed to his Cockney put-on. Careful viewers might have noticed a slight slurring in his speech, however.

That was because he'd had a good bit of Valium. As a result, he seemed a little loopy. He would get tongue-tied or lose his train of thought, and he never settled comfortably in his chair. When the

Jesuit asked Mick whether he was concerned about "corruption" in contemporary British society, he elicited a stream of gibberish.

> *Yes, I think it's always been in need of checking, the corruption, as you—I don't know what kind of corruption you're talking about exactly here, but um, but uh, today one's faced with a very different situation than in past centuries, perhaps because of communication for instance which is, nobody could've, none of us could have had the communication this, in any other century, that we have—instant communication—such as we're doing now. And this er, influences far more people. And with the small, with the small education even that one is allowed today, f-f freely, this also effects this—which makes this, this generation and all these—postwar thing. And the money, and everything else, very different to the others. And also this generation has had no, there was no America to go to, as such in the last century. If you really, you didn't like it here, you could go to America, start afresh.*

Mick was embarrassed by his performance. Probably he did very little to convince *World in Action*'s middle-aged viewers that he was not, in fact, on drugs. Some forty-odd years later, however, Rees-Mogg suggested that Jagger's remarks might have been more substantial than people first realized. One of Mick's claims that day was that people ought be permitted the freedom to do whatever they liked so long as they don't bring harm to others. It might not be wise to use drugs, he conceded, but it was not a crime against *society*, "any more than jumping out of a window is." However awkwardly it was expressed, Jagger championed a theory of social ethics that he may well have picked up at the London School of Economics. It owed a great deal to John Stuart Mill, and later it became an important characteristic of Thatcherism. "It was not the soft-liberalism of the Beatles but the libertarian Rolling Stones who best predicted the Anglo-American ideology of the 1980s," Rees-Mogg argued.

Perhaps Rees-Mogg ascribed too much significance to Jagger's youthful musings. Nevertheless, he raised an important point. Mothers might have deplored the influence of the Rolling Stones, but Establishmentarians had less cause for worry. Mick said he was dissatisfied with society, but he didn't bother trying to explain why that was so, and he did not commit himself to pursuing any sorts of reforms. In fact, he said he mostly wanted to be known for having "as good a time as possible . . . without any regard to responsibilities of any sort." In contrast to the stoicism and restraint of his parents' generation, Mick championed pure and simple hedonism. He did not declare an affiliation with the cultural radicalism of the hippies, and he did not endorse the strategic politics of the New Left. He was not interested in finding the right formulas for ending racism, halting the Vietnam War, or redistributing wealth. "I'm not a keen protestor at all," he told *World in Action.* "I don't go marching, or anything like that."

And yet somehow, amid the gauzy idealism and utopian strivings of the late-'60s youthquake, many youths continued to regard the Rolling Stones as radical folk heroes. The same thing happened to the Beatles; young people looked to them for political insight and guidance, even though the group normally tried to shy away from political controversy. Just a short while ago, both bands were known for catering to the fantasies of young fans. Now, millions of politically minded youths believed that the Beatles and the Rolling Stones—the biggest rock stars in the world!—should speak to them clearly and directly, about issues of contemporary significance, in a spirit of mutuality and from a vantage of authenticity. Young fans believed that rock culture was inseparable from the youth culture that they created, shared, and enjoyed. In some fundamental way, they believed themselves to be part of the same community as John and Paul, and Mick and Keith. They believed they were all fighting for the same things.

• • •

Although the Beatles are sometimes credited with expanding the expressive possibilities of pop music—thereby helping to turn it into "art"—it bears remembering that when the Fab Four landed in the States in 1964, music critics did not receive them warmly. In fact, establishment writers were so distracted by their shaggy hairdos and the hysterical reactions they elicited from teenage girls, that they barely discussed the Beatles' music at all. When they did, they frequently regarded it with degrees of condescension, suspicion, and contempt. In 1964, a *Newsweek* reviewer said this about the Beatles: "Musically, they are a near disaster: guitars slamming out a merciless beat that does away with secondary rhythms, harmony, and melody. The lyrics (punctuated by nutty shouts of 'yeah, yeah, yeah!') are a catastrophe, a preposterous farrago of Valentine-card romantic sentiments."

Even after the Beatles broadened their sonic and emotional palette with *Rubber Soul* and *Revolver,* some mainstream writers still regarded them as a puzzling cultural phenomenon. The first *New York Times* review of any Beatles record did not appear until June 1967, when the band released *Sgt. Pepper's Lonely Hearts Club Band.* Richard Goldstein, the paper's young pop critic, gave it a pan.

By contrast, underground press writers always lauded the Beatles, not just for their amazing creative powers, but also for their discernible intelligence, subversive charisma, and drug experimentation. Post–*Rubber Soul,* the Beatles were credited with helping to establish the byways of the emerging youth culture. The Beatles will "long abide as arbiters of a new aesthetic, missionaries for an emerging lifestyle and resident gurus to a generation," effused a writer for the *San Diego Door*. Others claimed that underground journalism and rock 'n' roll both helped to "dissolve many of the tensions" between the political radicalism of the New Left (made up of determined activists) and the aesthetic radicalism of the counterculture (made up of lackadaisical dropouts). "Even those who did not share the profound cultural alienation of the hippies were likely to share a liking for the Beatles, some respect for their collective visibility, and a desire to at least experiment with marijuana," said sociologist Dick Flacks.

Curiously, the Beatles garnered this respect even though they were not very political during most of the '60s. True, the group sometimes delighted in unmasking snobbery and puncturing class pretensions. But the Beatles never joined the crusade to ban atomic weapons or got involved in the civil rights movement. In fact, their manager, Brian Epstein, was constantly reminding them to avoid making controversial statements of any kind, for fear that they might alienate part of their audience. The Beatles may have been annoyed by this restriction, but for the most part, they acquiesced.

Their approach to American race relations was revealing. The Beatles' extant performance contracts from 1965 and 1966 all contain a rider stating that the group would not perform in front of racially segregated audiences. That provision probably was not in place during their earlier appearances, but that was just because no one had thought to include it. A September 11, 1964, concert at the Gator Bowl might have alerted the Beatles to the desirability of doing so in the future. A week or so before their performance, the Beatles got word that its Jacksonville-based promoter had planned to order seating according to race. Radio journalist Larry Kane asked McCartney for his thoughts:

KANE: What about this comment I heard from you Paul, about racial integration at the various concerts?

MCCARTNEY: We don't like it if there's any segregation or anything because we're not used to it, you know . . . it just seems daft to me. I mean it may seem right to some people, but to us it just seems a bit daft.

KANE: Well, you're gonna play Jacksonville, Florida. Do you anticipate any difference of opinion?

MCCARTNEY: I don't know really, y'know, because I don't

know what people in America are like. I think they'd be a bit silly to segregate people . . . cause you know . . . I don't think colored people are any different, y'know, they're just the same as anyone else. But, y'know, over here there are some people who think that they're sorta animals or something, and I just think that's stupid, y'know.

KANE: Yeah . . .

MCCARTNEY: You can't treat other people like animals. And so, y'know—I wouldn't mind 'em sitting next to me. Great, y'know, 'cause some of our best friends are colored people.

These are the remarks of a young man with an intuitive (you could almost say "childlike") objection to racism. Seeing as Paul was just twenty-two at the time, with only limited exposure to the United States, we can forgive his wince-worthy turns of phrase. His sentiments were laudable. It would be a mistake, however, to regard these as the remarks of an *activist*. During the civil rights movement, those who were actively committed to toppling segregation almost always used morally charged language to discuss the topic; they would have referred to segregation as grievously wrong, not merely "silly" or "a bit daft." The Beatles made a principled decision not to accommodate racism when they visited the US, but they did not work to abolish it. (Ultimately, the Gator Bowl concert was not segregated.)

The Beatles also opposed the Vietnam War. For a while, they tried to avoid talking about it. Then in 1966, they started answering questions on the topic, but they never left anyone with the impression that they were poised to join the ranks of the antiwar movement. "We don't agree with it," Lennon once told a journalist. "But there's not much we can do about it. All we can say is we don't like it." *The New York Times* reported that when the Beatles were asked about Vietnam at a press conference, they said, "We don't like war, war is wrong"—

but they kept their voices unusually "low," and were "nearly inaudible." Another time, in Toronto, a reporter began to ask the Beatles why, if they opposed the war, weren't they doing anything to try to stop it? But he couldn't finish his question before Lennon interrupted. "Because someone would shoot us," he snapped. Tariq Ali, a leader of the Vietnam Solidarity Campaign, said, "We'd heard rumors that some of the Beatles were quite anti-war, but attempts to contact them failed" and they never showed up at any antiwar events.

The following year, the Beatles came out in favor of pot legalization. At Paul's suggestion, they paid for, and signed their names to, a full-page newspaper advertisement in *The Times* that was headlined "The Law Against Marijuana Is Unworkable in Principle and Unworkable in Practice." (The ad was spearheaded by the drug organization SOMA. Sixty-one others signed as well, including fifteen doctors and two MPs.) Fearing bad publicity, the Beatles hoped to keep the fact that they financed the advertisement under wraps, but the word got out. And that was the full extent of their involvement in the campaign to legalize marijuana—just their names signed to a petition. Arguably, the only overt protest song the Beatles ever recorded was George Harrison's "Taxman," an acid complaint about the huge amount of Beatles' earnings that were going to the Inland Revenue.

Nevertheless, through the mid-1960s, enthusiasm for the Beatles was all but ubiquitous in the New Left. A new Beatles album "was an event," memoirist Geoffrey O'Brien recalls. "Friends gathered to share the freshness of the never-to-be-recaptured first hearing." The Beatles also provided an alluring soundtrack for many activists. Todd Gitlin, a former president of Students for a Democratic Society (SDS), the New Left's premier organization, recalled that once after a long meeting in 1966, a group of Berkeley students joined hands and clumsily attempted to sing the old labor standby, "Solidarity Forever," but it quickly became clear that hardly anyone knew the words. A moment later, the group erupted with a joyous rendition of "Yellow Submarine"—a new song from their own culture. "With a bit of effort," Gitlin remembered, "the song could be taken as the communion of hippies and activists, students and nonstudents, who at long last felt they could express their beloved single-hearted community." Another memoirist recalls that when he helped to occupy a Columbia University building during the vertiginous spring of 1968, hundreds of students bonded over the Beatles just before they were arrested. We "were no longer strangers . . . but brothers and sisters weaving in ritual dance. We sang the words of the Beatles' songs [and] danced round and round in a circle."

Beatles albums were frequently scrutinized for profound or hidden meanings, and a few went so far as to imbue the group with superhuman stature and mystical significance. In 1967, a young writer for Milwaukee's *Kaleidoscope* plausibly claimed that no other artist in history had ever commanded "the power and audience of the Beatles. The allure, the excitement, the glory of Beatlemania," he continued, "is the suspicion that the Beatles might succeed just where the magicians of the past have failed." Even though the Beatles rarely spoke about politics, a *Willamette Bridge* writer observed that youths turned to "the Beatles myth"—the idea that the Beatles possessed some secret insight, shamanic influence or untapped reservoir of power—for solutions to problems as diverse and intractable as the Vietnam War, the atomic bomb, the civil rights struggle, and campus unrest. Writing in the *Berkeley Barb* in early 1967, activist Marvin Garson remarked, "At idle moments more imaginative men in government must be haunted by a persistent nightmare . . . [that] Lennon and McCartney will go on to lead an antiwar sit-in at the Pentagon."

• • •

Of course, some left-wing youths more closely identified with the Rolling Stones. In 1965, Emmett Grogan, who later helped to form an important Haight-Ashbury hippie collective called the Diggers, distributed mimeographed flyers declaring the Stones to be "the embodiment of everything we represent, a psychic evolution . . . the breaking up of old values." No doubt that was part of the Stones' appeal. Many rebellious youths looked up to them just because they seemed so dangerously cool. "I went with the Stones once they started writing songs like 'Under My Thumb' and 'Satisfaction,' remembers cultural critic John Strausbaugh. "I didn't have the slightest idea what those songs were about. I just knew they were somehow bad, and bad's what I wanted to be."

To some radicals, the Stones also seemed more accessible. On May 16, 1965, Ken Kesey's group, the Merry Pranksters—who were just then emerging as the West Coast's premier LSD proselytizers—drove from San Francisco to Long Beach, where they partied with the Stones and plied Brian Jones with a fistful of acid. By contrast, when the Beatles completed a US tour at San Francisco's Cow Palace in 1965, the Pranksters tried to host a party in their honor, but of course the band didn't show.

In 1966, when London's new underground paper *International Times* threw a launch party, Jagger and Marianne Faithfull showed up and celebrated, while McCartney lurked around in a disguise. Actor Peter Coyote recalled that when a group of twenty-odd politically minded "rockers, bikers, and street people" visited the Beatles at their Apple headquarters in London, the Beatles and their handlers "were kind of afraid of us."

The Stones also inadvertently won some radical bona fides in 1967, when Jagger and Keith Richards were busted for drugs at Richards' country home in Sussex. The raid and its drawn out aftermath put the Stones at the center of a polarizing national debate about drug policy, youth culture, the courts, and the media. Ultimately, however, the Stones' ordeal only served to strengthen their reputation as anti-establishment icons. According to an acquaintance, "Mick's case had made him into a martyr, a hero, a spokesman for his generation, and he reveled in this newfound power."

The problems began when two enterprising reporters from the lowbrow *News of the World* started looking into some wild LSD parties that the Moody Blues were rumored to be hosting at their communal home. ("Roehampton Raves," they were called.) Their investigation led them to stake out Blaises, a private basement club in Kensington that sometimes attracted members of the pop aristocracy. One night, Brian Jones walked in. Whether he was just in a voluble mood, or had already lowered his inhibitions with drugs, is impossible to say. But reporters watched him consume about six bennies right on the spot. "I just wouldn't be able to keep awake in places like this if I didn't have them," Jones told them. On the topic of LSD, he said "I don't go much on it now [that] the cats (fans) have taken it up. It'll just get a dirty name." Finally, while still in the presence of the reporters, he pulled out a lump of hashish and invited some friends up to his flat for "a smoke." All of this soon appeared in the second installment of the Sunday tabloid's multi-part write up, "Pop Stars and Drugs: Facts That Will Shock You."

The only problem was, the piece contained a major factual error: the reporters thought they were talking to *Mick Jagger*. They couldn't tell the difference between the Rolling Stones' wispy, wide-mouthed singer and its dissolute, blond-haired guitarist. (Then again, Jones may have sent them down a confused road; he always liked to tell strangers that he was the group's "leader.") Jagger was livid, and rightly so. When the *News of the World* reporters collected their quotes, he had been on vacation in the Italian Riviera. Besides, Mick had always been cautious about his drug use, which anyhow was very moderate compared to Keith's or Brian's.

As it happened, on the very day that the story hit newsstands, the Stones taped an appearance on British TV's *Eamonn Andrews Show*. After they performed "She Smiled Sweetly" from *Between the Buttons*, Jagger sat for an interview, and it was there that he made "the Oscar Wilde mistake." He confidently announced that he would sue *News of the World* for libel. Just like the flamboyant nineteenth-century writer and poet, Mick was hardly in a position to feign indignation. After all, he *did* occasionally take drugs, and lots of people knew that to be so. Now *News of the World* just had to prove it in order to derail his powerful lawsuit against them.

The newspaper must have gotten to someone in the Stones' camp to act as an informant. (Keith later suspected it was his driver at the time, a Belgian known only as "Patrick.") Whoever their source was, the *News of the World* learned that Richards would soon be hosting a weekend party at his new country home, called Redlands, and that Mick and Marianne would be there. Most of the other guests were part of a tightly knit group. They included the Mayfair gallery owner Robert Fraser and his Moroccan "servant" (actually his lover) Mohammed Jajaj; the Chelsea interior designer Christopher Gibbs; and rock photographer Michael Cooper. George Harrison and his wife, Pattie Boyd, dropped by the party, too.

Then there were a couple guests who were not so well known to the others. One was Nicky Kramer, a foppish King's Road hanger-on. No one could quite remember inviting him in the first place; he just sort of attached himself to the group and Keith kindheartedly let him tag along. The other mysterious character was David Snyderman (sometimes spelled Schneiderman), aka "David Britton," aka "David Jove," aka "The Acid King"—a Canadian-born Californian. Keith had met him in New York City about a year earlier. Now he'd recently shown up in London, wanting to be everyone's drug supplier. He supposedly carried around fake identification and a monogrammed briefcase full of DMT and varieties of acid: White Lightning, Orange Sunshine, and Purple Haze.

On Sunday morning, Acid King Dave went around to everyone's room, serving them breakfast tea and acid. Some in the group were put off by his loony LSD evangelism: "This is the tao of lysergic diethylamide, man. Let it speak to you, let it tell you how to navigate the cosmos"—but as Marianne put it, "he *did* have the goods." A while later they all went out to the West Wittering Beach and larked around the sandy flats, enjoying the winter sunshine and watching the salty waves dissolve into surf on the shore. Then they set out on a

Sunday country drive, looking for the groovy mansion belonging to Edward James, a wealthy patron of the surrealist movement whose huge art collection was sometimes open to the public. Unfortunately, they wound up getting lost and by the time they arrived, the estate was closed. Still, they'd had a great day.

After they got back to Redlands, George Harrison and his wife paid a visit. Since they had not taken LSD that day, they might have found it hard to relate to the others. They stayed for only about an hour or two before driving off together in George's customized Mini Cooper. Shortly after they'd left, the drug squad arrived. Later, it was widely assumed that the raiding party had been staked outside Redlands for some time, *waiting* for Harrison to leave. According to Richards, the police took malicious, voyeuristic detail in busting the Stones, but at that point they dared not arrest *a Beatle.* Harrison agreed: "There was the kind of social pecking order . . . in the pop world," he said. First, they "busted Donovan [in mid-1966] . . . then they busted the Rolling Stones, and then [in 1969] they worked their way up and they busted John and Yoko, and me."

Keith recalled the bust: "There's a big knock on the door. Eight o'clock. Everybody is just sort of gliding down slowly from the whole day of sort of freaking about. Everybody has managed to find their way back to the house. TV is on with the sound off and the record player is on. Strobe lights are flickering. Marianne Faithfull has just decided that she wanted a bath and has wrapped herself in a rug and is watching the box."

(That late morsel of a detail—that Marianne was naked beneath a fur rug while in the company of a group of men—would become tantalizing to the prosecutors and the tabloids. There was also a rumor about a Mars Bar.)

Keith continues: " 'Bang, bang, bang,' this big knock at the door and I go answer it. 'Oh look, there's lots of little ladies and gentlemen outside.' . . . We were just gliding off from a twelve-hour trip." Later he said that in his acid-infused mind, the invading policemen looked like a nefarious band of goblins from *The Hobbit*. "Poor Mick—he could hardly believe his luck," Marianne added. "The first day he ever dares take an LSD trip, eighteen policemen come pouring in through the door."

For all their trouble, the cops didn't come away with much on the Stones. In a green velvet jacket belonging to Mick they found four pep pills, which actually belonged to Marianne. She'd recently picked them up in Italy, where they could be easily purchased at any *farmacia*. Keith wasn't charged with possessing anything, but rather with allowing people to smoke pot on his property. The police seized a pipe and a bowl from his house that were both found to contain traces of cannabis. They also detected an unusual odor when they arrived, although some of the officers couldn't agree on what it was—one said it was "sweet" and another called it "acrid." Finally, the police claimed that Marianne was acting without a normal young lady's inhibitions—a sure sign, they figured, of cannabis intoxication. The Stones' friend Robert Fraser, however, had much worse luck. He was found with twenty-four heroin jacks (pills) in his trousers.

Almost every account that has ever been written or spoken about the raid holds that Snyderman somehow got off scot-free. Supposedly, just when an officer was about to rifle through his attaché case, Snyderman piped up and said, "Please don't open the case! It's full of exposed film." And so, improbable as it sounds, the officer agreed not to open it. When Snyderman skipped the country two days later, never to return, everyone concluded that he was a police plant.

Only that is not what happened. Journalist Simon Wells has recently produced an authoritative examination of the Redlands bust, *Butterfly on a Wheel*. Surviving police records indicate that one Detective Constable Thomas Davies got all kinds of incriminating stuff off Snyderman. "In his right-hand breast pocket, two pieces of a brown substance weighing 66 grains [4.3 grams] were discovered. In another jacket pocket, an envelope was discovered that contained a powdery substance with one of his pseudonyms, 'David Britton,' written on it. Elsewhere, the detective found a cigarette tin that contained three pieces of a brown substance; a decorated wooden pipe with a stem with traces of a substance; a fairly large ball of a brown substance; a blue and white vial containing white pills; an orange colored pill; and numerous other items." All of this was confiscated and taken back to the police lab for analysis. It is true that Snyderman quickly fled England, but he probably did so in order to save his own skin.

On February 19, a week after the bust, *News of the World* ran a front-page story headlined "Drug Squad Raids Pop Stars' Party." Legally, the paper was prohibited from revealing anyone's name, but they otherwise provided a detailed and accurate account of what had happened, suggesting a quid pro quo: in return for the tipping off the police, the *News of the World* got the exclusive, inside scoop. The story's appearance also indicated that a £7,000 bribe that Jagger, Richard, and Fraser had paid to the police, via Tony Sanchez, had not worked. (That was equivalent to about £100,000 in today's money, or $155,000.) "That's what I feel most bitter about," Keith said years later. "In America, you pay off the cops as a matter of course. It's business. But in Britain, you pay them off and they still do you."

Jagger and Richards got Michael Havers to represent them. He was one of London's finest attorneys (later he became Lord Chancellor). Mick and Keith both remember being surprised when, in a private conversation, Havers told them that it looked as if the prosecutors and the court were seeking to make an example of the two Stones. Some regarded the judge who was assigned to the case, Leslie Block, as an old-style reactionary. Everyone became even more concerned when the police raided Brian Jones's London apartment on May 10, 1967. He was found to be in possession of pot, cocaine, and speed, and put under arrest.

The Stones thought they understood what was behind the sudden crackdown. "First they don't like young kids with a lot of money," Keith surmised. "But as long as you don't bother them, that's cool.

But we bothered them because of the way we looked, and the way we'd act. Because we never showed any reverence for them whatsoever. Whereas the Beatles had. They'd gone along with it so far, with the MBEs and shaking hands. Whenever we were asked about things like that, we'd say, 'Fuck it. Don't want to know about things like that. Bollocks. Don't need it.' That riled 'em somewhat."

Jagger must have figured that he had a strong defense. Although he did not have an official written prescription for the pills, his doctor testified that once he learned that Mick possessed them, he had verbally authorized their use (in order that he could stay up and work). Also, Havers stressed how exceedingly minor Jagger's offense was. Every year in England, the same types of pills that Jagger was found with were widely prescribed as appetite suppressants, for hay fever, and for motion sickness.

The judge, however, instructed the jury that whatever Jagger's doctor may have told him, it did not amount to a legal prescription. Six minutes later, Jagger was declared guilty. Hearing the news, he put his head in his hands and struggled to stifle his sobs. He was handcuffed and sent to Lewes Prison to await sentencing.

Richards's trial, held the next day, was a bit more complicated. He testified that the odor the police detected was incense, and that it wasn't used to cover-up marijuana smoke, but rather just to perfume the room. The pipes containing cannabis resin, he said, were not originally his; they were a gift from an American road manager. Then he was asked about Marianne Faithfull, who was known in court documents as "Miss X."

> PROSECUTION LAWYER: There was, as we know, a young woman sitting on a settee wearing only a rug. Would you agree, in the ordinary course of events, you would expect a young woman to be embarrassed if she had nothing on but a rug in the presence of eight men, two

of whom were hangers-on, and the third a Moroccan servant?

KEITH: Not at all. She doesn't embarrass easily, nor do I.

PROSECUTION LAWYER: You regard that, do you, as quite normal?

KEITH: We are not old men. We are not worried about petty morals.

When Judge Block gave his instructions to the jury some of his remarks seemed gratuitous. He asked them to purge from their minds anything they might have heard about others at Redlands admitting to, or being convicted of, possessing certain drugs. "Finally," he said, "I would ask you disregard the evidence as to the lady who was alleged by the police to have been in some condition of undress, and not let that prejudice your minds in any way."

After about an hour of deliberation, the jury found Richards guilty. Next, the judge handed down everyone's punishment. Keith was sentenced to a year in prison, and Mick got three months. Robert Fraser, who had used a different lawyer than the others, had pled guilty and was sentenced to six months in prison. All three were also fined toward the cost of their prosecution.

As Jagger was hauled off to Brixton, and Richards and Fraser were taken to Wormwood Scrubs, fans in the public gallery moaned, yelled, and wept. Later that night, hundreds of supporters thronged into the narrow streets that ran around the *News of the World* headquarters and chanted "Free the Stones! Free the Stones!" Elsewhere, fans passed out leaflets begging the police, the tabloids, and "outraged magistrates" to demonstrate "sanity." *Oz*, a countercultural magazine, circulated a broadside denouncing the sentences as "vicious." The Stones' most visible supporters in the pop world were the Who. They promptly announced they would begin putting out a series of Jagger-Richards cover songs as a form of protest, and their drummer, Keith Moon, showed up on Fleet Street with a sign reading "Stop Pop Persecution!"

Allen Ginsberg, who was visiting London at the time, said, "The Rolling Stones are one of Britain's major cultural assets, who should be honored by the kingdom instead of jailed."

The most significant show of support, however, came from an unlikely source. In 1967, perhaps the most highly respected figure in British journalism was William Rees-Mogg (later Baron Rees-Mogg), the aforementioned *Times* editor. Known for his erudition and upper-crust mannerisms, this former president of the Oxford Union was an absolute pillar of the establishment. Nevertheless, he was disquieted by what had occurred in the Chichester courtroom, and on July 1, he published the most famous editorial of his long career. Its headline (set in capital letters) was borrowed from Alexander Pope: "WHO BREAKS A BUTTERFLY ON A WHEEL?" Though Mick and Keith had each been granted bail the day before the editorial appeared, the appeals bench had yet to review their cases. As a result, Rees-Mogg assumed a substantial risk when he published his exquisitely worded opinion; if the court had wanted, it could have held him in contempt.

> *. . . In Britain, it is an offense to possess [amphetamine pills] without a prescription. Mr. Jagger's doctor says that he knew and had authorized their use, but he did not give a prescription for them as they had already been purchased. His evidence was not challenged. This was, therefore, an offense of a technical character. . . . If after a visit to the pope, the Archbishop of Canterbury had bought proprietary air sickness pills at the Rome Airport and imported the unused tablets into Britain on his return, he would have risked committing precisely the same offense.*
>
> *. . . Judge Block directed the jury that the approval of a doctor is not a defense in law to the charge of possessing drugs without a prescription, and the jury convicted.*
>
> *. . . We have therefore, a conviction against Mr. Jagger purely on the grounds that he possessed four Italian pep pills, quite legally bought, but not legally imported without a prescription.*

> *Four is not a large number. This is not a quantity which a pusher of drugs would have on him, nor even the quantity one would expect in an addict. . . . It is surprising therefore that Judge Block should have decided to sentence Mr. Jagger to imprisonment, and particularly surprising as Mr. Jagger's is about as mild a drug case as can ever have been brought before the courts.*
>
> *It would be wrong to speculate on the judge's reasons, which we do not know. It is, however, possible to consider the public reaction. There are many people who take a primitive view of the matter, what one might call a pre-legal view of the matter. They consider that Mr. Jagger has "got what was coming to him." They resent the anarchic quality of the Rolling Stones performances, dislike their songs, dislike their influence on teenagers and broadly suspect them of decadence . . .*
>
> *. . . As a sociological concern, this may be reasonable enough, and at an emotional level, it is very understandable, but it has nothing to do with the case.*
>
> *. . . If we are going to make any case a symbol of the conflict between the sound traditional values of Britain and the new hedonism, then we must be sure that the sound traditional values include those of tolerance and equality. It should be the particular quality of British justice to ensure that Mr. Jagger is treated exactly the same as anyone else, no better and no worse. There must remain a suspicion in this case that Mr. Jagger received a more severe sentence than would have been thought proper for any purely anonymous young man.*

Following Rees-Mogg's commentary, much of the country became engulfed in a debate over whether or not the two Stones had been treated unfairly. The *Sunday Express* said that Jagger's punishment was "monstrously out of proportion" to his offense, while the *Sunday Times* called the trial a "show trial." After the *News of the World* admitted that it had, in fact, tipped off the police about the Redlands party (claiming it was their "plain duty" to do so, they said), it earned rebukes from two members of parliament, as well as from John Osborne, the iconoclastic playwright. "Are we expected to accept the principle that newspapers' editors consider it their 'plain duty' to pass random tip-offs from informers about what may or may not be going in someone's house?" Osborne asked.

The Stones' appeal was heard on July 31. Keith couldn't attend because he had come down with chicken pox. When it was over, his conviction was overturned, and Mick was given a one-year conditional discharge. Though all of this court drama unfolded during the summer of 1967—the fabled Summer of Love—the Stones had missed out on the era's good hippie vibes. They were too busy fighting off their drug convictions and trying to hold their band together. The widespread perception that the establishment had targeted the Stones, however—not for any reasons having to do with maintaining the public order, but rather to make them pay for the insolent attitudes and louche behavior—only managed to enhance their popularity with politically motivated youths. "We weren't thinking of the Beatles at that period as radical in any way," remembered Tariq Ali, the young British activist. "They just made pleasing music. But Jagger we felt—there was more of an edge to him and his music at that period and he didn't like what was going on—sexually and politically—and that became very obvious."

• • •

Something like the Summer of Love would have happened even without the Beatles. Too many flower-power myth makers had too much to gain. Chet Helms, a Bay Area music promoter, was known to boast that nearly 50 percent of the world's population would soon be under twenty-five, and "they got twenty billion irresponsible dollars to spend." Many thousands of youths flocked to San Francisco, where psychedelic bands like the Grateful Dead, Big Brother and the Holding Company, and the Jefferson Airplane commanded the local scene. On a weekend in June, some 50,000 colorfully costumed youths descended on the seaside resort town of Monterey, California, for a three-day hippie music festival.

Some have pedantically argued that in London, there were *two* Summers of Love (in 1967 and 1968). Youths were kept abreast of hip happenings in underground publications such as *International Times* and *Oz*, which hippies peddled on street corners around King's Road. The Indica bookstore and gallery (named after a species of marijuana) was an important gathering place, as was the UFO Club (pronounced "yoof-oh"), which is where new bands such as Soft Machine and Pink Floyd performed alongside sensory-overloading lightshows and bubbling oil-slide projections.

No one disputes, however, that the Beatles' *Sgt. Pepper's* album was the soundtrack to the remarkable summer of 1967. It may not have been the greatest record the Beatles ever made, but when it was released on June 1, 1967, in England, and on June 2 in America, it evoked more triumphal fanfare than any other album in history. A young rock writer at the time, Langdon Winner, recalled driving across the US on Interstate 80 that summer. "In each city where I stopped for gas or food—Laramie, Ogallala, Moline, South Bend—the melodies wafted in from some far-off transistor radio or portable hi-fi," he said. "For a brief while the irreparably fragmented consciousness of the West was unified, at least in the minds of the young." Later on, pop critic and historian James Miller made a similar observation: "Everywhere one went, from Los Angeles to London, from Paris to Madrid, from Rome to Athens, snatches of the album drifted out of open windows, faded in and out of consciousness as cars passed by, came in and out of focus in tinny tones from distant transistor radios, the songs hanging in the air like a hologram of bliss."

Even the *Sgt. Pepper's* cover was enthralling. A masterpiece of Pop Art, designed by Peter Blake, it featured a gatefold sleeve, printed lyrics, and a kitschy cutout sheet insert suitable for children. (Among other items, it contained a fake moustache; the Beatles were now sporting moustaches as well.) It was the cover image, however, that drew the most attention. The Beatles were photographed wearing neon-colored satin uniforms that looked like they might belong to a Victorian Era military band, surrounded by a collage of more than sixty life-size cardboard cutouts of cultural and intellectual figures (Marilyn Monroe, Fred Astaire, William Burroughs, Sonny Liston, Stu Sutcliffe, and so forth). It rewarded hours of stoned scrutiny. Eventually everyone noticed what appeared to be marijuana plants in the garden. Off to the side, a cloth Shirley Temple doll is wearing a tiny knitted sweater that reads "Welcome Rolling Stones."

A few weeks after they released *Sgt. Pepper's*—"a decisive moment in the history of Western Civilization," said *The Times*'s Kenneth Tynan—the Beatles debuted their new single, "All You Need Is Love," on a program called *Our World*, the first global satellite television broadcast. Commissioned by the BBC, their performance reached approximately 350 million people across five continents. If some of the tracks on *Sgt. Pepper's* seemed a bit gimmicky or overproduced, "All You Need Is Love" was simple, nonspecific, and repetitive—and that made it perfect for sloganizing the era. The Beatles also pulled off yet another dazzling visual representation of the Summer of Love. They played while perched on stools in a half-circle (with Ringo off to the side) in a flower-strewn studio that was festooned with balloons, streamers, and posters. Meanwhile, a dozen or so friends—all of them gussied up in the finest hippie fashions—sat on the floor around them and gazed up like acolytes. Mick Jagger was among them. At one point in the broadcast, the camera cuts away to a two-second shot of him clapping and singing along in a purple silk jacket.

Beatles assistant Tony Bramwell had been tasked with recruiting most of the studio audience. To do so, he simply trawled London's up-market clubs the night before the broadcast and asked various friends to drop in. "Mick said he'd come, no hassle, but he was a bit put out that the BBC hadn't asked the Stones" to be on the broadcast, Bramwell recalls. "At the time they were doing their album, *His*

[sic] *Satanic Majesties Request* and he said you couldn't buy that kind of publicity."

Narcissistic as he often was, it is hard to imagine Mick saying such a thing. After all, he knew that he was due in court two days after the broadcast. Surely he ought to have understood that when it came to deciding which music group should represent Great Britain to the entire world, BBC executives had an easy decision. Besides, the Stones didn't have any promising new material to unveil at the time. They were at another low ebb.

Although they had a recent hit single with "Let's Spend the Night Together," they had been disappointed by the response to their last album, *Between the Buttons*. They were also terribly worried about everyone's drug hassles; if anyone in the group had gotten convicted, it would become difficult for the Stones to tour outside of the UK.

Meanwhile, Brian Jones continued deteriorating. The other Stones had been tolerating his addlepated and neurotic behavior on account of the fact that he was making salutary contributions to the group's music. Now, they wondered what to do with him. Whenever inspiration struck, Brian was still a skilled dabbler, but more often he was dead weight, a nuisance, an albatross. Certainly it did not help things when, in March, Keith Richards stole Brian's alluring fashion-model girlfriend, Anita Pallenberg, while they were all on holiday together in Morocco. In fact, Keith and Anita abandoned Brian there, sneaking away at night while he was on an errand, and leaving him behind at the El Saadi Hotel. Brian was devastated by the betrayal, but he had little ground to stand on. Everyone knew he had treated Anita terribly, even to the point of being physically abusive.

Andrew Oldham had also developed a nasty drug habit (mostly uppers and downers). After Scotland Yard's drug squad starting going after pop stars like Donovan and then the Stones, he thought it wise to flee the country. Thus it was that during the most precarious months of the Rolling Stones' career, when the band's key members were adrift in a sea of troubles—fighting, scheming against one another, and trying to stay out of jail—Oldham was in Monterey and Bel-Air, getting wasted.

Then again, it probably wasn't any great loss. Mick and Keith were thinking about cutting him loose anyhow when, to their annoyance, Oldham suddenly reappeared in London, firing on all cylinders and raring to get back to work. The Stones discovered they couldn't easily break their management contract, but they also learned that Oldham was responsible for paying all of their studio bills. And so they started bleeding him. They'd book huge blocks of studio time and then fail to show up. Or they'd show up hours late or rent two studios at once. Often when they *were* present they'd just screw around or invite their friends over and make it a party. "Olympic became the nightclub that was open after all the other ones closed," lamented George Chiantz, a sound engineer. Once when Oldham was there they squandered an entire recording session on purpose, just to piss him off. They kept going into these long, intentionally sloppy improvisational blues jams, winking at one another and waiting for Oldham to explode. Finally, it dawned on them that Oldham was so oblivious that he didn't even realize was he getting punked.

Only when Lennon and McCartney showed up at Olympic Studios one night did the Stones finally have a productive session. "Prior to their arrival the atmosphere in the studio had been akin to a bunch of relatives waiting graveside for a priest to do the honors," said Oldham. The Stones were trying to record a zeitgeist-catching summer anthem of their own, a hippie hymn called "We Love You"—but they couldn't get it off the ground. After hearing the work in progress, however, John and Paul quickly restructured the entire song around their own high backing vocals.

Record executive Tony Calder was in the studio that night as well. "Lennon said, 'Set the mike up,' and they went in and put the falsetto voices on," he remembered. "I had tears in my eyes; it was magic, that, absolute magic. It rescued the record—no, it made the record. It was phenomenal."

Many years later, when Oldham published his recollection of that night, his purple prose pulsed with enthusiasm.

> *The two Beatles didn't listen to the "We Love You" track for much longer than they'd spent running down "I Wanna Be Your Man" to my songless Stones just two and one half years before. They picked up the [headphones] and sniffed each other out like two dogs in heat for the right part. . . . John and Paul just glided in and changed a runway into an airplane with wings. Their voices locked and smiled like brothers, creating the signposts to give the disarray, the [song's] fractured parts and rhythms something to belong and cling to. Everybody, my gobsmacked Stones as well, straightened up as vision became reality. We'd just have another major lesson from the guv'nors as to what this recording thing was all about. In plain English, I'd just seen and heard a fuckin' miracle.*

It *did* turn out well. When "We Love You" was finally released in August, it was widely interpreted as a "thank you" to the many fans that had supported the Stones during their trials. A top ten hit in England, it featured a blazing piano lead from session player Nicky Hopkins and the rhythmic blasting of old Mellotron played by Brian Jones. It even contained a bit of sound vérité: before the song gets underway, listeners hear a heavy chain dragging across the concrete and then a jail door slamming shut. Everyone got the reference immediately. Lennon and McCartney's high harmonies were largely disguised in the mix, but careful listeners could discern Lennon's distinctive nasal vowels—We *luuuv youuu*—after the middle eight and again toward the end of the song.

In a 1967 interview, Mick seemed to half-apologize for the song. "It's just a bit of fun," he said. "I'm not involved in this 'Love and

Flowers' scene, but it is something to bring the people together for the summer—something to latch on to."

It was a questionable statement, coming from Mick. He wasn't involved in the love and flowers scene? As a gesture of thanks to John and Paul for their contribution, Mick sent huge bouquets of flowers to their homes in Weybridge and St. John's Wood (respectively). Biographers agree that by then, he and Marianne had both become interested in flimsy counterculture pursuits like astrology and the *I Ching*, and Mick's reading diet was increasingly devoted to studies on magic and the occult, paranormal phenomena, and books about "fairies, goblins and elves." For a time, he even kept a Native American teepee set up inside the Rolling Stones' Maddox Street office, into which he would occasionally go and sit for peaceful contemplation. A week after "We Love You" came out, the couple made yet another excursion into fashionable hippiedom when they joined the Beatles in North Wales for what was supposed to be a ten-day seminar in spiritual enlightenment led by the Maharishi Mahesh Yogi. John and George were particularly smitten with the Maharishi's glittery promise of cosmic consciousness. Their sojourn was cut short, however, when the Beatles got word that their faithful manager, Brian Epstein, had died from a sleeping pill overdose at his home in London.

The Stones finally released *Their Satanic Majesties Request* in December 1967—just in time for Christmas. Needless to say, the album was widely panned as ersatz Beatles. Over the years, this aberrational collection of lackadaisical songs and weird sounds has gained some notable defenders, who argue that the Stones ought to have been praised for their experimental brio. Back in 1968, however, the negative consensus around *Satanic Majesties* was widely held. It has been called a parody, a put-on, an imitation, a washout, an oddity, "a lovely puddle of psychedelic mumbo-jumbo," and a dog.

Writing in *NME*, Keith Altham called it a "strange electrical holocaust." *Rolling Stone*'s publisher, Jann Wenner, said it was "the prototype of junk masquerading as meaningful." Even the Stones soon disavowed the record. Sounding a bit like a drunk after a bad night, Keith Richards later claimed amnesia: "I can remember virtually nothing of those sessions. It's a total blank."

Somewhere in the midst of the *Satanic Majesties* recording sessions, Oldham resigned. "You have lost the plot," he tartly told them. Oldham understood that however much they tried, the Stones were unconvincing as hippies, and besides, the psychedelic era had already passed its high water mark. The Stones did find the wherewithal, however, to see that *Satanic Majesties* got a really groovy record sleeve. Just like *Sgt. Pepper's*, it was designed by Peter Blake and photographed by Michael Cooper. It was shot with a special Japanese camera, however, which gave it a 3-D effect; the cover image shifts and changes as it's viewed from different angles, and carefully hidden in a flowerbed are images of all four Beatles. But posed as they were in a mystical landscape out of Tolkien—sitting cross-legged, with Jagger wearing a purple robe and a crescent-emblazoned wizard hat—the Stones looked ridiculous.

The rock critic Jim DeRogatis has optimistically called *Satanic Majesties* "the first psychedelic rock album to satirize the prevailing optimism about LSD and to hint that there could be a dark side to the psychedelic experience." But of course satire implies social criticism. If the Stones seemed acid-fuddled, it was because they were eating LSD, not ridiculing it. They were glomming onto a trend. Besides, other bands—arguably including the Beatles—had already alluded to LSD's harrowing aspects.

DeRogatis is correct, though, that the Stones were never fully aligned with the era's incense-scented idealism and flower-powered frippery. (Keith: "I'm quite proud that I never did go and kiss the Maharishi's goddamn feet.") Probably that was good for their ensuing fortune, because shortly after *Satanic Majesties* came out, the political landscape began shifting yet again. The Vietnam War intensified in 1968; by the end of the year, the US had more than half a million troops there. In Paris and Chicago, popular rebellions were met with tear gas and billy clubs; in Prague, the students were met with tanks; in Mexico, they faced guns. In America, FBI and local police forces illegally harassed, surveilled, and in some cases physically attacked civil rights and youth culture activists. In Chicago, the police murdered two Black Panthers in cold blood. After Martin Luther King, Jr., was assassinated, major urban rebellions—marked by arson, looting, and shooting—broke out in more than one hundred American cities. There is some likelihood that on June 5, 1968, when Senator Robert F. Kennedy was killed in California—at the very moment that Sirhan Sirhan's bullet went into RFK's brain at the Ambassador Hotel—the Rolling Stones were at Olympic Studios, in London, recording "Sympathy for the Devil."

• • •

"Even beyond the usual hysterical interest attracted by any new Beatles record," *Time* magazine announced, "Hey Jude" / "Revolution" was "special." Released in the US on August 26, 1968, it soon became one of the bestselling 45s in music history. Many were drawn to "Hey Jude" for its infectious chorus and unconventional four-minute fade out, but it was Lennon's raucous "Revolution," on side B, that captured the attention of American radicals that summer. "That's why I did it," Lennon said later, "I wanted to talk, I wanted to say my piece about revolution."

"Revolution" opens with Lennon screaming abrasively over heavily distorted guitars, but it quickly settles into a bluesy romp, and it soon becomes apparent that Lennon's sonic epistle to the New Left does not express solidarity, but disaffection. Though Lennon says he shared the goals of many radicals ("We all want to change the world") he disavows their tactics ("When you talk about destruction / Don't you know that you can count me out?"). Elsewhere, he expresses skepticism of the New Left's overwrought rhetoric ("Don't you know it's gonna be alright?") and he says he's tired of being pestered for money for leftwing causes ("You ask me for a contribution, well you know / We're doing all we can"). The final verse amounted to an endorsement of the apolitical counterculture, and a toxic kiss-off to the Movement's ultra-radicals:

You say you'll change the constitution, well you know
We all want to change your head.
You tell me it's the institution, well you know
You'd better free your mind instead
But if you go carrying pictures of Chairman Mao
You ain't gonna make it with anyone anyhow!

Anyone in the late '60s who was unfamiliar with the controversy the song provoked would have to be a "Cistercian Monk," remarked one underground journalist. "The Beatles have said something and what they have said is not going to be popular with a great many," announced Ralph Gleason, an influential music critic who helped found *Rolling Stone*. "The more political you are, the less you will dig the Beatles' new song 'Revolution.'" But Gleason approved of the song's message. Countercultural politics, he believed, would ultimately prove more transformative than "real" politics. Instead of presenting another ineffectual "Program for the Improvement of Society," he argued that the Beatles had taken up a more noble task; they were teaching youths to transform their entire consciousness. Wrote Gleason: "The Beatles aren't just more popular than Jesus, they are also more potent than SDS," the New Left's leading student group.

Distributed through Liberation News Service (LNS), the radical news agency that served hundreds of American underground newspapers, Gleason's essay was much-discussed. But it was a small radical British newspaper—*The Black Dwarf*—that was the locus of an even more spirited debate about Lennon's "Revolution." Edited by Tariq Ali, the paper's first issue, dated October 13, 1968, contained a little-noticed essay in which a writer maintained that the Rolling Stones represented "the seed of the new cultural revolution," whereas the Beatles were interested in "safeguarding their capitalist investment."

Two weeks later, another item in *The Black Dwarf* drew a lot more attention. It was "An Open Letter to John Lennon," written by an otherwise obscure socialist named John Hoyland. The fact that it appeared shortly after John and Yoko had themselves been busted for drug possession was not a coincidence. Hoyland later said that when Sgt. Pilcher's drug squad goons stormed into Lennon and Ono's apartment and found 219 grains of cannabis, it made "the inadequacy of [Lennon's] philosophy . . . even more evident."

The last thing radicals needed to do, Hoyland stressed, was change their *heads*. Instead, it was time to pursue an aggressive politics of confrontation: "In order to change the world, we've got to understand what's wrong with the world. And then—destroy it. Ruthlessly." Hoyland also lampooned the Beatles' recent ventures into hip capitalism, as represented by Apple Corps. "What will you do when Apple *is* as big as Marks and Spencer and one day its employees decide to run it for themselves?" he asked. "[W]ill you call in the police—because you are a businessman, and Businessmen Must Protect Their Interests?" Finally, Hoyland impertinently told Lennon, "Recently your music has lost its bite," whereas "the music of the Stones has gotten stronger and stronger." The Stones, "helped along a bit by their experiences with the law . . . refuse to accept the system that's fucking up their lives," he maintained.

Lennon was so disturbed by the letter that he phoned Ali to complain; Ali encouraged him to write a rebuttal, which appeared in January. It was not terribly coherent. Lennon began by saying, "I don't worry about what you, the left, the middle, the right or any fucking boys club think," which (as Peter Doggett has observed) raised the question as to why he was even bothering to reply in the first place. Next, Lennon labored to defend the position he enunciated in "Revolution" while simultaneously trying to maintain his radical cred. "I'm not only up against the establishment, but you too, it seems," he said. "I'll tell you what's wrong with [the world]—People—so do you want to destroy them? Ruthlessly? Until you/we fix your/our heads there's no chance." Lennon added that Apple Corps was less a money-making venture than a vehicle for the Beatles' creative experimentation, and he professed not to care much about it. But Lennon was disingenuous; "Look man, I was/am not against you," he said, even though Hoyland—who championed the revolutionary overthrow of the State—was exactly the type of person that "Revolution" targeted. But after radicals like Hoyland objected, Lennon pandered to them by suggesting that the song didn't really mean what it seemingly meant. Still, he was pissed. "Instead of splitting hairs about the Beatles and the Stones," Lennon added, "think a little bigger . . ."

Though Hoyland's reply seemed to be written in the first person, it was actually written by the *Black Dwarf* editorial collective, which maintained that "Revolution" amounted to a betrayal.

> *The feeling's [sic] I've gotten from songs like "Strawberry Fields Forever" and "A Day in the Life" are part of what made me into the kind of socialist I am. But then you suddenly kicked us in the face with "Revolution." That's why I wrote you—to answer an attack you made on us, to criticize a position you took . . . in relation to the revolutionary socialist movement—knowing that what you said would be listened to by millions, whereas whatever reply we make here is read by only a few thousand.*

During this period, countless other rock enthusiasts turned volte-face against the Beatles. The underground press "ate the Beatles alive," one journalist remarked. A writer from the *Berkeley Barb* disparaged "Revolution" as an "unmistakable call for counter-revolution." *Village Voice* writer Robert Christgau was likewise disappointed that the Beatles went out of their way to criticize the political left. A writer for *New Left Review* called the song a "lamentable petty bourgeois cry of fear." In *Ramparts,* Jon Landau called the song a "betrayal." Even a

Moscow-based newspaper, *Sovetskaya Kultura*, chided the Beatles for their "indifference to politics."

Balanced against this, a few others read a more complicated message in Lennon's song. Some held that its musical textures overwhelmed its lyrical content. "Revolution isn't the strumming of a folk guitar, it is the crashing explosions of a great rock 'n' roll band," wrote Greil Marcus. "There is freedom in the movement, even as there is sterility and repression in the lyrics." "We owe an apology to the Beatles," said another left-wing writer. "However shitty the lyrics of 'Revolution' may be, the message"—that is, the question of whether a revolution was desirable or necessary, and how to go about effecting one—had at least provoked a useful conversation. Another writer credited the song with generating "more thought and discussion over the whole question of violence and revolution among young people than any other single piece of art or literature." Yet another fan simply would not be deterred. "The Beatles' politics are terrible," he said, "but they're on our side."

• • •

Contra to "Revolution" was "Street Fighting Man," the Stones' new single from *Beggars Banquet*, which was released in the US on August 30, 1968, just four days after "Revolution" (thereby violating the much vaunted agreement that the Beatles and the Stones wouldn't put their records in direct competition with each other). The original record sleeve (very quickly withdrawn) shows a photo of an LA cop with his boot on the back of a young protestor who is lying, defeated, in the street. Fearful that the song would further inflame the passions of militants who had been involved in the chaos surrounding the Democratic National Convention, most Chicago radio stations refused to play it. Jagger supposedly penned its lyrics after attending a March 17, 1968, rally that began at London's Trafalgar Square, which drew a crowd of about twenty-five thousand. After listening to speeches, many of the protestors clashed with mounted policemen outside the US Embassy in Grosvenor Square. Cops charged at the protestors with their batons, while youths swung back with tree branches and fence posts and showered them with debris. Half of the fifty people who wound up being hospitalized were police officers. By some accounts, Jagger was in the thick of the action; one remembers him "throwing rocks and having a good time," while another recalls him "hiding [and] running." A Michael Cooper photograph taken at the event shows Jagger surrounded by demonstrators, keenly observing what was happening, but not quite participating.

To his regret, Jagger had to abandon the protest after being recognized by too many fans. The song's refrain was thought by some to evoke his feelings of impotence and frustration. ("But what can a poor boy do? / Except to sing for a rock 'n' roll band? / 'Cause in sleepy London town / There's just no place for a street fighting man.") Others saw the refrain as a hedge against the song's more provocative lyrics.

Soon after "Street Fighting Man" was released, New York City's most militant newspaper, the *Rat*, printed its lyrics in a sidebar. A little later, the *Black Dwarf* reprinted a handwritten copy of the lyrics that Mick Jagger had given them: "Everywhere I heard the sound of marching, charging feet, boy / 'Cause summer's here and the time is right for fighting in the street, boy." Some regarded the song as a clarion call. SDSer Jonah Raskin recalls marching up New York City's Fifth Avenue in December 1968, protesting the recent police murder of two Black Panthers. When someone beside him started whistling the song's tune, Raskin writes, "I chanted the words myself: 'The time is right for violent [sic] revolution.' I arched one stone after another; the whole plate glass window collapsed." During many shows on the Stones' 1969 US tour, Mick wore a shirt with an Omega symbol on the front: the symbol of Resistance, an American antidraft group. When the Stones played Madison Square Garden that year, a group of New York radicals called Mad Dogs draped a nine-by-twelve-foot National Liberation Front (NLF) flag from the top of a balcony. When they played Chicago in November 1969, Jagger dedicated "Street

Fighting Man" to the people of that city, "and what you did here last year." When the tour reached Seattle, members of Weatherman crashed the gates and passed out leaflets. In Oakland, a group of anarchists distributed a broadsheet:

> *Greetings and welcome Rolling Stones, our comrades in the desperate battle against the maniacs who hold power. The revolutionary youth of the world hears your music and is inspired to even more deadly acts. We fight in guerilla bands against the invading imperialists in Asia and South America, we riot at rock 'n' roll concerts everywhere. We burned and pillaged in Los Angeles and the cops know our snipers will return.*
>
> *They call us dropouts and delinquents and draft dodgers and punks and hopheads and heap tons of shit on our heads. In Viet Nam they drop bombs on us and in America they try to make us war on our own comrades but the bastards hear us playing you on our little transistor radios and know that they will not escape the blood and fire of the anarchist revolution.*
>
> *We will play your music in rock 'n' roll marching bands as we tear down the jails and free the prisoners, as we tear down the State schools and free the students, as we tear down the military bases and arm the poor, as we tattoo BURN BABY BURN! on the bellies of the wardens and generals and create a new society from the ashes of our fires.*
>
> *Comrades, you will return to this country when it is free from the tyranny of the State and you will play your splendid music in factories run by workers, in the domes of emptied city halls, on the rubble of police stations, under the hanging corpses of priests, under a million red flags waving over million anarchist communities. In the words of [André] Breton, THE ROLLING STONES ARE THAT WHICH SHALL BE! LYNDON JOHNSON—THE YOUTH OF CALIFORNIA DEDICATES ITSELF TO YOUR DESTRUCTION! ROLLING*

STONES—THE YOUTH OF CALIFORNIA HEARS YOUR MESSAGE! LONG LIVE THE REVOLUTION!!!

Still spooked after nearly being sent to prison after his 1967 drug arrest, Jagger had declared on *World in Action*, "I don't really want to form a new code of morals or anything like that. I don't think anyone in this generation wants to." But in 1969, he left some believing that he did, in fact, endorse a general uprising. Asked about "Street Fighting Man" being boycotted by Chicago radio stations, Jagger mused, "They must think a song can make a revolution. I wish it could."

• • •

"America, with its ears turned to its transistors, has been following what it imagines to be an ideological debate between the Beatles and the Rolling Stones," observed a London writer. Although both bands were culturally influential in ways that are difficult to quantify, on close examination the supposed ideological differences between them are harder to discern. Their albums were not, to borrow a phrase, "wax manifestos." They were more like Rorschach inkblot tests, upon which youths projected their own interpretations. Although Jagger allegedly developed a left-wing critique of capitalism when he was briefly enrolled at the London School of Economics, an acquaintance observed that later, "he grew rather fond of capitalism as first one million, then the next poured into his account." The notion that he was "radicalized" by his drug arrest seems equally specious; after all, he apparently only attended part of one demonstration in his entire life. Jagger's friend Barry Miles even suggested that when Mick showed up at Grosvenor Square, he did so at least in part because he thought of it as a social event. "[Jagger] did have a genuine revulsion against the Vietnam War. But I think much more than that it was also the thing to do. That's what everybody in Chelsea was doing that week, going to that demonstration."

In 1968, the Stones appeared in Jean-Luc Godard's *Sympathy for the Devil* (also called *One Plus One*). Before he started filming, Godard announced his creative intentions with a series of non sequiturs that, even in the heady atmosphere of the late '60s, must have been off-putting to anyone who was rationally minded. "What I want above all is to destroy the idea of culture," he boasted. "Culture is an alibi of imperialism. There is a Ministry of War. There is also a Ministry of culture. Therefore, culture is war." What he wound up producing instead was an utter catastrophe of a film that blended documentary-style shots of the band working in the studio interspersed with clips of Black Panthers spouting ugly rhetoric and murdering white women in a South London junkyard. In one scene, a female character named "Eve Democracy" wanders around aimlessly in the forest and, no matter what question she is asked, answers only "yes" or "no." In another, a girl walks into a porno store and gives a Nazi salute. At one point an off-camera narrator announces that he is waiting on the beach for "Uncle Mao's yellow submarine," obviously a reference to the Beatles' song. No one had even the slightest idea what the hell it was supposed to mean, but it certainly *seemed* radical.

On their 1969 tour, however, the Stones refused to allow the Black Panthers to appeal for funds from their stage. In hindsight, it is hard to regard the Rolling Stones' radicalism as anything but a fad. After all, the band had already been moddish during the mid-'60s, and psychedelic during the Summer of Love; in the mid '70s, the Stones would dally with reggae, and after that, they would enter a brief disco phase.

Meanwhile, Lennon's political thinking in the late 1960s and early 1970s can only be described as muddled. Not long after "Revolution" came out, he launched a series of whimsically flavored avant-garde peace protests with Yoko Ono—beginning with their March 1969 Bed-In in Amsterdam—that seemed to endorse pacifism and flower power. They also sent "acorns for peace" to various world leaders, lobbied for peace while cloaked in a white canvas bag, and commissioned billboards in major cities across the globe, announcing "War Is Over—If You Want It."

The following year, after the Beatles broke up, he told Jann Wenner that he resented "the implication that the Stones are like revolutionaries and the Beatles weren't," but he never explained what he meant. In the same interview, Lennon disavowed his previous belief that "love [will] save us all" and professed (whether literally or metaphorically) to be wearing a Chairman Mao badge. "I'm beginning to think he's doing a good job," Lennon said. When asked about the possibility of a "violent revolution," Lennon tartly announced, "If I were black, I'd be all for it." In August 1971, he even turned up at a rally with a sign proclaiming "Victory for the IRA Against British Imperialism." (The Irish Republican Army, of course, was a terrorist group.) Asked how he squared his pacifism with his support for the IRA, Lennon said, "it's a very delicate line." That same year, he placed yet another phone call to the *Black Dwarf*'s Tariq Ali, only this time it was to play for him (literally over the phone) a didactic new song called "Power to the People," which seemed to refute "Revolution." ("We say we want a revolution / Better get on it right away.") Later on he would change course again. In one of his last interviews, Lennon said, "The lyrics [in 'Revolution'] still stand today. They're still my feeling about politics. . . . Don't expect me on the barricades unless it's with flowers."

Despite the confusion and half-heartedness with which the Beatles and the Stones regarded the exigencies of their day, both bands held such clout over young music fans that their songs, lyrics, behavior, and mannerisms continued to provoke robust debate. Even those who turned against the Beatles after "Revolution" never doubted their influence. But this stirred another complaint: why didn't they do more? "They could own television stations," remarked John Sinclair, the notorious Detroit radical. "They could do anything they want to do. They are in a position to carry out a total cultural assault program, the effects of which would be incredible," and instead they frittered away their energy on embarrassing hobbies like the Apple Boutique, a trendy retail store in downtown London. "I think it may be safely said that they have more power and influence over the 'revolutionary' generation . . . than anyone else alive," said another young writer. If they "*really* wanted to change the world, the world would feel it."

Instead, the Beatles' politics lagged. "For a long time the Beatles were oracles for our generation," said a wistful writer for Houston's underground newspaper, *Space City!* "Whatever the state of the world was, they seemed to be able to make their music expressive of it; when we began to look analytically at our society they began to tell us what we saw."

On the one hand, that was off base. Hardly any social criticism can be found in mid-'60s Beatles lyrics. And yet by 1968, one could plausibly argue that the group had fallen out of step with radical youths. "Revolution" was "probably an honest statement," rock critic Richard Goldstein remarked. "They probably don't understand what *we* mean by revolution." Recalling that the Beatles had received MBE awards from Queen Elizabeth in 1965, a writer for Milwaukee's *Kaleidoscope* newspaper called them "confirmed institutionalists," adding, "[they] may yet become the Walt Disneys of their day."

By contrast, radicals continued to regard the Stones as more militant and more authentic than the Beatles, and it was a perception that Mick Jagger encouraged.

At a Rolling Stones press conference in 1969, a reporter asked, "What do you think about John Lennon returning his [MBE] medal" in protest of the Vietnam War?

"At last!" Jagger exclaimed, his Cockney accent back in force. "He should have done it as soon as he'd got it."

"I don't dig hero cults," sniffed Dave Doggett, editor of Jackson, Mississippi's *Kudzu*, "and the Beatles are beginning to smell of that sort of thing." Jon Landau maintained that the Stones "strive for realism in contrast to the Beatles' fantasies." Another writer observed that Beatles songs were frequently elliptical—one had to *search* for meaning—whereas, "When you hear a Stones song, there is no question in your mind as to what they are trying to accomplish." "The Stones sing to and for the 'Salt of Earth,' reflecting their backgrounds," added a clueless writer for Detroit's *Fifth Estate*. Meanwhile, "the Beatles live in their beautiful, self-enclosed Pepperland."

But the Stones' bloom was brief; soon radicals charged them with elitism and aloofness, especially during their 1969 US tour, when they played in gargantuan arenas and gouged fans with exorbitant ticket prices. This was a new thing; until then, the world's most popular bands often played halls that held one or two thousand people, in part because the infrastructure and technology for facilitating arena concerts did not yet exist. Oftentimes, the Stones kept fans waiting until late in the night before they started their show, and the best seats weren't even available for fans; they were reserved for music industry big shots. Youths who believed they shared some commonality of outlook and purpose with the Stones were quick to register their frustration.

After the Stones played Philadelphia, they were denounced in a lengthy, humorous front-page *Free Press* article. "A small band of daring fast-moving bandits . . . pulled off one of the cleanest and biggest hauls in recent history at The Spectrum. . . . Operating before almost 15,000 eyeball witnesses, the bizarrely dressed gang . . . made a clean getaway with cash and negotiable paper believed to be worth in the neighborhood of $75,000." The paper revealed embarrassing details of the Rolling Stones' contract (remarkable for its "sheer audacity") and complained that little of the economic activity around the Stones' show redounded to the community's benefit. Worse still, the Stones acted like prima donnas, refusing interviews and traveling with a rough security team ("goons") who made sure fans kept their distance. According to Philip Norman, "Promoters in almost every city attacked them for the huge percentage [of the gate] they had taken, [and] their egomaniacal Rock Star arrogance. . . . To amass their two million gross, it was suggested, the Stones had systematically and callously ripped off teenagers all across America."

In 1970, editors at Chicago's *Rising Up Angry* completely revised their opinion about the Stones. The previous year, they wrote that, "Unlike the Beatles and their passive resistance with 'All You Need Is Love,' and ['Revolution'], the Stones take a different look at things. They know you can't love a pig to death with flowers while he kicks the shit out of you." Though "only a rock group," the Stones address "real life and how to deal with it, not meditation and cop-out escape." But fallout from the 1969 tour convinced them that the Stones deserved more critical scrutiny. "They should no longer be able to sing about revolution and give clenched-fist salutes, making money hand over fist unless they actively support what they sing about."

> *To give an example, when the Stones were in Chicago,* [radical activist] *Abbie Hoffman went backstage to see them. He talked to Mick Jagger and they both congratulated each other on their accomplishments. Abbie then asked Jagger if he could donate money to the Conspiracy (trial defense). Jagger said they had upcoming trials, too. After the uneasy moment, Jagger told Hoffman to ask their business manager, who said no.*

"If the Rolling Stones are part of the family," antiwar activist Todd Gitlin asked, "why don't they turn their profits into family enterprises?" Even Liberation News Service—which had once run an inadvertently humorous article headlined "LNS Backs Stones in Ideological Dispute with the Beatles"—turned on the Stones with a scorned lover's fury. "[C]lapping hands, cutting up, busting loose, fucking, blowing weed, and breaking windows is a far cry from seizing state power," they observed. "And a lot of the Revolution so far is just a hip ego trip. What do groupies, pimps, PR men and ticket-takers have to do with Revolution? Mick Jagger is . . . a half-assed male chauvinist prick."

Having recorded songs like "Under My Thumb," "Yesterday's Papers," and "Back Street Girl," the Stones were overdue for condemnation on the sexism charge. But for many Movement politicos, it was the Altamont disaster that precipitated their final break. Nettled by criticisms about all the money they were making, the Stones boasted that they would show their gratitude to American fans by headlining a hastily organized "free" outdoor concert at Altamont Speedway, some forty miles north of San Francisco. (In fact, they expected to cash in indirectly since they knew their performance would be featured in the forthcoming concert film *Gimme Shelter*, directed by Albert and David Maysles.)

Altamont was a dirty, bleak space for a rock festival, almost completely lacking in amenities for the three hundred thousand concertgoers. Asked to guard the stage, the Hell's Angels motorcycle gang went on a drug-and-booze soaked rampage, assaulting countless hippies with weighted pool cues and kicks to the head. "Their violence united the crowd in fear," one journalist remarked.

When the Stones played "Under My Thumb," the Angels set upon an African American teenager, Meredith Hunter. While trying to escape a beating (possibly a stabbing), Hunter whipped out a pistol and held it high over his head; in an instant, the Angels stabbed and beat him to death. Ever since, historians have presented the Altamont disaster—along with the Manson Gang murders and the Weather Underground's town house explosion—as the youth movement's death knell. "It would take a little while longer for the message to filter through to the rest of the world," Tony Sanchez wrote. But at Altamont, on December 6, 1969, "all the beautiful fantasies of the sixties withered and died like flowers beneath the shower of paraquat."

• • •

Rock 'n' roll had always been a popular and a performative art—based in part on the commercial exploitation of the blues—and even the most ostentatiously "radical" acts of the 1960s understood this. Neither the Beatles nor the Stones were very radical, however. Both of these immensely talented bands helped to construct images of youth culture that generated powerful confidence, self-awareness, and libidinal energy among their listeners, and as a result, they stimulated a great amount of change. But neither group articulated, or proved willing to defend, a coherent political cosmology. The supposed "ideological rift" between the two bands was nearly as stylized as the contrasting costumes they wore on *The Ed Sullivan Show*.

The controversies and discussions generated by the Beatles and the Stones remind us, however, that there was a time when rock's artifice was frowned upon and its commercial logic was muted. To rock fans in the '60s, the idea that the Rolling Stones would go on to gross hundreds of millions of dollars playing on gargantuan stages, in outdoor stadiums, while under corporate sponsorship, and as senior citizens, would have seemed unfathomable. Nor could they have imagined (not even in a stoned moment) that Mick Jagger would accept a knighthood, at the Queen's behest, at Buckingham Palace in 2003. The idea that Michael Jackson would purchase a considerable chunk of the Lennon-McCartney songbook and authorize "Revolution" to be used for a Nike commercial would never have been entertained. As music writer Fred Goodman observed, "Just a few decades ago rock was tied to a counterculture professing to be so firmly against commercial and social conventions that the notion of a 'rock and roll business' seemed an oxymoron." That sentiment was captured in a 1969 letter to the editor of Seattle's underground newspaper, *Helix*: "Why does it cost $50,000 to book the Rolling Stones for a concert? Why does *Abbey Road* list at $8.98?"

> *Why can't rock groups who want to do free gigs just go ahead and do them . . . And why do rock entrepreneurs . . . make hundreds of thousands of dollars charging high prices for "festivals"? . . . I say FUCK 'EM! FUCK the record companies! Fuck the culture vultures and all those hypocritical assholes who "bring the music!" Fuck the rock groups who have "made it" and feel totally justified in screwing us! Don't buy their trash! Show the [rock promoter]*

> *Bill Graham's [sic] and the Beatles of the scene that they no longer belong.*

As the rock constituency that fueled the New Left and the counterculture faded into memory, so too did the radical newspapers that once printed such clamorous rhetoric. In their place arose the "alternative press," today's network of weekly newspapers that are sometimes distributed for free in metropolitan vending boxes or stacked in piles in cafes and bars. Unlike the underground papers, these metropolitan weeklies—which are now on hard times—were always meant to be commercially successful. The "alternative" label they embraced was in fact a transparent bid for respectability, meant to underscore their distance from the political radicalism that sullied the underground press. In return for advertisements in these papers, record companies regularly receive flattering articles, record reviews, and concert listings promoting their artists. Meanwhile, market-savvy researchers and niche advertisers helped to shape a rock culture that is not only older, but is also increasingly heterogeneous. As a global phenomenon, and a multibillion-dollar industry, rock 'n' roll holds considerable capitalist clout, but today no one thinks of it as a generation's lingua franca.

Of course, youths will always turn to rock 'n' roll as an outlet for their energies, frustrations, rebellions, desires, and as a way of making sense of their lives. But the underground press coverage of the Beatles and the Stones reminds us just how much the audience for rock music has changed. Perhaps, though, we ought not be *so* cynical. No matter how fractious the New Left may have seemed in the late 1960s, many radicals and hippies continued to regard rock 'n' roll as their one common denominator, the single force around which they could unify and extend their communal culture. In this context, even the era's most tepidly political rock heroes—the Beatles and the Rolling Stones—could present themselves as avatars.

CHAPTER SIX

WHEEL-DEALING IN THE POP JUNGLE

In 1967, the Beatles spent the last weekend in August in North Wales, attending a conference on "spiritual regeneration" hosted by the Maharishi Mahesh Yogi. Their entourage—wives, assistants, and friends, including Mick Jagger and Marianne Faithfull—numbered about sixty people, all of whom were housed in an otherwise empty student college dormitory. Everyone slept in tiny rooms with bunk beds and plain furniture, and everyone paid the same standard rate for lodging: £1.50 per night, including breakfast. Members of the press were forbidden from the campus, and since only one person from the Beatles' management team had a phone number with which to reach the group—to be used only in case of an emergency—it was expected to be a quiet weekend. But on the afternoon of August 27, the pay phone in the dormitory lobby just kept ringing and ringing.

The news was devastating: Brian Epstein was dead. At that point, the cause of his demise had not yet been officially determined, but authorities noticed that his bedside table was cluttered with eight pill bottles. He was thirty-two years old.

"It was simply terrible how lost, how heartbroken, the Beatles were," Marianne recalled. "They kind of went into close family mode from the sorrow and the pain."

The Maharishi tried assuaging the Beatles' grief with his boring homilies. Brian had not *really* died, he told them. Rather, he had merely departed the earthly, physical realm; now he was gliding toward some other plane of existence. As they headed out of town, John and George—both glum and visibly shaken—spoke briefly with press. "Meditation gives you comfort enough to withstand something like this, even the short amount we've had," said John. George added, "There's no real such thing as death anyway." Of the four Beatles, these were the two who were the most committed to Eastern teachings, but they didn't sound terribly convincing. Later, Lennon revealed what was truly on his mind. "I *knew* that we were in trouble then," he said. "I didn't really have any misconceptions about our ability to do anything other than play music. And I was *scared* you know, I thought 'we'd fucking had it now.' "

• • •

Before he poisoned himself with sleeping pills, Brian had become highly adept at cultivating press relations. One of the Fleet Street newshounds to whom he'd become especially close was Don Short, a reporter for London's *Daily Mirror*. Although Short was known as a tenacious journalist, he and Brian had reached an understanding: when it came to covering the Beatles, there were certain "no-go" areas—things that he might become privy to, like Brian's homosexuality or the Beatles' drug use—that he would not report on. If, on the rare occasion, Epstein felt the need to vent about the Beatles, or to talk about them in a way that was not entirely flattering, he could do so with Short, confident that his remarks would not show up in the press.

One evening over drinks at his Chapel Street town house, Brian asked Short to hazard a guess: Which of Beatles do you think is the hardest to manage?

Short quickly assumed it was John Lennon. He was the most volatile and sharp-tongued member of the group, the one most likely to go off script at a press conference or get ensnared in some kind of embarrassing shenanigan.

"In fact, Brian's answer was McCartney," Short recalled. "Paul wanted to project himself as the nice guy, but in terms of arranging Beatles business, he was the problem." Paul frequently pestered Brian with questions and concerns about the Beatles' business affairs, and he wasn't shy about reminding Brian that it was his job to keep the Beatles happy. Usually McCartney got whatever he wanted by relying on his wooing and soft-selling skills, but sometimes he could be domineering and pushy—a bit of a control freak, even—and Brian would be intimidated. "John may have been the loudest Beatle, but Paul was the shrewdest," claimed the group's PR man, Tony Barrow.

In 1965, the pop music industry was abuzz about an audacious American accountant by the name of Allen Klein, who renegotiated the Rolling Stones' record contract with Decca to the tune of $1.25 million in advance royalties. (That may not sound like much today, but it was unheard of at the time.) He did it with a bit of panache as well. Keith Richards recalls that he summoned the Stones and said, "We're going into Decca today and we're going to work on these motherfuckers. We're going to make a deal and we're going to come out with the best record contract ever. Wear some shades and don't say a thing. Just troop in and stand at the back of the room and look at these old doddering farts. Don't talk. I'll do the talking."

When Klein barreled into Decca's boardroom with the Stones following behind him, he dispensed with any pleasantries. "The Rolling Stones won't be recording for Decca anymore," he announced.

Decca's sixty-five-year-old chairman, Sir Edward Lewis, was appalled by the scene. When he reminded Klein that the Stones were already under a contract, Klein shot back that he did not care. ("A contract is just a piece of paper," he was known to say.) According to Keith Richards, Sir Edward was literally drooling while Klein went through his spiel. ("I mean not over us, he was just drooling. And then somebody would come along and pat him with a handkerchief.")

When it was over, Richards said, "They crumbled and we walked out with a deal bigger than the Beatles'."

Paul was annoyed. If the Beatles were the most successful act in show business, he reasoned, why didn't their record contract with EMI reflect that? Paul understood, of course, that when the Beatles were first getting going, Epstein's career guidance had been invaluable. Epstein had managed the group with all-consuming devotion and uncanny prescience. But it was becoming increasingly apparent that Epstein lacked Klein's sharklike mentality, as well as his deep knowledge of contractual law and music industry accounting practices.

Then again, so did just about every other pop group's manager. In the mid-'60s, Klein was an acknowledged force in the fast-growing music business. He'd made his reputation by performing aggressive, small-print audits on behalf of his clients, including Bobby Darin, Lloyd Price, and Bobby Vinton, and then recovering unpaid royalties. In 1963, he renegotiated soul singer Sam Cooke's contract with RCA, and won him $110,000 worth of back payments. Before long, record labels seemed almost fearful of Allen Klein. Others in the music industry, however, admired him. Klein's personality was gruff (almost gangsterlike); he had a stout frame, oily hair, and one of his favorite words was "motherfucker." But he also had a deep and abiding love for pop music, and he was unquestionably good at what he did. In some quarters, Klein's sybaritic lifestyle—his fancy yacht and his high-rise office—enhanced his reputation.

After the Beatles quit touring, Epstein's responsibilities on their behalf had greatly diminished. What the group most needed now, some people said, was a disciplined and hawk-eyed moneyman who could oversee their increasingly complicated finances. All eyes pointed toward Klein. Not only had he gotten the Stones a huge advance payment, he also increased the group's royalty rate to 25 percent of the wholesale prices of each LP they sold (about 75 cents per album). When Epstein renegotiated the Beatles' contract with EMI in late 1966, he must have tried to get a similar deal, but he fell short. The

Beatles received only 15 percent per album sold in England, and 17.5 percent for each LP they sold in the US on the Capitol label.

Klein and Epstein met in London in 1964, ostensibly to discuss the possibility that Sam Cooke might support the Beatles on an upcoming tour. Soon after the two began talking, however, Klein broached a different topic: the possibility of a business relationship. Epstein's assistant, Peter Brown, recalled the meeting. "Klein said that he heard the Beatles' low royalty rates from EMI were 'for shit' and that he could renegotiate their contracts. Brian was royally offended at the suggestion that someone else should do his job for him, and he had Klein shown to the door."

If Epstein had hoped to discourage Klein, or embarrass him, then he underestimated the man. Klein soon began telling people that it was only a matter of time before he would "get" the Beatles. "[Epstein] always thought Klein was a big threat to him," said Danny Betesh, a music industry veteran.

As if to make Brian even more insecure, Paul used Klein's success against Epstein. One time in a crowded elevator, surrounded by the other Beatles, Paul said to him, "Yeah, well Klein got the Stones a quarter and a million, didn't he? What about us?"

It was a fair question, but Paul later regretted the cutting way he put it across. Epstein was always so sensitive, and he desperately craved the Beatles' approval—but perhaps never more so than during the last months of his life. His five-year management contract with the group was set to expire in October, and among his associates, he fretted endlessly about the possibility that the Beatles might cut him loose. Few of those in Epstein's circle thought he had much cause for worry—probably he would have just been asked to take a lower commission—but who could say for sure?

In November 1966, Epstein was forced to swat down a newspaper rumor saying that the Beatles had already begun meeting with Klein to discuss their future management. Then in early 1967, Klein ensconced himself at London's Hilton Hotel and boasted to reporters that he was destined to manage the Beatles. His remarks caused such a stir that Epstein denounced them with a formal press statement. Still, the Stones' new manager never gave up. "The whole time Allen was with the Stones he was trying to get the Beatles interested in him," said Sheila Klein Oldham (Andrew's ex-wife). Mickie Most, the British record producer, said much the same. "Allen got very obsessed with signing the Beatles. The Stones were much more aggravation than he counted on."

About seven weeks before Brian died, the Beatles released "Baby, You're a Rich Man," the B-side to their number one hit "All You Need Is Love." George Harrison dubiously claimed that the song touted an uplifting, Eastern-tinged message: the idea that anyone can be "rich" because richness comes from within. But Brian likely surmised that "Baby, You're a Rich Man" was an unfriendly song, intended specifically for him. One can only hope (perhaps faintly) that he didn't notice the despicable way that Lennon corrupted the song's chorus as it faded out. Instead of singing "Baby you're a rich man too," he sang, "Baby you're a rich fag Jew."

Baby you're a rich fag Jew. It wasn't the first time Lennon had attacked Brian that way, but that didn't make it any less outrageous, especially considering everything that Brian had done for the Beatles. Though it is hard to imagine now, showbiz managers in the 1960s looked after their clients a bit like parents did their children. That was considered normal. In fact, the Beatles were so dependent upon Brian that they hardly ever carried their own money. Instead, whenever they wanted or thought they needed something—whether it was new set of guitar strings or a fancy new car—they would have to ask their manager. Brian controlled the entire group's purse strings. He ensured that everyone was taken care of and, when possible, he allowed for this or that extravagant expense. It was also his responsibility to be "fair" when he doled out the money (some got more than others) and to be mindful of his clients' long-term financial health.

The Stones had a similar relationship with Klein, only Klein tried to ingratiate himself with his clients by presenting himself as the "cool dad" on the block—the most understanding, generous, and indulgent of all possible managers. "If you wanted a gold-plated Cadillac, he'd give it to you," Richards marveled. "When I rang and asked for £80,000 to buy a house on Chelsea Embankment near to Mick's, so that we could wander back and forth and write songs, it came the next day."

What the Stones did not realize, however, was that they had already been swindled. When Klein came on board as comanager of the Stones in August 1965, the Stones (plus Oldham) had already set up their own company in the UK called Nanker Phelge Music. Klein then promptly set up his own company, called Nanker Phelge USA—he was its president and sole stockholder—and it bore no relation whatsoever to the other Nanker Phelge. When Klein won that widely publicized $1.25 million advance from Decca, the money went to *his* coffers, not theirs. Furthermore, according to the fine print, Klein wasn't required to release that money to the Stones for twenty years. (Meanwhile he invested it in General Motors stock and kept the enormous profits to himself.) Even more substantially, Klein tricked the Stones into surrendering the publishing rights to all of their recordings. It was an incredibly audacious scam. One would be hard-pressed to imagine a scenario in which a group as hugely successful as the Rolling Stones would knowingly surrender control of the copyright and master tapes of all of their songs. But Klein wound up owning the North American rights to everything the Stones produced until their contract with Decca expired in 1971. In fact, it was Klein—not the Rolling Stones—who made a fortune from the Stones' all-time best-selling record, the compilation double album *Hot Rocks 1964–1971*. Later on, when Klein was forced to justify what he had done, he said it was a protective measure to shield the Stones from the British income tax.

The Stones eventually launched numerous lawsuits against Klein and his company, ABKCO (the Allen and Betty Klein Company), and it would take seventeen years before they reached a final settlement. Long before then, Klein cut off their golden spigot. In his memoir, Bill Wyman produced a series of telex exchanges from 1968 that show just how vexed and frustrated the Stones became over their inability to get Klein to release any of their money. A lengthy June 19 missive from Fred Trowbridge, the band's London bookkeeper, indicated that the Stones' travel agents were threatening legal action if they weren't paid, that they owed money to their publicist (Les Perrin) and, to top it off, various overdraft fees were piling up. "We have made numerous attempts to contact you on the telephone," Trowbridge wrote. "The position has now reached [a] crisis point. I need money now. . . . Yes Allen I need £12,995.10 (pounds), now."

Later that summer, the Stones' road manager and pianist, Ian Stewart, had to buy a new Hammond organ to replace his old one, which had been destroyed in a fire. But he couldn't get Klein's office to reimburse him. In August, Jagger formally asked Klein to put £125,000 in his account for a house he was trying to buy, but two months later the money still hadn't been received. "What is happening on Mick's checks re his properties[?]," read one communiqué, "these are most urgent." By the fall, the cables from London to New York were growing increasingly frantic. On October 15, Brian Jones "urgently" requested £6,000 he needed to pay his lawyers. On October 21, Charlie Watts wrote, "I have not yet received my $5,000. Please telephone me back." On October 26, Trowbridge wrote again: "Berger Oliver [a London law firm] are screaming for the balance of Bill's money. What is happening to those checks? What about Brian's £6,000?" An October 28 letter to Klein said, "We are still awaiting . . . funds in order to settle the £13,000 tax liability that is now overdue in respect of the past remunerations for Rolling Stones Ltd." The most derisive cablegram, however, came directly from Mick: "The phone and electricity will be cut off tomorrow. Also the rent is due. I am having to run the office despite your wishes. If you would like to remedy this, please do so."

When Klein introduced himself to the Stones in 1965, everyone in the band was still in their early twenties, except for Bill Wyman, who was nearly thirty. As Wyman later explained in his memoir, he was the only one in the group who was initially skeptical of Klein. "I didn't trust him and he knew it. 'Why don't you like me, Bill?' he would say on many occasions. 'Because I don't trust you, Allen,' I would reply." But before long, Wyman was mollified (at least temporarily) by a "fat check . . . the biggest payout [he'd] ever had," which he delightedly showed his wife.

The only other Rolling Stone from whom one might have expected a bit of wariness was Jagger, the former economics student who nowadays is well known for his business acumen. But Marianne always felt that Mick became savvy about money only later on, as a result of the problems Klein caused. Initially, Allen struck Mick favorably. Mick was perhaps a wee bit uneasy about Allen's gauche personality—his abrupt manners, slovenly appearance, and thick New Jersey accent—but it wasn't a deal breaker. In fact, it has been said that Mick was so pleased with Allen Klein that he recommended him to the Beatles. Derek Taylor, Apple's press officer, remembers Jagger telling the group, "Well, maybe you wouldn't want to go on holiday with Allen, but he'll take care of you."

Marianne Faithfull likewise remembers Jagger speaking positively about Klein to the Beatles, only she alleges that he did it falseheartedly. "Mick's strategy in dealing with Allen Klein was fairly diabolical," she wrote. "He would fob Klein off on the Beatles. Mick called up John Lennon and told him, 'You know who you should get to manage you, man? Al-len Klein.' And John, who was susceptible to utopian joint projects such as alliances between the Beatles and the Stones said, 'Yeah, what a fuckin' brilliant idea.' It was a bit of a dirty trick, but once Mick had distracted Klein's attention by giving him bigger fish to fry, Mick could begin unraveling the Stones' ties to him. It was just a matter of time before the relationship was severed."

Was Mick capable of pulling off such a Machiavellian power

move? Of course he was. (After all, this is a guy who once denied paternity of his own daughter and enlisted lawyers to give the runaround to the child's mother, Marsha Hunt.) Besides, one only needs to look at the dates of the angry cablegrams that the Stones sent from London to New York to see that Faithfull's account is completely plausible. Several requests for funds were sent in late 1968: just a few months before Klein met any of the Beatles. Also, the Stones' accountants were not merely requesting money from Klein in this period. They also wanted information about the Stones' tax returns (which likewise was not forthcoming). And why? Because the Stones had hired a London law firm, Berger Oliver & Co., to look into their financial situation. They had grown to distrust Klein so much that they decided they needed an outside appraisal of their financial situation. Around the same time, Mick was introduced, via his society friends, to Prince Rupert Loewenstein, a merchant banker who descended from the Bavarian royal family. After they became friendly, Mick hired him as his personal financial advisor. Loewenstein said that Mick felt that the Stones were in Klein's "grip," and that he had "done them in financially." And Loewenstein agreed: "I was equally certain that he had been taken for a ride, and that I represented for him a chance to find a way out of a difficult situation." He aimed to help the Stones extricate themselves from Klein as soon as such a move became feasible.

Klein and John Lennon met for the first time on the set of *The Rolling Stones Rock and Roll Circus*, a film that the Stones released in December 1968, and that they hoped would be broadcast on the BBC. A year earlier, the Beatles had put out *Magical Mystery Tour*, an hour-long TV special in which they filmed themselves roaming the English countryside in a garishly painted charter bus with an assortment of oddball characters. The Beatles hoped that viewers would find the film clever and offbeat, but in fact, most people found it disconcertingly weird. One problem was that although *Magical Mystery Tour* was filmed in color, the BBC transmitted it in black and white. Another was that it aired in primetime on Boxing Day (the day after

Christmas in England). Well-fed families that had gathered contentedly around their television sets expecting light entertainment from the Fab Four were witness, instead, to a largely improvised, phantasmagoric film with no discernible structure or plot. In one scene, Lennon—his hair slicked back with Brylcreem, wearing a crimson waiter's jacket and sporting an off-putting pencil-thin moustache—uses a garden shovel to dump a huge mound of spaghetti onto an obese woman's table. It was gross.

When the Stones decided to make *Rock and Roll Circus*, they must have seen it as an opportunity finally to outperform the Beatles. They would just have to make a *successful* Christmas TV special. Michael Lindsay-Hogg, the Oxford-educated director who had already done promo clips for both the Beatles and the Stones, came up with the conceit: the Stones would simply put on a rock show in a circus environment. Mick thought it was a fabulous idea. Originally, they hoped to make Brigitte Bardot the circus ringmaster (in part because they figured it would have been a fine excuse to put her in a sexy costume and have her fondle a whip). She proved unavailable, however, so Mick assumed the role. Along with jugglers and clowns, the Stones were supported by host of musical acts, including the Who, Taj Mahal, Jethro Tull, and (most intriguingly) rock's first bona fide supergroup, the Dirty Mac. That was the roguish moniker that Lennon chose for a group that featured himself along with Eric Clapton, Keith Richards (on bass guitar), and drummer Mitch Mitchell, from the Jimi Hendrix Experience. ("Dirty mac" was a slang expression, used to describe the type of trench coats favored by perverts.)

It was the first time since the Beatles began that Lennon had played in public with anyone else besides the Beatles, and they did just two songs: "Yer Blues" (from *The White Album*) and then a five-minute blues jam that was supposed to be a showcase for Ivry Gitlis, the legendary Israeli violinist. Shortly after their song got underway, however, Yoko Ono wriggled out of a black canvas bag near the side of the stage and (with John's encouragement) started screaming into the microphone—*Aaaaaaaaaaahhhhhhhhh! Yeeeeeeeeeee-eedeeeaaaaaaaah-hhhhhhhhh! Aaaaaaahhhh Aaaaaahhhhh*. Giltis tried to smile as he played along, while Clapton and Richards mostly just looked away. Later the filmmakers gave the song a title, "Whole Lotta Yoko," as if she had been a planned performer. It was an unbelievably rude stunt—one that John and Yoko would never have dreamed of pulling on the Beatles—yet no one in the Stones' camp said a word edgewise.

Unfortunately, the filming was also marred by long delays—some of the cameras that Lindsay-Hogg imported from France kept malfunctioning, and several performances had to be shot and then reshot. The Stones didn't take the stage until about 4:00 a.m., by which point many in the studio audience—who had been brought in around noon the day before—had left; those who remained were exhausted. The Stones were tired as well, and in addition to being tired they were rusty, having performed together only once in the previous eighteen months. Most agreed that show's climactic song came off well: Mick sang "Sympathy for the Devil" with diabolic intensity, whirling and kneeling and ripping off his shirt to reveal a configuration of devilish tattoos that had been painted on his chest and biceps. Otherwise, however, the band seemed listless. Peter Swales, newly hired as an assistant to the Stones, recalls seeing a preview of the film at a Soho movie theater. "Allen Klein sat next to Jagger and—right there—killed the movie. He said, 'I don't like it. Why? Because the Who blew you off your own stage!' It was all he had to say." (*Rock and Roll Circus* was finally made available to the public in 1996, when it was released on home video.)

Curiously, when Klein met Lennon on the set, they didn't talk about any financial matters; they just exchanged brief and perfunctory hellos. A few weeks later, however, Lennon gave a revealing interview to *Disc and Music Echo* about the sorry state of Apple Corps (pronounced "core"), the multimedia company the Beatles had founded a year earlier. They started Apple partly as a tax-avoidance scheme. In January 1968, EMI was scheduled to hand the Beatles about £2 million in accrued royalties, and at that time England's highest tax rate on earned income was 83 percent (and dividend and interest income was taxed at a staggering 98 percent). When the Beatles' accountants told the group they could either give almost all that money to the Inland Revenue or do something else with it, they figured it was an easy choice. First, they opened up the Apple Boutique at 94 Baker Street, which traded in high-end hippie gear, most of it designed by an Anglo-Dutch design collective called The Fool. But the handsome storefront was a poorly managed money pit. In fact, it hemorrhaged money so rapidly that the Beatles abruptly decided to close it for good just seven months later. Instead of trying to sell off the remaining merchandise at a discount, they just gave it all away.

Even as the boutique was collapsing, however, Apple Corps expanded into film, electronics, publishing, and music divisions. In June 1968, the Beatles bought an impressive, five-story building at 3 Savile Row for £500,000, installed a recording studio in the basement, and made it their new headquarters.

Although Apple would never have existed if the Beatles hadn't desired to shield themselves from the Labour government's high personal income tax, the enterprise was also fueled by an eager determination to prove that "business" didn't always have to be stodgy, starchy, and serious. Instead, the Beatles insisted that business could be *fun*—a worthy outlet for the group's boundless creative energy. Apple was also propelled by an extraordinary generosity of spirit. The Beatles boasted that it would provide an unprecedented opportunity for other creative types. By signing with Apple, they said, newbie artists would be allowed to pursue their visions without having to compromise, beg for nickels, or worry about pleasing their corporate masters. "We're in the happy position of not really needing any more money," announced twenty-five-year-old Paul McCartney, "and so for the first time the bosses aren't in it for the profit."

To prove the point, Paul helped design a full-page advertisement that ran in *NME* and *Rolling Stone*, which showed their trusty assistant, Alistair Taylor, as a one-man band: he's pictured with a big bass drum strapped onto his back and guitar in his hands, and he appears to be singing like a loon. "This man has talent . . . " the copy reads up top. "This man now owns a Bentley . . . " it says at the bottom. The accompanying text provided instructions for people to send in their demo material. Within a few days, Apple was inundated with demo tapes featuring all varieties of music, as well film scripts, poetry, novels, fashion designs, and ideas about electronic gadgets. And yet not a single person who sent material this way wound up getting signed.

The Beatles unwisely put numerous Liverpool friends on Apple's payroll, and meanwhile, they hired several business professionals who failed to serve the company well. Department heads ran up astronomical expense accounts by flying first-class, staying at luxury hotels, and conducting business at trendy restaurants and nightclubs. Lower-level employees lived large, too. One of them, Richard DiLello (aka the "house hippie") wrote an insider account of Apple's rise and fall called *The Longest Cocktail Party*—an apt title, since one of his responsibilities was to ensure that the place was always well stocked with cartons of cigarettes, Cokes, high-end liquor, and Kronenbourg lager. Derek Taylor, recently rehired as the Beatles' press agent (after resigning in 1964), turned his office into a veritable salon for journalists and touring musicians. "I remember going [there]," said publisher Sean O'Mahony, "and the entire room was a haze of cannabis. It was ridiculous—you could hardly breathe." Apple was also a destination spot for down-on-their luck tourists and burnt-out hippies. Someone said the building's lobby resembled "the waiting room of a Haight-Ashbury VD clinic."

To top it all off, crackpots and scam artists were always calling up Apple's headquarters on the telephone. One staffer remembers overhearing a phone call.

"What did she want?"

"Mick's home phone number and some acid."

"Mick's home phone number and some acid? Christ, what the fuck do they think this place is! Why do they always come *here*?"

In an interview that ran in the January 1969 issue of *Disc and Music Echo*, journalist Ray Coleman asked Lennon whether he was "happy" with Apple? Lennon seized the opportunity to vent his frustration with unusual candor.

> *No, not really. I think it's a bit messy and it needs tightening up. We haven't got half the money people think we have. We have enough to live on, but we can't let Apple go on like it is. We started off with loads of different ideas of what we wanted to do, an umbrella group for different activities. But, like one or two Beatle things, it didn't work out because we aren't practical and we weren't quick enough to realize that we needed a businessman to run the whole thing. . . . It's been pie-in-the-sky from the start. Apple's losing money every week because it needs closely running by a businessman. We did it all wrong, you know, Paul and me running to New York [to appear on* The Tonight Show] *saying we'll do this and encourage this and that. It's got to be a business first, we realize that now. It needs a new broom, and a lot of people have to go. It needs streamlining. It doesn't need to make vast profits, but if it carries on like this, all of us will be broke in the next six months.*

Lennon's last comment was a bit hyperbolic; none of the Beatles were in imminent danger of going broke. Then again, how could anyone be expected to know otherwise? All around the world, newspapers picked Lennon's remarks off the wire services and put them into print. He was the first Beatle to confirm, in even a minor way, what so many others already suspected and feared: without Epstein at the helm, the Beatles were in real trouble. They seemed flaky. First, they were flirting with the Maharishi, next came the *Magical Mystery Tour* fiasco, and now this. Apple was a boondoggle, a shit show, a fiasco.

When Lennon aired out the Beatles' business in the media, the others were aghast. It wasn't just that they were all heavily financially invested in Apple Corps (although that was the case); they were also invested creatively, time-wise and ego-wise. It was an exceedingly audacious endeavor, and they had launched it with no small amount of fanfare. Of course, they knew Apple was floundering, and badly. But they were trying hard to fix it. Now Lennon had just created another infuriating distraction.

About a week after the piece ran, while visiting Apple's headquarters, Coleman had the misfortune to cross paths with Paul McCartney in a hallway. Paul lashed out: "You know this is a small and young company, just trying to get along," he exclaimed. "And you know John always shoots his mouth off. It's not that bad. We've got a few problems but they'll be sorted out." (By now, Coleman's back was pressed against a wall.) "I'm surprised it was you—we thought we had a few friends in the press we could trust."

In fact, Coleman had long been magnanimous toward the Beatles. Oftentimes he had sat on juicy stories that he knew would embarrass the group, cause them trouble, or disrupt their families. This, however, was truly newsworthy. Lennon had provided an accurate, firsthand appraisal of Apple's problems in an interview that both parties understood to be on the record. Moreover, Coleman was certain that Lennon knew what he was doing. He was well practiced at giving interviews, and he put his remarks across sharply precisely because he wanted them to land with big impact. "The day we spoke he was as clear-minded as he had ever been," Coleman said.

• • •

In 1971, Klein gave an interview to *Playboy* that focused heavily on his personal and business relationships with the Beatles and the Stones.

PLAYBOY: Why did you want the Beatles?
KLEIN: Because they're the best.
PLAYBOY: Why did you feel you'd have them?

KLEIN: Because I'm the best. I can even tell you the moment when I knew for sure I was going to be their manager. I was driving across a bridge out of New York and I heard on the radio that Epstein had died and I said to myself, "I got 'em." Who else *was* there?

PLAYBOY: Did you get in touch with John or did he call you?

KLEIN: I called John. Sometime in early 1969 I read that he had made a statement to the papers saying that if the Beatles didn't do something soon, Apple would be broke in six months. That was my opening.

Peter Brown, who was made executive director of the newly formed Apple Corps in 1967, remembers that Klein called frequently. On one occasion, Brown even agreed to a meeting between himself, Klein, and Clive Epstein (the late Brian's younger brother). But nothing was accomplished. "[Klein] was so foul-mouthed and abusive, I ended the meeting in a few minutes and had him shown the door—just as Brian had done years before," Brown recalled. After reading Lennon's comments about Apple, however, Klein redoubled his efforts to make inroads on the Beatles. "I would dutifully return the calls," Brown said, "but Klein was now insisting that he would only speak to one person—John Lennon. I told him that was impossible."

Refusing to be stymied, Klein then reached out to Tony Calder, a business partner of Andrew Oldham's who was also friendly with Derek Taylor. Over a couple of afternoon vodkas in Derek's office, Calder passed along a high-priority message: Klein was staying at the Dorchester Hotel, and he wanted to have John and Yoko over for dinner.

Derek did as he was asked. Years later, he seemed a bit sheepish about it. "Klein is essential in the Great Novel as the Demon King," he quipped. "Just as you think everything's going to be alright, here he is. I helped to bring him to Apple, but I did give the Beatles certain solemn warnings."

Although Klein would become widely disliked in the music industry, his early success in pop music management was not hard to understand. Among other skills, he was said to be brilliant at sizing a person up. In just a few moments, he could locate someone's seductive points or their vulnerable ones. Back in 1963, when soul singer Sam Cooke was having troubles with his record label, RCA, Klein told him: "Sam, I think they're treating you like a nigger, and that's terrible—you shouldn't let them do it." When Klein met Lennon in January 1969, he pressed a different button: He stressed that there were *four* Beatles. Paul McCartney wasn't anybody's leader! Where did he get off, treating the others as if they were merely sidemen? It was just what John wanted to hear.

Lennon also believed that Yoko was fully his equal as an artist, and that she wasn't being paid proper mind—neither by the other Beatles, nor by the broader society. And so Klein prearranged to have the hotel serve Yoko the macrobiotic rice that he knew she favored, and he lavished attention upon her throughout the entire dinner. He told Yoko he would find funding for her art exhibitions, and he would get her avant-garde films distributed by United Artists. Not only that, he predicted they would pay her a million dollar advance (a preposterous claim).

When Klein discussed his background, he stressed the uncanny ways that his own rough childhood had paralleled John's. Allen never knew his mother; she died when he was very young. His father, a Hungarian immigrant, worked in a butcher shop, and since he couldn't afford to raise four kids on his own, he placed infant Allen in an orphanage, where he remained until he was at least nine (some sources say older). Eventually he was placed in the custody of an aunt (just like John had been). Klein had graduated from high school, but it had not been easy: teachers found him difficult to handle, and he'd been expelled numerous times. Later he put himself through tiny Upsala College, in East Orange, New Jersey, by working all day and taking courses at night.

And now? He owned a yacht and he worked from a plush corner office on the forty-first floor of a West Side office building. He could afford to gloat about his success because he had earned it. It came as a result of his calculator brain, his tenacious work ethic, and his utter fearlessness. On his desk, he kept a plaque that parodied Psalms 23: "Yea, though I walk through the valley of the shadow of death, I shall fear no evil *for I am the biggest motherfucker in the valley.*"

Some speculated that Klein, a nondrinker, neurotically channeled his energy into work; that he was what we would nowadays call a "workaholic." That may be so (it is impossible to say), but he certainly had other passions as well. He was said to be a devoted family man and a gifted tennis player, and he had an extraordinary love for popular music. During his dinner with John and Yoko, he made a point of demonstrating his enthusiastic knowledge of soul, pop, and rock 'n' roll by quoting various song lyrics from way back. Of course, he also underscored his deep understanding of the Beatles. "He knew every damn thing about us, the same as he knows everything about the Stones," Lennon said. "He's the only businessman I've met who isn't grey right through his eyes to his soul."

Klein assured Lennon that initially he wouldn't charge him a penny. He just wanted permission to look into his affairs and see what he could do on his behalf. The next morning, Lennon sent a memo to EMI's chairman, Sir Joseph Lockwood: "Please give [Klein] any information he wants and full cooperation."

That came as alarming news to McCartney. Although Paul had once had a favorable view of Allen Klein, he had recently revised his thinking as a result of his new connection with the Eastman family. Paul was introduced to the American photographer Linda Eastman in May 1967. He was still seeing Jane Asher at the time, but their relationship was rocky, and he found himself drawn to Linda's good looks and charming self-confidence. At first, Paul and Linda didn't see much of each other, but about a year later they reconnected, and in March 1969 they were married in a shotgun wedding. Linda came from a privileged background. She grew up in Scarsdale, New York, where artwork by Picasso and Matisse decorated her family's home. Her father, Lee, was a hugely successful showbiz attorney, and her brother, John, was being groomed to take over the family law firm. Both men were posh, debonair, and expensively educated.

The Eastmans advised McCartney to stay far away from Klein. Not only was he gross and unlikeable, they said, he was also now under investigation in the US by the SEC (Securities and Exchange Commission) over an alleged stock-kiting scheme involving Cameo-Parkway Records, a nearly defunct label that he'd purchased in July 1967. When Paul asked Lee and John Eastman if they'd be willing to help the Beatles straighten out their finances, they said they would be happy to oblige. And perhaps they would have done a fine job. But McCartney should have realized that the other Beatles weren't about to let him put his own relatives in charge of the group's finances.

Shortly after Klein won over John and Yoko, he called for another meeting, this one between all the Beatles plus Klein (representing Lennon) and John Eastman (representing McCartney). Right away, the two businessmen in the room began sparring, and before long, McCartney and Eastman became so fed up with Klein's pugnacious attitude that they fled the room. From a tactical point of view, it was a grievous error. After they'd left, Klein told the other three Beatles that they were getting screwed six ways to Sunday, but he knew how to put a stop to it all. He said he'd audit EMI's books, renegotiate their record contract, and get Apple Corps going again by removing all its dead weight. And he promised he'd act in *all* of their interests, rather than defer to Paul. The other Beatles were so impressed that they told Klein they were ready to sign with him, right there on the spot. Klein said it wasn't necessary. "I didn't want to appear too anxious," he explained later.

Alarmed at what had transpired, Lee Eastman flew to London for another meeting with the four Beatles (plus Klein and a few others).

In preparation, he'd brought along a copy of Cameo-Parkway's annual proxy statement (presumably because he found it misleading) as well as a sheaf of newspaper clippings that portrayed Klein negatively. Klein, however, had done some research of his own, and he'd made an odd discovery: Lee Eastman, a descendant of Jewish parents who emigrated to the US from Russia, was using a surname that was different from the one he'd been given at birth. Originally, he was Leopold Vail *Epstein.* Like many ambitious young men, he'd changed his last name so it sounded more Anglo. According to Peter Brown, who was present at the meeting, John and Allen both taunted Eastman by referring to him as "Epstein." Furthermore, Klein wouldn't let Eastman get a word in edgewise. He "began interrupting everything [Eastman] said with a string of the most disgusting four-letter words he could tick off his tongue." Finally, Eastman exploded in such a furious rage that he only managed to discredit himself in front of the others.

Lennon, however, remembered differently: he claimed that Eastman was the bully. "We hadn't been in there more than a few minutes when Lee Eastman was having something like an epileptic fit, and screaming at Allen that he was 'the lowest scum on earth,' and calling him all sorts of names." When Paul began chiming in as well, making snarky comments about Allen's poor style of dress, he further undermined his position. Lennon was not always a polite man, but he loathed snobbery and class condescension. Now, for once, he was horrified by Paul's poor manners.

By that point, there were probably only a couple of people on the planet who, if they had so desired, *might* have been able to keep the Beatles from fracturing. One was Yoko Ono, with whom John was spending nearly all of his waking hours (often in a junkie stupor). Now embarrassed about his earlier infatuation with the Maharishi, Lennon freely admitted that he was relying on Yoko as his personal "advisor." Later on, when Paul asked John to explain why he was so drawn to Klein, John shrugged and said, "Well, he's the only one Yoko liked." But she wasn't the least bit savvy about the music business either. Nor was it at all clear that Yoko even wanted the Beatles to stay together. If the schism over Klein portended the Beatles' demise, she might have been pleased. (Such was the nature of her and John's bizarre codependency.)

Then there was Mick Jagger. Did he feel in any way responsible for the Beatles' current predicament? Earlier, he had recommended Klein to the Beatles; now it was clear from his own actions that he distrusted Klein. When Jagger learned that Allen was making headway into the Beatles' organization, he had a rare opportunity to do the Beatles a huge favor. He could easily have approached all four of them—his supposed good friends—and said, "Look, I know how convincing Allen can be—we trusted him too!—but we were wrong, man. He's a shady actor. He's screwed us up royally, and now we're trying to get rid of him."

It is sometimes claimed that Mick tried to do precisely that, but the far greater likelihood is that he did not.

First, none of the Beatles has ever publicly said that they received such a message from Jagger. Although they all wound up regretting their involvement with Klein, none of them has ever expressed remorse over their failure to heed Jagger's advice. Not only that, but the two key players in the whole dispute, John and Paul, both suggested the opposite: Mick failed to properly warn them about Klein. In a February 1969 interview, Lennon said, "We know [Klein] through Mick Jagger and we trust him—as much as we trust any businessman." The following year, Lennon remarked, "I had heard about all these dreadful rumors about [Klein], but I could never coordinate it with the fact that the Stones seemed to be going on and on with him and nobody said a word. Mick's not the type to just clam up, so I started thinking he must be all right."

In his authorized biography, McCartney said he invited Mick over to Apple's headquarters and requested his unvarnished perspective. "We, the Beatles, were all gathered in the big boardroom there, and we asked Mick how Klein was, and he said, 'Well, he's all right if you like that sort of thing.' He didn't say 'He's a robber,' even though Klein had already taken the *Hot Rocks* copyrights off them by that time."

By some accounts, when Klein heard that Mick was scheduled to talk with the Beatles, he made a point of showing up at the meeting as well, obviously aiming to intimidate his own client. McCartney doesn't mention Klein being there, but if he was, it would have been a clever move. Mick knew better than most just how fixated Klein was on bagging the Beatles; it was to be his greatest coup, his pièce de résistance. And so long as Klein wielded such immense control over the Rolling Stones' interests, Mick would have reasoned that there wasn't any point in antagonizing him.

McCartney later said in an affidavit that when John, George, and Ringo outvoted him three to one in favor of Klein, it was "the first time in the history of the Beatles that a possible irreconcilable difference had appeared between us." At the time, music publisher Dick James and his business partner Charles Silver owned nearly 35 percent of the Beatles' song publishing company, Northern Songs. James's business relations with the late Brian Epstein dated back to 1963, and the Beatles had made him a fantastically wealthy man. By the late 1960s, however, James had grown anxious about the future worth of Northern Songs. He was put off by the drug culture that the Beatles had become immersed in and by Lennon's eccentricity. He worried whether the Lennon-McCartney songwriting partnership would endure. He had also grown to dislike the Beatles personally, no doubt in part because the Beatles plainly despised *him.* John and Paul regarded Dick James as the worst kind of capitalist pig. He'd never done much of anything on the Beatles' behalf, they reasoned, and yet he'd managed to become extraordinarily rich off their accomplishments.

It was not until Klein got involved with the Beatles, however, that James finally decided to sell all of his Northern Songs stock to

Lew Grade, the media mogul who owned ATV (Associated Television). "James knew of Klein's propensity for lawsuits and tearing up contracts," remembered Peter Brown. "This was clearly the time to abandon ship."

The transaction was carried out abruptly and privately on March 28, 1969, and it left John and Paul in the lurch: James did not even offer them the chance to buy his share of the company that owned their songs. Furthermore, having just acquired 35 percent of Northern Songs, Grade went in hot pursuit of 15.1 percent more—just enough to put him in control. Meanwhile, McCartney and Lennon decided that *they* wanted to own Northern Songs. Holding the balance of power between Lennon and McCartney and their allies (on the one hand) and Lew Grade (on the other) stood a consortium of brokers and hedge fund investment managers.

In the midst of all this, Klein's reputation in England took a seismic hit. On April 13, 1969, the *Sunday Times* printed an investigative report on Klein, "The Toughest Wheeler-Dealer in the Pop Jungle." The paper attributed Klein's success to "a startling blend of bluff, sheer determination, and financial agility, together with an instinct for publicity and the ability to lie like a trooper." It also revealed that he had been involved in no fewer than forty lawsuits, that the SEC was prying into his affairs, and that the Rolling Stones' North American publishing royalties were paid directly into Klein's own company, Nanker Phelge USA.

All of this made the remaining Northern Songs shareholders so skittish that Klein was forced to publicly pledge that, should the Beatles win control of the company, he would not join its board or interfere with its management in any way. Nevertheless, after about six months of complicated negotiations and maneuvering, it was Grade who won the controlling share of the Beatles' publishing company. And if that wasn't depressing enough to the Beatles, amidst all of this it was revealed that Paul had been secretly buying shares of Northern Songs in his own name; he owned 751,000 shares compared to Lennon's 644,000. That was flagrantly in violation of a verbal agreement the two had made to keep their shares on equal footing. When Lennon discovered the double-cross, he grew more hostile toward Paul than ever.

Of course, it would be fallacious to say that Klein caused the Beatles' dissolution. Other factors contributed as well. When the Beatles released the double LP known as *The White Album* (officially, *The Beatles*) in November 1968—before any of them had even met Klein—it was clear that they were moving in different artistic directions. *The White Album* was hugely successful, but people often remarked that it sounded more like a collection of solo projects than a coherent group effort. And it did.

The White Album also indicated that George was rapidly maturing as a songwriter. Nevertheless, John and Paul continually stymied his attempts to take an enhanced role in the group. George became particularly resentful after they turned away his recent material around the very time that Paul was subjecting the group to laborious recordings of some of his corniest songs, like "Ob-La-Di, Ob-La-Da" and "Maxwell's Silver Hammer." George also felt that Paul had ceased seeking any creative input from the others. A scene in *Let It Be* captured Harrison's mood: he and McCartney are seated across from each other, working on the arrangement for "Two of Us," when Paul makes a suggestion that causes George to snap. "I'll play whatever you want me to play," he says through clenched teeth. "Or I won't play at all, if you don't want me to play. Whatever it is that will *please you*, I'll do it!"

Paul's ill-timed jocularity likewise grated on the others. Again, the *Let It Be* documentary is revealing. McCartney is frequently shown trying to summon up a spirit of mutuality and *esprit de corps* when it was plainly obvious that nobody else was in the mood. Paul's chirpiness was particularly annoying to Lennon. And yet John must have realized that he had little ground to stand on, since he had largely absolved himself of any responsibility for the Beatles. When he wasn't at home snorting heroin, he would frequently stalk around the studio in a volatile mood, shooting people dirty looks or verbally smacking down anyone who dared cross him. Or he would completely disengage from the others. The Beatles would be trying to build a consensus on something important (like "should we perform live again?") and John would flout his disinterest by staring into space, or doodling in his notebook.

The entire time, John and Yoko subsumed themselves into each other. The Beatles had never before allowed wives or girlfriends in the recording studio, and now Yoko was present at nearly every session. The others did their best to make her feel uncomfortable and de trop, but to no avail. Yoko's effrontery had no limits, they complained. She was always whispering conspiratorially in John's ear or sitting imperiously on an amplifier—as if she were supervising the Beatles' recording sessions. (McCartney: "We were always wondering how to say, 'Could you get off my amp?' without interfering with their relationship.") Worst of all, she would sometimes make comments and suggestions about their music, as if (the audacity is breathtaking) she were now a part of the group. And although Yoko made little effort to get to know the Beatles' friends and helpmates, she was quick to order them around, as if they were her own personal errand boys.

Yoko also kindled Lennon's smoldering interests in avant-gardism and political activism, which only further alienated him from the group (and that may have been the point). In November 1968, the couple released *Unfinished Music No. 1: Two Virgins*, a spontaneously recorded experimental record that hardly anyone heard, but everyone talked about: its cover was made from a photograph that showed John and Yoko in the nude, full frontal and hairy (John's uncircumcised penis and all). Neither of them looked terribly healthy. They must have thought they were making an important artistic statement, perhaps having something to do with innocence, honesty, and vulnerability. But it was scarcely the paradigm buster that John and Yoko imagined it to be. About thirty years later, George said, "What

I thought about the sleeve then was the same as I think now. It's just two not very nice looking bodies, two flabby bodies naked."

It must have been exhausting, putting up with John and Yoko. Lindsay-Hogg tells an anecdote about filming *Let It Be* in January 1969—right around the time Lennon brought Allen Klein into the picture. The Beatles had just endured a long and dreary meeting, and as it was drawing to a close, John produced a sound recording that he wanted the others to hear. It was something he and Yoko had made.

> *He got up and put the cassette into the tape machine and stood beside it as we listened.*
>
> *The soft murmuring voices did not at first signal their purpose. It was a man and a woman but hard to hear, the microphone having been at a distance. I wondered if the lack of clarity was the point. Were we even meant to understand what was going on, was it a kind of artwork where we would not be able to put the voices into a context, and was context important? I felt perhaps this was something John and Yoko were examining. But then, after a few minutes, it became clear. John and Yoko were making love, with endearments, giggles, heavy breathing, both real and satirical, and the occasional more direct sounds of pleasure reaching for climax, all recorded by the faraway microphone. But there was something innocent about it too, as though they were engaged in a sweet serious game.*
>
> *John clicked the off button and turned again to look toward the table, his eyebrows quizzical above his round glasses, seemingly genuinely curious about what reaction his little tape would elicit.*
>
> *However often they'd shared small rooms in Hamburg, whatever they knew of each other's love and sex lives, this tape seemed to have stopped the other three cold. Perhaps it touched a reserve of residual Northern reticence.*
>
> *After a palpable silence, Paul said, "Well, that's an interesting one."*

When Lennon asked the others what they thought, it's easy to imagine that his mannerisms might have been a bit contrived. Surely, he was dissembling. He wasn't really interested in their feedback or their critique or their opinion. No, this was just his way of informing the rest of the group that he wasn't interested in being a Beatle anymore.

• • •

When the Beatles broke up in 1970 they also nixed the tantalizing possibility that they might form some kind of an alliance with the Rolling Stones. However febrile the idea sounds in retrospect, it was once a live possibility. "There was always a 'movement' wanting to put the Stones and the Beatles together in any way possible," Wyman recollected. A couple months after Epstein died, McCartney and Jagger bruited about the idea of merging the two groups' business interests. Mick even went so far as to have a lawyer register the name "Mother Earth" as a possible moniker for a jointly owned recording studio. Paul was known to muse about how cool it would be to have a heliport on top of their headquarters. A statement from the Beatles' press office said, "the prospect of some professional tie-up between the Beatles and Stones is very intriguing. What the boys are contemplating is a separate business project for opening up a joint talent center that will build up on other people's talents, produce and distribute their records."

In other words, they were talking about collaborating on something a bit like Apple's record label. Left to their own devices, it's impossible to know if the Beatles and the Stones would have followed through. But Klein was naturally quite horrified by the possibility of a merger, and on October 17, 1967, he ordered Les Perrin, the Stones' PR guy, to throw a wet towel over the whole idea. McCartney and Jagger had only had "preparatory conversations of a purely exploratory nature," Perrin's statement said. "These conversations have not been resolved and any assumption to the contrary should be considered premature." A few years later, however, the Stones went on to form their own label, Rolling Stones Records, headed by Marshall Chess and distributed in the US by Atlantic Records. Although the Stones never wound up signing many artists, at the outset they had wanted it to resemble the Apple label, only without all of the grandiosity, chaos, and attendant headaches.

On December 31, 1970, McCartney filed suit against the other three Beatles to dissolve their partnership. Along with almost everyone else, the Rolling Stones were disappointed by the news. No doubt that was partly because they would miss their extraordinary music. In a 1971 interview with *Rolling Stone*, Keith Richards expressed his gratitude toward the Beatles, as well as his dismay about their demise. "When they went to America, they made it wide open for us," he said. "We could never have gone there without them. [They were] so fucking good at what they did. If they'd kept it together and realized what they were doing, instead of . . . disintegrating like that in such a tatty way. It's a shame."

Then again, Mick and Keith might also have been disappointed that the Beatles parted ways at the very time that the Stones seemed poised to overtake them as the world's most important band. For about a six-year span in the 1960s, when both groups were churning out records at roughly the same pace, the Beatles' efforts were generally better appreciated. When the Stones released *Beggars Banquet* in 1968, however, they showed they were no longer using the Beatles as a template; instead, they were concentrating their energy in their strongest medium: blues-inflected rock. Then in 1969, the Stones showed even more improvement with *Let It Bleed.* The smartest critics said that *Let It Bleed* surpassed the Beatles' *Abbey Road.* Then in 1971, the Stones—now featuring wunderkind Mick Taylor on guitar (replacing Brian Jones)—put out *Sticky Fingers*, a thrilling and wide-ranging album with an Andy Warhol cover. The following year they left Mother England for southern France, where they lived an even more decadent and perilous lifestyle than ever before, and yet somehow managed to record *Exile on Main St.*—perhaps the finest album of their brilliant career. Even if the Beatles had stayed together, some find it hard to imagine that their output in the very early 1970s would have matched what the Stones accomplished. Of course, we'll never know.

It was in this period that some of the goodwill between the two groups seemed to evaporate. In 1969, Jagger declared, "I don't really like what the Beatles have done very much." *The White Album*, he said, was "ordinary." Jagger was also horrified that the Beatles had allowed their ceaseless bickering and internal power struggles to become press fodder, and he vowed his group would never devolve into such a tawdry spectacle. When a reporter asked Mick if the Stones would ever break up, he answered, "Nah. But if we did, we wouldn't be so bitchy about it.

". . . We'll remain a functioning group, a touring group, a *happy* group."

Lennon shot back in a famously cranky interview with *Rolling Stone*'s Jann Wenner. "I was always very respectful about Mick and the Stones, but he said a lot of tarty things about the Beatles, which I am hurt by, because you know, I can knock the Beatles, but don't let Mick Jagger knock them."

But his complaints against Mick ran much deeper than just that: "I would like to just list what we did and what the Stones did two months after, on every *fuckin'* album and every *fuckin'* thing we did, Mick does exactly the same. He imitates us. And I would like one of you underground people [sic] to point it out, you know, *Satanic Majesties* is *Pepper*, 'We Love You'—it's the most fuckin' bullshit—that's 'All You Need Is Love.'

"I resent the implication that the Stones are like revolutionaries and the Beatles weren't," Lennon continued. "They're not in the same class, music-wise or power-wise. Never were. And Mick always resented it. I never said anything. I always admired them because I like their funky music and I like their style. I like rock and roll and the direction they took after they got over trying to imitate us."

Lennon still was not through: "[Mick] is obviously *so* upset by how big the Beatles are compared to him; he never got over it. Now he's in his old age [he was twenty-seven] and he is beginning to knock us, you know. And he keeps knocking. I resent it, because even his second fuckin' record ['I Wanna Be Your Man'], we wrote it for him."

In a rarely seen interview, filmed sometime in the mid-'70s when Keith Richards was etiolated from heroin, someone asked the Stones' guitarist for a response to Lennon's outburst. Richards didn't hold back.

"I think John's, uh, John's just a little bitter, you know? Always has been, and [he] could never take another band coming up and doing things better than him maybe? Or you know, some things, they could do—when they were together—they could do things better than we could. And there was [sic] other things that we can do better than they can. John Lennon is probably past his golden period. Unless he does something soon, I don't think anyone's going to take much notice of what John Lennon says or does. Because musically he hasn't turned out anything approaching six or seven years ago, what he was doing with the Beatles. None of them are."

"Not even McCartney," the interviewer said, with a touch of sadness.

"Not even McCartney," Keith agreed.

EPILOGUE

At least the Beatles didn't break up because they started to suck. Fans have long debated what a final "Beatles album" would have sounded like, if only the group had stayed together long enough to record the best songs from everyone's early solo projects. Naturally, people disagree over which songs would have made the final cut, and the question raises numerous imponderables: Who would have produced the album—George Martin, Phil Spector, or someone else? How much would John and Paul have tried to shape each other's songs? Would the two of them have finally granted George more space to feature his blossoming talent? Historians tend to shy away from these types of counterfactuals. Nevertheless, it is easy to imagine that if the Beatles had lasted just a short while longer, they might have produced another masterpiece.

For a long time after the Beatles disbanded, the former members dealt with pesky questions and rumors about whether they would reunite. Some have even speculated that on a few occasions the group came tantalizingly close to doing so. But that was probably wishful thinking. The last time all four Beatles even appeared in the same room together was for a business meeting in September 1969. And with each passing year, the odds for a Beatles reunion may well have been dwindling. In late 1980, John Lennon taped an interview with

Playboy magazine in which he ridiculed the idea that grown men should even *want* to carry on in a rock 'n' roll group. It struck him as a pathetic thing to do. He also lashed out against fans who were still clamoring for a Beatles reunion.

LENNON: They want to hold on to something they never had in the first place. Anybody who claims to have some interest in me as an individual or even as part of the Beatles has absolutely misunderstood everything I've ever said if they can't see why I'm with Yoko [instead of the Beatles]. And if they can't see that, they don't see anything. They're just jacking off to . . . it could be anybody. Mick Jagger or somebody else. Let them go jack off to Mick Jagger, OK? I don't need it.

PLAYBOY: He'll appreciate that.

LENNON: I absolutely don't need it. Let them chase [Paul McCartney's group] Wings. Just forget about me. If that's what you want, go after Paul or Mick. I ain't here for that. If that's not apparent . . . I'm saying it in black and green, next to all the tits and asses on page 196. Go play with the other boys. Don't bother me. Go play with the Rolling Wings.

PLAYBOY: Do you . . .

LENNON: No, wait a minute. Let's stay with this a second; sometimes I can't let go of it. (*He is on his feet, climbing up the refrigerator.*) . . . You know, they're congratulating the Stones on being together 112 years. Whoooopee! At least Bill and Charlie still got their families. In the Eighties, they'll be asking, "Why are those guys still together? Can't they hack it on their own? Is the little leader scared someone's going to knife him in the back?" That's gonna be the question. That's a-gonna be the question. They're going to look back at the Beatles and the Stones and all

> those guys as relics. . . . They will be showing pictures of the guy with lipstick wriggling his ass and the four guys with evil black makeup on their eyes trying to look raunchy. That's gonna be the joke in the future. . . . It's all right when you're sixteen, seventeen, eighteen, to have male companions and idols, OK? It's tribal and it's a gang and it's fine. But when it continues and you're still doing it when you're forty, that means you're still sixteen in the head.

Lennon's remarks sound harsh, but it's important to remember that back then, there simply wasn't any precedent for middle-aged men playing rock 'n' roll. Cameron Crowe made the point in his beautifully evocative film *Almost Famous*, which is set in 1973. A gung-ho music manager, Dennis Hope (played by Jimmy Fallon), tries to persuade the fictional band Stillwater that they mustn't squander their opportunities—that they need to strike while the iron is hot. And why? Because rock 'n' roll is a young person's art form. "If you think Mick Jagger will be out there trying to be a rock star at age fifty, you are sadly, sadly mistaken," he says. And yet the Rolling Stones have now outlasted the Beatles by a staggering forty-three years.

Not only that, but there was a brief period when it seemed like the Stones could do no wrong. Almost everyone agrees that they had a five-year stretch, beginning in 1968 and ending in 1972, during which time they knocked out four of the most enduring and ass-kicking rock records in history: *Beggars Banquet*, *Let It Bleed*, *Sticky Fingers*, and the double LP *Exile on Main St.* It was a "run of albums against which all other rock 'n' roll will be forever measured," averred one critic. Another called it "a series of roughly perfect albums." This was the Stones' "imperial phase," and they capped it off with a legendary series of concerts. Nowadays, their 1972 North American tour (also called the *S.T.P.* tour, for "Stones Touring Party") is often remembered as a carnival of lubricity. But it was also the bookend to an era. If the

Rolling Stones had simply disbanded after it was over—without ever releasing another album or appearing on a stage again—surely they would be widely regarded today with the same kind of mystical reverence that is often reserved for the Beatles.

Instead, the Stones soldiered on (though eventually at a much slower pace), and over the years critics have noticed an obvious decline in the quality of their recorded work. In the '60s, it was Establishmentarians who complained that the Stones were god-awful and graceless and tacky. Eventually, insightful rock fans began saying many of the same things. That is not to say that the twelve studio albums the Stones have made since 1973's *Goats Head Soup* haven't all contained at least a couple of admirable songs (surely they have) nor is it even to make an aesthetic judgment. It is just a plain statement about how their work has been received. For a long stretch in the '70s, Mick's immersion in the high society jet set seemed to eclipse his interest in making music, and Keith got so strung out on smack as to be nearly useless. The only thing that complicates the Stones' declension narrative is 1978's *Some Girls,* an eclectic and wittily priapic album that was justifiably hailed as a return form. After that, the Stones languished in mediocrity.

Complaints about the Stones reached a pitch in the summer of '89, when they launched their *Steel Wheels* tour. They didn't have a lot going on musically, so as if to compensate, they put on the most freakishly bombastic rock production the world had ever seen. The stage was some kind of dystopian megastructure: an asymmetrical tangle of scaffolding, catwalks, and balconies that was fitted with blinking lights, fog machines, and flame-shooting turrets. When the Stones played "Honky Tonk Women," gigantic inflatable dolls swelled up alongside the stage. When Mick sang "Sympathy for the Devil," he stood from a ledge over one hundred feet high, shrouded in smoke, as the structure beneath him appeared to burst into flames. Every show ended with a coruscating fireworks display.

Bill German, a Stones fanatic who used to publish the pre-

Internet fanzine *Beggars Banquet*, saw the Stones as often as he could on that tour, and he noticed an "interesting irony" in their approach. "As much as Mick professed his love for the new music and as much as he despised the 'retro rocker' label, he was hesitant about adding the band's new songs to the repertoire."

> *Mick wanted each song, be it "Brown Sugar," "Tumbling Dice," or "You Can't Always Get What You Want" to sound exactly like the original album version. By seeing a lot of new and commercially successful acts . . . Mick got a sense of what was going on in the music industry. He learned the way to reach the vastest audience . . . was to play the hits the way people remembered [as opposed to experimenting with the songs' arrangements]. . . . Most baby boomers want "Gimme Shelter" the way they heard it in their dorm room twenty years ago, so that's how we'll give it to them. It was more a business decision than an artistic decision, but it worked.*

Meanwhile, the Stones took the corporate sponsorship of rock 'n' roll to gaudy new heights. In 1981, they inked a deal with Jovan, a perfume company. The group's main benefactor during the *Steel Wheels* tour was Anheuser-Busch, the brewing conglomerate, which paid them at least $6 million (some sources say more). Now the Stones' expensive concert gear was available at department stores, including Macy's and JC Penney. You could buy *Steel Wheels* boxer shorts, wallets, and commemorative coins. The Glimmer Twins even appeared on the cover of *Forbes*. "What Will They Do With All That Money?" the magazine asked.

Their age was becoming an issue as well. It wasn't that anyone held a grudge against the Stones for getting older, but rather that they were so outlandishly undignified about it. In the mid-'80s, when Mick began attending to his solo career, he was plainly aping the music and mannerisms of much younger acts, like Prince, Michael Jackson, and

Duran Duran. In 1989, Bill Wyman, aged fifty-two, married eighteen-year-old Mandy Smith. And of course, people sniggered about the Rolling Stones' nostalgia-peddling "Steel Wheelchairs Tour."

Again, that was *twenty-five years ago*. Other artists who have remained popular with baby boomers have always continued to evolve, whether for better or worse. (Bob Dylan and Bruce Springsteen are both prime examples.) But the Stones haven't seemed musically audacious for a very long time—not since they experimented with some of the trendy disco sounds of the late '70s and early '80s. (And even the hits they had back then, like "Miss You" and "Emotional Rescue," now seem like duds.) Nor did the Stones return to their roots in blues music, which—unlike rock—is something that old men (if they are talented enough) can perform with dignity. Instead, the Stones drenched themselves in self-parody and inflated ballyhoo.

Nowadays, the Rolling Stones scarcely bother trying to make new music—they've recorded only two completely new songs since 2005—but in 2012 they made an awfully big deal about their fiftieth anniversary. To help out with all the celebrative merchandising, they hired graphic design artist Shepard Fairey to update their infamous lips and tongue logo. They put out a coffee table book (*The Rolling Stones Fifty*), a biographical film (*Crossfire Hurricane*, directed by Brett Morgan), and they released yet another career retrospective of old hit singles, titled *GRRR!* Depending on how one counts it is perhaps the twenty-fifth Rolling Stones compilation album.

And of course the Stones launched their *50 & Counting* tour, which began in Paris and London in late 2012, and came to the United States shortly thereafter. Way back in 1975, Jagger said, "I'd rather be dead than sing 'Satisfaction' when I'm 45," but now he and Keith were both just shy of seventy. Naturally, they played "Satisfaction" at nearly every stop. (It was an encore song.) On some nights, their set lists did not contain a single number that was written after 1981.

Most concert reviewers gave the Stones solid marks. The standard rap was that even in their dotage, the Stones were still capable of delivering an exciting performance. They played their old hits to a surefire audience, and everyone had a good time. Nevertheless, some fans found it hard to regard the *50 & Counting* tour as much more than a sordid money grab. On average, the Stones charged $346 per ticket. For the most part, only very affluent adults could afford to attend. The Stones wound up grossing about $100 million from just eighteen shows.

Then again, music is a powerful memory cue; it can summon nostalgia like little else, and that can be a potent and wonderful thing. Certainly many Beatles fans remain deeply disappointed that they never got a chance to hear another studio album or see the group perform. The Portuguese have a fine word for that feeling: *saudade.* It's a kind of longing for something that one has never experienced, or a keen desire for something that cannot exist.

Paradoxically, however, by refusing to reunite, the Beatles may have actually enhanced their legacy. Unlike so many other fabled pop and rock acts from the '60s and '70s, the Beatles retired while they were near the top of their form. They didn't dilute their catalogue with a string of mediocre records, and they didn't reinvent themselves as a touring act, hawking their hits from thirty and forty years ago to well-heeled baby boomers.

True, Apple continued putting out invaluable Beatles material long after the Beatles dissolved their partnership, including *Live at the BBC* in 1994 and *The Beatles Anthology* in 1995 (which was at once a documentary television series, six CDs worth of unreleased material, and an oral history). As part of that ambitious project, Paul, George, and Ringo even released two "new" Beatles songs—"Real Love" and "Free as a Bird"—which were built around Lennon's singing voice on some old demo recordings that Yoko Ono had been safekeeping. All of the ex-Beatles went on to have successful solo careers, and recently, Paul McCartney has been putting on some magnificent, nostalgia-filled concerts of his own. But of course the Beatles never carried on *qua* Beatles. In a sense (and unlike the Stones) the Beatles never even grew old.

They didn't have the chance.

Hollow-point bullets are designed to expand as they hit their target, causing maximum tissue damage. In New York City, on December 8, 1980, two of them pierced the left side of Lennon's back, and two more entered his left shoulder. They were "amazingly well-placed," said Dr. Stephen Lynn, who treated Lennon at the emergency room at Roosevelt Hospital. "All the major blood vessels leaving the heart were a mush, and there was no way to fix it."

SHOUT OUTS

So many people helped out with this book, whether by reading parts of the manuscript, answering questions, pointing me toward sources, or talking with me at length about the Beatles and the Stones. They include Willie Marquis, Allan Kozinn, David McBride, Dave Rick, Bill Higgins, Steven Stark, Alex Cummings, Joe Perry, Larry Grubbs, Michael Castellini, Jeff Toeppner, Bill Mahoney, Griff, Juan Carlos, Ingrid Schorr, Rebecca O'Brien, Michael Lydon, Christine Ohlman, Steve Biel, Gary Shaprio, Naomi Weisstein, Lizzie Simon, Laurie Charnigo, Anastasia Pappas, Kate Taylor Battle, Andrew Loog Oldham, Todd Prusin, Brendan O'Malley, Eddie Stern, Aaron Buchner and Stef Haller, Brandon Tilley, and J. D. Buhl. Dave Brolan kindly let me reprint a couple of rare Michael Cooper photos at a reasonable price, and Phil Metcalf meticulously copyedited the manuscript.

As always, my three best friends in this profession, Jeremy Varon, Mike Foley, and Tim McCarthy, were tremendously helpful. So too was Whitney Hoke. Special thanks are also due to my old pal Jason Appelman, Heretics of the North Productions, and to to some of my newer Atlanta friends: John Bayne, Stephen Currie and Teresa Burke, and Paul Herrgesell and his lovely family.

I began this book while teaching at Harvard, where Lee and Deb

Gehrke gave me with a charming little office at Quincy House, and the Division of Continuing Education supplied an outstanding research assistant, Arwen Downs. I finished it while teaching at Georgia State University, where the department of history supplied me with summer funding and yet another talented and diligent research assistant: Zac Peterson. At the last minute, I received some crucial proofreading assistance from GSU grad student Katie Campbell, and from Lela Urquhart. This book grew out of an essay I wrote for *The Believer* magazine way back in 2007, where editors Heidi Julavitz and Andrew Leland were both exceedingly helpful.

Special shout outs are owed to Gustavo Turner, Geoff Trodd, and Nick Meunier, all of whom took a special interest in this project and provided feedback on almost the entire manuscript. I deeply appreciate their generosity and kindness. I'm likewise grateful to Peter Doggett for his insightful in-house review of the manuscript and for saving me from several howling errors.

I was fortunate to work with three editors. Amber Qureshi enthusiastically signed this book up, Alessandra Bastagli helped me to finish the first draft, and Jofie Ferrari-Adler saw the project to completion. Jofie has been an outstanding editor: friendly, reliable, flexible, supportive, and smart. Thank you, Jofie! It has likewise been a pleasure working with Jofie's kind and efficient editorial assistant, Sarah Nalle, and with S&S's associate publicist, Erin Reback. My amazing agent, Chris Paris-Lamb, first planted the idea that I should write this book, and then he took me on as a client at just the right time. He's served me remarkably well, and I remain grateful for his friendship, advocacy, and advice.

This book is dedicated, with much love, to my wonderful parents, Harlon and Judy McMillian.

NOTES

INTRODUCTION

1 *"When it was over," Sanchez said*: Tony Sanchez, *Up and Down with the Rolling Stones* (London: John Black, 2011), 93–94. Paul McCartney and Marianne Faithfull have both told this anecdote as well, and the Beatles' press officer, Tony Barrow, has commented on it. But the date it occurred is in dispute. Sanchez claims the party took place on Mick's actual birthday, July 26. But "Hey Jude" was probably not finished then; it was mixed in stereo on August 2 and in mono on August 8.

2 *"It was a wicked piece"*: As quoted in O'Mahony, ed., *Best of the Beatles Book* (London: Beat Publications, 2005), 214.

2 *"You could dance"*: See http://www.scotsman.com/lifestyle/music/news-and-features/beatles-or-the-stones-choose-both-1-513103.

3 *"The Beatles want to hold your hand"*: As quoted in Peter Fornatale, *50 Licks: Myths and Stories from Half a Century of the Rolling Stones* (New York: Bloomsbury, 2013), 45.

3 *Fans registered their loyalty*: Many other writers have dichotomized the Beatles and the Stones in a similar fashion; cf. Philip Norman's observation: "Whatever passing allegiance for this or that newly fashionable group, being a pop fan in 1964 Britain depended on one fundamental question: 'Are you Beatles or are you Stones?' asked with the searching ferocity of rival factions in a football crowd. Even football factions, though, had scarcely been as rife with implications of reflected character. To answer 'Beatles' implied that one was oneself similarly amiable, good-natured, a believer in

the power of success to effect conformity. To answer 'Stones' meant, more succinctly, that one wished to smash up the entire British Isles."

3 *And as most people understand*: "There is little friendship in the world," Sir Francis Bacon remarked, "and least of all between equals." Gore Vidal spoke to the same point when he admitted, "Whenever a friend succeeds, a little something in me dies." Both thinkers are quoted in Joseph Epstein's 2006 treatise, *On Friendship* (New York: Houghton Mifflin, 2006), 8.

5 *"the narcissism of small differences"*: See Sigmund Freud, *Civilization and Its Discontents* (New York: W. W. Norton, 1961), 58–63.

5 *the opposing qualities of the Beatles and the Stones*: That said, some interesting and whimsical takes on the Beatles versus the Stones can be found in the outer reaches of intellectual and pop culture. In 1997, philosopher Crispin Sartwell gained a bit of notoriety when he devised a tongue-in-cheek mathematical formula that he says proves, definitively, that the Stones were the superior band. In 2006, Marxist postpunk rocker Ian Sevonius subjected the groups to addlepated analysis in his chapbook *The Psychic Soviet* (Chicago: Drag City, 2006). ("The Beatles vs. Stones dialectic then, was actually Lennon/McCartney's industrial Sovietology vs. Mick and Keith's agrarian Maoism," he concludes.) In 2010, novelist Alan Goldsher published *Paul Is Undead* (New York: Gallery, 2010) a comic postmodern horror tale (in the form of an oral history) in which the Beatles are portrayed as zombies on a quest for world domination. The plot thickens as England's foremost zombie hunter, Mick Jagger, begins chasing after the Fab Four.

6 *"Vesuvio closed a couple"*: Marianne Faithfull, "As Years Go By," *The Guardian* (October 5, 2007).

1: GENTLEMEN OR THUGS?

7 *By December, he was selling*: See Andrew Loog Oldham, *Stoned: A Memoir of London in the 1960s* (New York: St. Martin's Press, 2000), 256.

8 *Since O'Mahony was already*: Oldham remembers meeting O'Mahony when the latter was working for Robert Stigwood, the future music impresario. And after Oldham introduced O'Mahony to Eric Easton, and the two became fast friends. See *Stoned*, 216, 266.

8 *In 1964, when journalist*: See Mark Lewisohn, "Foreword to the 1995 Reprint," in Michael Braun, *Love Me Do! The Beatles Progress* (New York: Penguin, 1995, c. 1964), 6.

8 *When publishing photos*: As quoted in Ray Coleman, *The Man Who Made the Beatles: An Intimate Biography of Brian Epstein* (New York: McGraw-Hill, 1989), 323.

9 *Many years later, though*: As quoted in *Stoned*, 256.

9 *"We were the ones"*: As quoted in *The Beatles Anthology* (San Francisco: Chronicle Books, 2002), 8.

9 *Yes, Stark points out:* Steven Stark, *Meet the Beatles: A Cultural History of the Band that Shook Youth, Gender, and the World* (New York: HarperCollins, 2005), 113.

10 *Only Ringo came from central Liverpool*: Hunter Davies, *The Beatles* (New York: Norton, 2002, c. 1968), p. 189.

10 *Their homes got very cold*: Steven D. Stark, *Meet the Beatles: A Cultural History of the Band That Shook Youth, Gender, and the World* (New York: HarperCollins, 2005), 42.

10 *"My father drove a bus"*: As quoted in David Pritchard and Alan Lysaght, eds., *The Beatles: An Oral History* (New York: Hyperion, 1998), 17.

10 *"the poor slummy kind"*: As quoted in David Sheff, "Interview with John Lennon and Yoko Ono," *Playboy* (January 1981). One of the first books about the Beatles, which *Record Mirror* journalist Peter Jones published under the pseudonym "Billy Shepherd," professed to the tell "the real story behind [the Beatles'] rise from the slums of Liverpool to skyrocketing fame." See Billy Shepherd, *The True Story of the Beatles* (Bantam, 1964), unpaginated first page.

10 *But by the standards*: When Ringo was six, his appendix burst and he developed peritonitis, sending him into a coma that lasted ten weeks. Then when he was thirteen, he developed chronic pleurisy, which kept him in the hospital for almost two years. All of this wreaked havoc upon his schooling, so the poorest Beatle was also the least educated. On an early press release, he spelled the word "anyone" as "enyone." And on the Beatles' first US tour, in 1964, a waiter who served the group at an upscale restaurant said that Ringo seemed incapable of ordering off a menu and was baffled by the word *oven* (as opposed to *cooker*). Ringo also did not come from an educated family; Freda Kelly, the Beatles' fan club secretary, recalls a time when Ringo asked her to help with his fan mail. "I told him he must be joking. 'Get your mum and dad to do it. All the other parents do.' But he just stood there pathetically and said, 'Me mum doesn't know what to put.'"

11 *According to the Stones' official*: Jon Wiener, *Come Together: John Lennon in His Time* (Champagne-Urbana: University of Illinois Press, 1990), 56.

11 *"One was proud"*: Victor Bockris, *Keith Richards: The Unauthorized Biography* (London: Hutchinson, 1992), 7.

11 *"Two nations between whom"*: As quoted in Stark, 40.

11 *"To Londoners," Steven Stark writes*: Stark, 40.

12 *"With us being from Liverpool"*: As quoted in Pritchard and Lysaght, *Beatles Oral History*, 51.

12 *"could spend night and day"*: As quoted in Pritchard and Lysaght, *Beatles Oral History*, 89.

12 *"We looked at them"*: As quoted in Debbie Geller (ed. Anthony Wall), *In My Life: The Brian Epstein Story* (New York: St. Martin's Press, 2000), 85.

13 *He was, by his own admission*: As quoted in Hunter Davies, *The Beatles* (New York: Dell, 1968), 59; as quoted in Stark, 53.

13 *"His work, erratically presented"*: Ray Coleman, *Lennon: The Definitive Biography* (London: Pan Books, 1995), 83.

13 *"He was the biggest micky-take"*: As quoted in Coleman, *Lennon*, 97.

13 *"he had a very small capacity"*: As quoted in Coleman, *Lennon*, 199.

13 *"came to be regarded"*: Pete Shotton and Nicholas Schaffner, *John Lennon: In My Life* (New York: Henry Holt, 1987), 61.

14 *Though Hunter Davies's authorized biography*: Hunter Davies, *The Beatles* (New York: W.W. Norton, 2010, c. 1968), 59.

14 *Somehow, he touched her breast*: Lennon: "I was just remembering the time I had my hand on my mother's tit in [One] Bloomfield Road. It was when I was about fourteen. I took a day off school, I was always doing that and hanging out in her house. We were lying on the bed and I was thinking, 'I wonder if I should do anything else?' It was a strange moment, because I actually had the hots for some rather lower class female who lived on the other side of the road. I always think that I should have done it. Presuming [or "Presumably"] she would have allowed it."

14 *"It was the worst thing"*: As quoted in Philip Norman, *John Lennon: The Life* (New York: Harper Collins, 2008), 146.

14 *"All I wanted was women"*: Geoffrey Giuliano, *Blackbird: The Life and Times of Paul McCartney*, 17.

14 *"Without question one"*: Giuliano, *Blackbird*, 15.

14 *"They let me stay out"*: As quoted in Geoffrey Giuliano, *Dark Horse: The Life and Art of George Harrison* (New York: Bloomsbury, 1989), 10.

15 *"From about the age of thirteen"*: As quoted in Bob Spitz, *The Beatles: The Biography* (Boston: Little, Brown, 2005), 120.

15 *"You kept your head down"*: As quoted in Spitz, *The Beatles,* 335.

16 *cries of* 'Seig Heil!' *and 'Fucking Nazis!'*: Philip Norman, *Shout! The True Story of the Beatles* (New York: Fireside, 2005, c. 1981), 92.

16 *"Shimmy Shake" as "shitty shitty"*: Richard Buskin, *The Complete Idiot's Guide to the Beatles* (New York: Alpha, 1998), 109.

17 *far more so than in England*: Speaking of sex in England, George Harrison reminisced that in the late 1950s, "it wasn't that easy to get. The girls would all wear brassieres and corsets, which seemed like reinforced steel. You could never actually get in anywhere. You'd always be breaking your hand trying to undo everything. I can remember parties and I'd be snogging with some girl and having a hard-on for eight hours till my groin was aching—and not getting any relief. That was how it always was. Those *weren't* the days."

17 *"two or three girls each night"*: As quoted in Geoffrey Giuliano, *Blackbird: The Life and Times of Paul McCartney* (London: John Blake, 1991), 46.

17 *"It was a sex shock"*: As quoted in *The Beatles Anthology*, 53.

17 *"Between the whores"*: As quoted in Giuliano, *Blackbird*, p. 38.

17 *"Virtually every night"*: As quoted in Giuliano, *Blackbird*, p. 38.

18 *"Within seconds the fellow"*: As quoted in Coleman, *Lennon*, 275.

18 *In another despicable episode*: Norman, *John Lennon: The Life*, p. 216.

18 *"They liked us because"*: As quoted in *The Beatles Anthology*, p. 57.

18 *"raw. . . .They were always"*: Liz Hughes, as quoted in Pritchard and Lysaght, *Oral History*, 72.

18 *"commanded the stage"*: As quoted in Andrew Solt and Sam Egan, eds., *Imagine: John Lennon* (New York: Macmillan, 1988), 37.

19 *"'Shurrup, you with the suits on'"*: Coleman, *Lennon*, p. 241

19 *"John . . . was always ready to have a go"*: As quoted in Gareth L. Pawlowski, *How They Became the Beatles: A Definitive History of the Early Years* (London & Sydney: Macdonald, 1990), 35.

19 *After Stuart Sutcliffe died:* Stuart's younger sister, Pauline, alleged in her memoir *The Beatles' Shadow: Stuart Sutcliffe and His Lonely Hearts Club* (London: Macmillan, 2002) that it was actually Lennon who made the fatal attack upon her brother, and that it occurred in Hamburg, not Liverpool. She also claimed that McCartney witnessed the vicious assault, and that she learned of it firsthand from Stu. But McCartney denies having seen such a fight, and Stu's lover, Astrid, doubts it happened, "because if it had, Stuart would have told me." Lennon was closer to Stu than anyone else in the Beatles, and all things considered the allegation does not seem very credible.

20 *"The Beatles when they lived"*: As quoted in Oldham, *Stoned*, 293.

20 *"He was a rebel"*: As quoted in Wyman, *Rolling with the Stones* (New York: DK Publishing, 2002), 19.

20 *Brian "sometimes talked of becoming"*: As quoted in David Dalton, ed., *The Rolling Stones: The First Twenty Years* (New York: Knopf, 1981), 12.

20 *"an old ladies' resting place"*: As quoted in Wyman, *Stone Alone* (New York: Da Capo, 1997), 77.

20 *"He started to rebel"*: As quoted in Philip Norman, *The Stones* (New York: Penguin, 1994), 54.

21 *"Brian was totally dishonest"*: As quoted in Wyman, *Stone Alone*, 103. Photographer Nicky Wright, who did the cover for *England's Newest Hit Makers*, remembered a time when Brian came to him and said, " 'Here you are—here's a present for you.' Inside were all these wonderful records—Howlin' Wolf, Lightnin' Hopkins, John Lee Hooker. Twenty years later I realized they belonged to Long John Baldry when I read a magazine interview where he mentioned he lent a stash of Chess records to Brian, and never got them back!"

21 *"Within two weeks Brian"*: As quoted in Wyman, *Stone Alone*, 107.

22 *"One night Brian punched"*: Wyman, *Stone Alone*, 82.

22 *"Brian fixed anyone with his big baby eyes"*: Norman, *The Stones*, 51.

22 *"Botticelli angel with a cruel streak"*: Christopher Sanford, *Keith Richards: Satisfaction* (London: Headline Books, 2003), 39.

22 *As a teenager, Michael Jagger*: cf. George Harrison, on his Liverpool childhood: "You couldn't get a cup of sugar, never mind a rock 'n' roll record."

22 *"I never got to have a raving"*: As quoted in Christopher Sanford, *Mick Jagger: Rebel Knight* (London: Omnibus Press, 2003), 16.

23 *"wasn't particularly impressed"*: As quoted in David Dalton and Mick Farren, eds., *The Rolling Stones: In Their Own Words* (London: Omnibus, 1980), 11.

23 *"Rock and roll got me"*: As quoted in A. E. Hotchner, *Blown Away: The Rolling Stones and the Death of the Sixties* (New York: Simon & Schuster, 1990), 52.

23 *Instead, Richards found himself*: Journalist George Melly described the British art schools of the 1950s as "the refuge of the bright but unacademic, the talented, the non-conformists, the lazy, the inventive, the indecisive: all those who didn't know what they wanted but knew it wasn't a nine-to-five job." The list of noteworthy rock musicians who spent time in art school is remarkable; in addition to John Lennon and Keith Richards, it includes Ray Davies, Eric Clapton, Jimmy Page, Pete Townshend, David Bowie, Roxy Music's Brian Ferry, and Dick Taylor, who very briefly played with the Stones before helping to start the Pretty Things.

23 *"free-spirited . . . pest"*: Christopher Sanford, *Keith Richards*, 34.

24 *"the most stylish young man"*: Wyman, *Stone Alone*, 91.

24 *"Charlie's concession to joining the Stones"*: James Phelge, *Nankering with the Stones: The Untold Story of the Early Days* (Chicago: A Capella, 224), 44.

24 *"The major difference between the Stones"*: Wyman, *Stone Alone*, 111.

24 *"The place was an absolute pit"*: Wyman, *Stone Alone*, 112.

24 *"I never understood why"*: Wyman, *Stone Alone*, 112.

25 *When the "Rollin' Stones"*: When their debut gig was announced in *Jazz News*, they were misidentified as "The Rolling Stones," but they meant to go by the "Rollin' Stones" (apostrophe after the *n*) and that is how they were known until they met Andrew Loog Oldham in the spring of 1963.

25 *"They seemed accomplished"*: As quoted in Oldham, *Stoned*, 207.

25 *"but on stage they were"*: Wyman, *Stone Alone*, 131.

26 *"R&B was a minority thing"*: As quoted in Stephen, *Old Gods Almost Dead: The 40-Year Odyssey of the Rolling Stones* (New York: Broadway Books, 2001), 52. Additionally, rock 'n' roll was associated with the working class. "Nice respectable grammar school boys preferred jazz," Peter Doggett wrote me in an informal email, "and so they might have reached the blues via that direction. Liking rock 'n' roll in the '50s was an admission that you were, or wanted to be seen as, a kind of hoodlum. Many boys from middle-class homes used to pretend they didn't like pop and rock 'n' roll because their friends would have laughed at them if they admitted that they did."

26 *"waffly white pop"*: As quoted in John Strausbaugh, *Rock Til You Drop* (London & New York: Verso, 2001), 40.

26 *"Liverpool's best-dressed bachelor"*: Ray Coleman, *The Man Who Made the Beatles*, 29.

27 *"They used to drive us crackers"*: As quoted in Coleman, *The Man Who Made the Beatles*, 76.

28 *"Inside the club it was as black"*: Brian Epstein, *A Cellarful of Noise* (New York: Doubleday and Co., 1964), 39.

28 *"fascinated" by their "pounding bass beat"*: Epstein, *Cellarful of Noise*, 39.

28 *"They were not very tidy"*: Epstein, *Cellarful of Noise*, 39.

28 *"This accusation has been"*: As quoted in *Brian Epstein: Inside the Fifth Beatle* (DVD, Passport, 2004).

28 *"he looked efficient and rich"*: *The Beatles Anthology*, 65.

29 *"The Beatles are going"*: As quoted in Pritchard and Lysaght, *An Oral History*, 86.

29 *Except for on one slightly infamous occasion*: One late night circa 1963, while the Beatles were working, Epstein unexpectedly showed up with one

of his paramours at Abbey Road Studios. No doubt eager to impress, he leaned into the intercom and made a suggestion about Paul's vocals. Lennon's voice boomed back at him: "You look after your percentages, Brian. We'll take care of the music." It was the type of remark that would have sent the Beatles' fragile manager reeling.

29 *"Brian wanted to be a star himself"*: As quoted in Geller, *Brian Epstein Story*, 58.

29 *"It was a choice of making it"*: As quoted in *The Beatles Anthology*, 67.

29 *"After that . . . I got them to wear sweaters onstage"*: As quoted in Pritchard and Lysaght, *An Oral History*, 87. So seemingly reluctant were the Beatles to wear Epstein's outfits that on April 5, 1962, they played the first half of a show at the Cavern Club in their old leather outfits; then they came out and played their second set in tailored suits.

29 *They must "stop swearing"*: As quoted in Geller, *Brian Epstein Story*, 43.

30 *"He was a director"*: As quoted in Pritchard and Lysaght, *An Oral History*, 49.

30 *"posthumous, wise-after-the-event"*: As quoted in Geller, *Brian Epstein Story*, 42.

30 *"It was really hot"*: As quoted in http://www.thebeatlesinmanchester.co.uk/page16.htm.

30 *"there we were in suits and everything"*: As quoted in Coleman, *Lennon*, 268.

30 *"Paul was keen on the changes"*: Cynthia Lennon, *John* (New York: Three Rivers Press, 2006), 106.

30 *"Brian Epstein made them behave"*: As quoted in Oldham, *Stoned*, 294–95.

31 *"I'd never seen anything like it"*: Oldham, *Stoned*, 191.

31 *"a new public personality"*: As quoted in Oldham, *Stoned*, 44.

31 *"a nasty little upstart tycoon shit"*: As quoted in James Miller, *Flowers in the Dustbin: The Rise of Rock and Roll, 1947–1977* (New York: Touchstone, 2000), 203.

32 *"He was the most concerned-about-clothes"*: Oldham, *Stoned*, 71.

32 *"he had all the confidence in the world"*: As quoted in Oldham, *Stoned*, 101.

32 *"I will always thank Mary"*: Oldham, *Stoned*, 95.

32 *"He didn't want me to be a model"*: As quoted in Oldham, *Stoned*, 99. Another time, while in a furious anger, Oldham apparently knocked his mother down a stairwell. According to one of his bosses, he was completely inconsolable for days afterward. Andrew says he doesn't remember hurting his mom but concedes that he might have done so and then suppressed the traumatizing memory.

33 *"were a nightmare together"*: As quoted in Oldham, *Stoned*, 169.

33 *some radio shows and press interviews*: This was the type of thing the Beatles learned to do assiduously, but only after being coached by Epstein. "Trying to get publicity was just a game," Lennon remembered. "We used to traipse round the offices of the local papers and musical papers asking them to write about us, because that's what you had to do. It was natural we should put on our best show. We had to appear nice for the reporters, even the very snooty ones who were letting us know they were doing us a favor. We would play along with them, agreeing how kind they were to talk to us. We were very two-faced about it."

33 *"Onstage, you could not hear the Beatles"*: Oldham, *Stoned*, 182–183.

34 *"I met the Rollin' Stones"*: Oldham, *Stoned*, 185.

34 *The first person he phoned for help was Epstein*: It is sometimes said that the story about Oldham offering to partner with Epstein is apocryphal, but in his latest book, *Stone Free,* Oldham affirmed it. "As for whether Brian might have had the Stones, it's true. He might have. Back when I first saw the Stones, I knew I would need an experienced partner. The band needed work above all else, and I was not a booking agent, nor at 19 could I have been legally licensed as such. I had terrible doubts about partnering up with my landlord, Eric Easton, who was a booking agent. Besides, it was my duty, based either on the ethic my mother had taught me or that I had picked up in the cinema, to call my present employer, Brian Epstein, and let him know what I was up to, and at least sort of offer him an interest in the Rolling Stones. I did, but I hoped he was not listening; he was not, so I made my bed with agent Eric Easton and the Stones jumped in with me."

34 *"Andrew was the young go-getter"*: As quoted in Oldham, *Stoned*, 217.

34 *"the most brilliant self-selling job"*: Norman, *The Stones*, 93.

34 *"He probably said, 'I am the Beatles' publicist'"*: As quoted in the Rolling Stones, ed. Dora Loewenstein and Philip Dodd, *According to the Rolling Stones* (San Francisco: Chronicle Books, 2003), 56.

35 *"was looking for an alternative to the Beatles"*: As quoted in Oldham, *Stoned*, 197.

35 *"looked more pop"*: Bockris, *Keith Richards*, 40. Richards restored the *s* in 1977.

35 *"marched us up to Carnaby Street"*: Wyman, *Stoned*, 192.

36 *"obvious" that "Andrew was"*: Wyman, *Stone Alone*, 136.

36 *"a jumbled assortment of jeans"*: As quoted in Wyman, *Stone Alone*, 162.

37 *"the band your parents loved to hate"*: Oldham, *Stoned*, 294.

37 *"made sure we were as vile as possible"*: As quoted in Strausbaugh, *Rock Til You Drop,* 39.

37 *"If people don't like us"*: As quoted in Hotchner, *Blown Away*, 100.

38 *"most vivid dreams"*: As quoted in *The Beatles Anthology*, 8.

38 *"salmon fisherman"*: Impressively, outside of music (and related activities), Lennon never once held steady employment in his life.

38 *"loved rock and roll"*: From www.robertchristgau.com/xg/music/stones-76.php.

39 *"more like [what] we'd done before"*: *The Beatles Anthology,* 101.

39 *"Sure, they were very creative"*: As quoted in Dalton and Farren, eds., *In Their Own Words*, 107.

39 *"We saw no connection between us"*: As quoted in Stark, *Meet the Beatles*, 202.

39 *"For the first time, London"*: Edward Luci-Smith, ed., *The Liverpool Scene* (London: Garden City Press, 1967), 5.

39 *"the center of the consciousness of the human universe"*: Luci-Smith, *The Liverpool Scene*, back cover.

39 *"They feel you don't tell"*: As quoted in Coleman, *The Man Who Made the Beatles*, 323.

2: "SHIT, THAT'S THE BEATLES!"

41 *Inside the venue, it was*: See Paul Trynka, ed., *MOJO's The Beatles: Ten Years That Shook the World* (USA & Great Britain: DK Publishing, 2004), 72.

41 *Still, the "fans loved it"*: As quoted in Pritchard and Lysaght, *An Oral History*, 126.

42 *the Beatles' press officer, Tony Barrow*: Tony Barrow to author, email, 2/21/10.

42 *"Certain groups are doing exactly"*: Here, Lennon was no doubt referring to Freddie and the Dreamers, who had scored a top-five hit with a cover of James Ray's "If You Gotta Make a Fool of Somebody," which the Beatles said had been swiped from their set-list. McCartney even maintained that he knew precisely where the "theft" took place: "Freddie Garrity saw us playing that song in the Oasis Club in Manchester and took it," he said. Though it may sound odd to hear the Beatles grumbling about other bands "copying" songs that they themselves had just gotten from American artists, they had a legitimate complaint. At the time, it was unusual for British groups to perform their own material; most acts put together set-lists that consisted almost entirely of obscure American numbers. Once a group discovered a song they liked, however, and then added it to the

repertoire, it was widely understood that in some sense, they "owned" that song.

42 *"And in a final blast, an angry Lennon said"*: Ray Coleman, "Boiling Beatles Blast Copy Cats," *Melody Maker* (October 1963).

43 *"the Liverpool-London controversy"*: As quoted in *MOJO's The Beatles,* 67.

43 *"a popular misconception"*: Wyman, *Rolling with the Stones*, 55.

43 *"it was always a very friendly relationship"*: Keith Richards, *Life* (New York: Little, Brown, 2010), 141.

43 *"very good friends of ours"*: As quoted in *MOJO's The Beatles,* 152.

43 *"I know it sounds daft"*: As quoted in *MOJO's The Beatles,* 154.

43 *"Our rivalry was always a myth"*: As quoted in Wyman, *Stone Alone*, 511.

44 "Art students have had this": "Peter Goodman," *Our Own Story, by the Rolling Stones* (New York: Bantam, 1965), 92. Emphasis added. The Stones continued with this line at least as late as February 1964. When Ray Coleman, the *Melody Maker* journalist, sat them down for an interview, he said, "There was a groan of horror at the mere suggestion" that the Stones' haircuts were Beatle-ish. "'Look,' said Keith, 'These hairstyles have been quite common down in London long before the Beatles and the rest of the country caught on. At art school, and years ago, ours had always been the same.' 'Look at Jimmy Saville,' urged Jagger. 'He had it like it is long before others started that style. It's the same with us.' 'And Adam Faith,' added Bill Wyman. 'He had hair like the Beatles years ago, didn't he?' 'I dunno,' Richard said to Wyman. 'I reckon your style came direct from the Three Stooges.'"

45 *"Brian Jones had been bending"*: As quoted in Strausbaugh, *Rock Til You Drop,* 41.

45 *But Gomelsky recalls that snow*: Gomelsky even claims to remember who the three attendees were. "They all joined the music business," he said. "One of them, Paul Williams, became a blues singer; another, Little H, [became] a famous roadie who worked for Jimi Hendrix and later died in the crash with Stevie Ray Vaughan; and the third started his own venue somewhere and became an agent. They were cool guys."

46 *"He was the kind of guy"*: As quoted in *According to the Rolling Stones*, 42.

46 *"Giorgio, there's six of us, and three of them"*: As quoted in Strausbaugh, *Rock Til You Drop*, 41–42.

46 *"detected a certain Neanderthal"*: Alan Clayson, *The Rolling Stones: The Origin of the Species* (Surrey: Chrome Dreams, 2007), 140.

47 *"two hundred pair of arms"*: As quoted in Strausbaugh, *Rock Til You Drop*, 42.

47 *"No one had seen anything"*: As quoted in *According to the Rolling Stones*, 50.

47 *"formula-ridden commercial popular music"*: As quoted in Oldham, *Stoned*, 203–204.

47 *"My motivation in all this"*: Gomelsky's partnership with the Stones attenuated after Andrew Oldham and Eric Easton swooped in and offered the group a manager's contract while Gomelsky was out of the country (at his father's funeral, no less). "Sure, I was broken up about what happened," Gomelsky later admitted. "Brian's betrayal was very underhand, he was my friend, supposedly. . . . I guess I didn't cut it with the vanity-driven mentality prevailing among those guys, particularly Brian and Mick." Soon after Oldham and Easton signed the Stones, they met with Gomelsky. Supposedly they wanted to talk about compensating him for the work he'd already put into the group, but Gomelsky figured their main goal was to see that the Stones wouldn't lose their precious Sunday-night gigs at the Crawdaddy. Magnanimously, Gomelsky let them continue their residency, even though he came to hold Oldham and Easton in poor regard. They were "two pretty low-flying characters with no interest in blues, underdog culture or social justice!" he said. "Dollar signs were pointing their way."

48 *"good, fluent band"*: As quoted in Strausbaugh, *Rock Til You Drop*, 44.

48 *"to bring about the still unperceived wit"*: Philip Norman, *The Stones*, 80–81. Beatlemania is difficult to date. After examining various regional newspapers, Beatles authority Mark Lewisohn concluded that "Beatles-inspired hysteria had definitely begun by the late spring [of 1963], some six months before it was brought to national attention by Fleet Street press officers." But the Beatles' press agent, Tony Barrow, prefers a more precise date for Beatlemania: October 13, 1963, when the group debuted on the hugely popular television program, *Sunday Night at the Palladium*. The word "Beatlemania" did not appear in print, however, until November 2, 1963, when a writer for London's *Daily Mirror* used it.

48 *"explosive enthusiasm as just another"*: As quoted in Strausbaugh, *Rock Til You Drop*, 47.

48 *"I suppose I should remember"*: As quoted in Strausbaugh, *Rock Til You Drop*, 47. Plans for the film were finally scotched when United Artists, the American film studio, swooped in and offered to finance three motion pictures with the Beatles. According to Clayton, Epstein "unethically" gave the synopsis they'd been working on to the American studio executives, and eventually it morphed into Richard Lester's *A Hard Day's Night*. But

it's hard to know if this really happened. Clayton also says that he misplaced the letter that Epstein sent him a couple of years later "in which he apologized. He said he didn't know, he was naïve, blah blah."

49 *"to find out what was happening"*: As quoted in *The Beatles Anthology*, 101.

49 *"Hey you guys, you've got to listen"*: As quoted in Dalton, *The First Twenty Years*, 26.

49 *Dylan "represented everything that Lennon"*: Miller, *Flowers in the Dustbin*, 226.

50 *"It was like meeting Engelbert Humperdinck"*: As quoted in Spitz, *The Beatles*, 583.

50 *"[W]e were provincial kids"*: As quoted in Barry Miles, *Paul McCartney: Many Years from Now* (New York: Holt, 1998), 100.

50 *who claims to be the "Mr. Jimmy"*: He could be correct, but more likely the reference was to Jimmy Miller, the Stones' producer when they recorded that song. The Chelsea Drugstore mentioned in the song was actually a chic King's Road shopping center that opened in 1968.

51 *but as musicologist Ian MacDonald points out*: Ian MacDonald, *Revolution in the Head: The Beatles' Records and the Sixties* (London: Fourth Estate, 1997), 53.

51 *Probably the Beatles got the idea*: Another song from the era that featured a harmonica, which the Beatles covered, was "I Remember You," which was a hit for Frank Ifield in 1962.

51 *Phelge recounts the scene this way*: Phelge, *Nankering with the Stones*, 29. Phelge claimed that the BBC show that captured Brian and Keith's attention was *Saturday Club*, which featured the Beatles on January 26, 1963. On that show, the Beatles played "Love Me Do," but they didn't follow up with a Chuck Berry number later in their set, as Phelge maintains. The Beatles also played "Love Me Do" on *Talent Spot* on December 4, 1962, and *Parade of the Pops* on February 20, 1963, but they didn't play Chuck Berry songs on those occasions either. Thirty-five years after the fact, it would be unusual if Phelge's memory of the Beatles set list was perfectly accurate. No one, however, has risen to dispute his general account.

52 *"It was an attack from the North"*: As quoted in Davis, *Old Gods*, 33.

52 *"They had long hair, scruffy clothes"*: Of course the Beatles were not, at that point, known for wearing "scruffy clothes."

53 *"That's when I told them"*: As quoted in Dalton, *The First Twenty Years*, 26.

53 *Gomelsky continues: "The club used to open"*: As quoted in Dalton, *The First Twenty Years*, 26.

53 *"Shit, that's the* Beatles!": Wyman, as quoted in Pritchard and Lysaght, *An Oral History*, 122; Wyman, *Stone Alone*, 127.
53 *"We were playing a pub"*: YouTube clip, "Keith Richards—Friends with the Beatles."
53 *"I didn't want to look at them"*: As quoted in Yoko Ono, ed., *Memories of John Lennon* (New York: HarperCollins, 2005), 105.
53 *"an intentionally intimidating image"*: Barry Miles, *The Beatles Diary, Volume One: The Beatles Years* (London and New York: Omnibus Press, 2001), 93.
54 *he said their long leather jackets*: Chris Hutchins, *Elvis Meets the Beatles* (London: Smith Gryphon, 1994), 66.
54 *they exuded a kind of "Fuck You"*: Oldham, *Stoned*, 171.
54 *"almost frightening-looking young men"*: *Boyfriend* magazine, 1963, n.d, n.p.
54 *"four-headed monster"*: As quoted in *MOJO's The Beatles: Ten Years That Shook the World*, 67.
54 *"They could do their stuff"*: As quoted in *The Beatles Anthology*, 101.
54 *"I remember standing in some sweaty room"*: As quoted in *The Beatles Anthology*, 101.
54 *"It was a real rave," he reminisced*: As quoted in Wyman, *Stone Alone*, 127.
54 *"carried themselves with the air"*: Phelge, *Nankering with the Stones*, 105.
55 *"Everyone was trying to find out"*: Phelge, *Nankering with the Stones*, 106.
55 *"John was really nice"*: As quoted in Ono, *Memories of John*, 105.
55 *"A harmonica with a button"*: As quoted in *The Beatles Anthology*, 101. Apparently under Jones's influence, Lennon came around to this point of view as well. Six weeks later, on June 1, 1963, the Beatles performed Chuck Berry's "I Got to Find My Baby" for the BBC show *Pop Goes the Beatles*, and this was the first time Lennon was recorded using a harp. What's more, when disc jockey Lee Peters tried introducing the song by mentioning that Lennon would be playing a "harmonica" on it, Lennon abruptly cut him off.

"Harp! It's a harp," he said pedantically.

"What's a harp?"

"The harp. I'm playing a harp on this one."

"You're playing a harp?"

"Harmonica I play in 'Love Me Do.' Harp in this one [unintelligible]."

Not understanding the difference, Peters said to Lennon (in mock frustration): "Do you want to do these announcements?" and then pretended to storm out of the studio. In all likelihood, Lennon had quickly absorbed Jones's predilection for playing a harp (and later, he would conclude that the harmonica he'd played on "Love Me Do" hadn't been "funky-blues enough" for his taste). Still, the distinction is rather silly, since all harps are also harmonicas.

56 *"Mick says [that meeting] is what made"*: As quoted in Barry Miles, *Many Years from Now*, 101.

57 *Only later would they discover*: Still, the Beatles' success was totally unprecedented. By 1964, they were making so much money (on an 83 percent tax rate) that Board of Trade president (later Prime Minister) Edward Heath quipped that they were propping up the entire national economy. (The Beatles responded in 1966 with George Harrison's song "Taxman.")

57 *Brian Jones asked them to autograph a magazine photo*: This is according to biographer Stephen Davis in his book *Old Gods Almost Dead.* But the story about Brian asking for an autograph and taping it to the wall does not seem to appear in any of the extant primary sources.

57 *"They were very cool guys"*: As quoted in *According to the Stones*, 55.

57 *"Brian read it again aloud"*: Phelge, *Nankering with the Stones*, 104.

57 *For months afterward, Wyman said*: Wyman, *Stone Alone*, 126.

58 *"We looked like this before"*: As quoted in Davis, *Old Gods*, 45. Emphasis added.

59 *"Mick was made up"*: Davis, *Old Gods*, 43. I have not been able to find this anecdote mentioned in any primary sources, or in any secondary literature that was published prior to Davis's book in 2001. When I sent a note to Davis through his publisher, he failed to reply.

59 *"In the end I just gestured into"*: George Melly, *Revolt into Style: The Pop Arts* (New York: Anchor Books, 1971), 73.

59 *"reached the threshold of pain"*: "POPS for Everyone," *Radio Times* (May 2, 1963), 39. Incidentally, a posed photo accompanying the *Radio Times* piece showed a delicately featured blonde teenager clenching her fists and screaming feverishly. It was Jane Asher, the beautiful London debutante and *Juke Box Jury* panelist to whom Paul McCartney would later become engaged but never marry. She was just seventeen.

59 *"And there's a bunch of girls"*: As quoted in Strausbaugh, *Rock Til You Drop*, 45.

60 *"This is what we* like*"*: As quoted in Wyman, *Stone Alone*,128.

60 *According to a rumor, for years*: See *MOJO's The Beatles,* 32.

60 *"Nobody had* ever *played the Philharmonic"*: Harrison was correct to say that the Philharmonic wasn't in the business of hosting rock acts. But he was mistaken when he said that *no* rock act ever played there. Buddy

Holly and the Crickets had performed at the Royal Albert Hall on March 20, 1958, when George was just fifteen. Though none of the future Beatles attended, biographer Jonathan Gould says Lennon and McCartney both "became completely caught up in the enthusiasm generated by Holly's appearance."

61 *"At the height of 'Pool mania"*: Melly, *Revolt into Style*, 82.

61 *The Liverpool scene had been*: Performers at the Lancashire and Cheshire Beat Group Contest played under the apprehension that the winner would receive a Decca recording contract. After it was over, though, the winners—a group called the Escorts—were informed that the prize was merely a Decca *audition*. The Escorts never made a proper album during their four-year career, though in 1983 (supposedly at the behest of Elvis Costello), Edsel Records reissued the twelve songs the group recorded as singles before they split up in 1967, on the LP *From the Blue Angel.* On one of the tracks, Paul McCartney played tambourine.

61 *"I'd really had my backside"*: Dick Rowe, audio recording, "The Rolling Stones Past and Present," Mutual Broadcast System, Broadcast dates: September 30–October 3, 1988. Hour one.

61 *"When George turned around"*: Norman, *The Stones,* 95.

61 *"He took the next train to London"*: Spitz, *The Beatles*, 407.

61 "drove *all day to be at the"*: Davis, *Old Gods*, 56. Emphasis added.

62 *"Upon his return [from Liverpool]"*: Email to author, 2/14/2011.

62 *"When we arrived"*: Email to author, 2/14/2011.

63 *"There wasn't a girl to be seen"*: Dick Rowe, audio recording, "The Rolling Stones Past and Present," Mutual Broadcast System, Broadcast dates: September 30–October 3, 1988. Hour one.

63 *"crowds of boys, rising"*: Norman, *The Stones*, 207.

63 *"the most logical place"*: Oldham, *Stoned*, 210.

63 *"I remember taking [the Stones' audition tape]"*: Rowe, audio recording, "The Rolling Stones Past and Present," Mutual Broadcast System, Broadcast dates: September 30–October 3, 1988. Hour one.

64 *"He had us totally beaten there"*: As quoted in Oldham, *Stoned*, 212.

64 *"Who has been most helpful"*: As quoted in *Rolling Stones Book,* No. 1, June 1964, 11.

65 *"Giorgio, Giorgio,* that's *what I want"*: Strausbaugh, *Rock Til You Drop*, 45.

65 *"In these hectic days of Liverpool"*: As quoted in George Tremlett, *The Rolling Stones Story* (London: Futura Publications, 1974), 61.

65 *"It's good, punchy, and commercial"*: As quoted in Nicholas Schaffner, *The*

British Invasion: From the First Wave to the New Wave (New York: McGraw-Hill, 1982), 60.

66 *"would sit for hours composing letters"*: As quoted in *According to the Rolling Stones*, 43.

66 *"When we left the club scene"*: As quoted in Wyman, *Stone Alone*, 171.

66 *"was the most uneasy of all"*: Wyman, *Stone Alone*, 171.

67 *"From the moment I joined"*: Wyman, *Stone Alone*, 172.

67 *"You're on the road 350 days"*: As quoted in *According to the Rolling Stones*, 101. Richards was of course exaggerating about the extent of the Stones' touring schedule.

68 *"Brian could be sweet—he was intelligent"*: Rob Chapman, "Brian Jones," *MOJO* (July 1999).

69 *Sometimes when the Stones performed*: "For Charlie I think that was the most frustrating time," Keith remarked. "He was a serious musician, a jazz drummer, and all of a sudden he's playing to a load of thirteen-year-old girls wetting themselves and Brian's doing 'Popeye the Sailor Man.' "

70 *"Brian embarrassed himself first"*: As quoted in David Robson, "As Soon As I Saw the Stones, A Wave Came Over, My Life Was Fulfilled," *The Express* (May 30, 2000).

70 *"Rubbing shoulders with the Beatles"*: Wyman, *Stone Alone*, 128.

70 *"idolized the Beatles"*: Wyman, *Stone Alone*, 173.

70 *Dick Rowe called them "ghastly"*: Rowe, audio recording, "The Rolling Stones Past and Present," Mutual Broadcast System, Broadcast dates: September 30–October 3, 1988. Hour two.

71 *"The dialogue," Oldham said*: As quoted in Norman, *The Stones*, 90.

72 *"I remember teaching it to them"*: It was a kind gesture, but not quite an altruistic one. At the time, Lennon and McCartney had more songs than they knew what to do with, and in addition to receiving royalties from each song they donated to other artists—people like Cilla Black, Billy J. Kramer and the Dakotas, and Tommy Quickly—they both received a bit of pleasure from seeing their compositions touted in music magazine record advertisements: "Another Smash Hit from the Sensational Song Writing Team John Lennon and Paul McCartney." (Of course, whoever recorded John and Paul's material likewise got to wallow in some prestige.)

72 *"So Paul and I went off to"*: *The Beatles Anthology*, 101.

72 *"We liked the song"*: Richards, audio recording, "The Rolling Stones Past and Present," Mutual Broadcast System, Broadcast dates: September 30–October 3, 1988. Hour two.

72 *"that John and Paul would be"*: As quoted in Wyman, *Stone Alone*, 151.

72 *"We weren't going to give them"*: As quoted in Keith Badman, ed., *The Beatles: Off the Record* (London: Omnibus Press, 2008), 66.

72 *"Instead of patting myself"*: Oldham, *2Stoned* (New York: Vintage, 2003), 66.

72 *"A songwriter, as far as"*: As quoted in Oldham, *Stoned*, 250–251.

73 *"Look at the other boys"*: *According to the Rolling Stones*, 84.

73 *"The Beatles had set this trend"*: As quoted in Oldham, *Stoned*, 249–250.

73 *"We spent the whole night"*: Richards, *Life*, 142.

73 *"Keith likes to tell the story"*: *According to the Rolling Stones*, 84.

74 *"I saw an angel"*: As quoted in Davis, *Old Gods*, 80.

74 *Had Jagger and Richards*: Arguably, the best Jagger-Richards composition from this period was "So Much in Love." As recorded by the Mighty Avengers, a Coventry band that Oldham also managed, it was a catchy, twangy pop song, but lyrically it was quite caustic, and in that way it presaged some of what the Stones would do later. It was a very minor hit in the UK.

74 *Jagger-Richards composition*: Two more original songs appear on the record, however. One is "Now I've Got a Witness," an instrumental that is credited to the group under the pseudonym "Nanker Phelge." The other, "Little by Little," was credited to Nanker Phelge and Phil Spector.

75 *"Even though people"*: Dalton, *The First Twenty Years*, 31.

76 *Others remember him toiling*: http://www.earcandymag.com/rrcase-brian jones.htm.

76 *"but out of hand"*: Wyman, *Stone Alone*, 177.

76 *"quite upset, almost crying"*: http://www.earcandymag.com/rrcase-brian jones.htm.

76 *"Now there was no distance"*: Oldham, *Stoned*, 245.

76 *"Until that time Brian"*: As quoted in Wyman, *Stone Alone*, 179.

77 *"Brian wasn't really a writer"*: As quoted in *According to the Rolling Stones*, 86.

79 *"all in our smart new clothes"*: As quoted in Miles, *Paul McCartney*, 120.

3: A PARTICULAR FORM OF SNOBBERY

81 *Andrew Oldham recalls puckishly*: "Would You Let Your Sister Go with A Rolling Stone?" *Melody Maker*, March 14, 1964. See also "But Would You Let Your Daughter Marry One?" *Evening Standard* (April 1964).

81 *"I've made sure the Stones"*: As quoted in Wyman, *Stone Alone*, 192.

82 *"Don't for heaven's sake say"*: As quoted in Braun, *Love Me Do*, 14.

82 *At the time, the group's popularity*: People sometimes forget just how young the Beatles' core audience was. In November 1963, the knowledgeable British critic George Melly said "the average age of the fanatic Beatles fan today is about twelve." In 1964, a disc jockey who was master of ceremonies at a Beatles concert in Vancouver estimated that 80 percent of the audience was between the ages of thirteen and sixteen.

82 *By the time they ventured*: The Beatles are thought to have performed 150 different songs, at least once, before they released *Please Please Me* in March 1963. Although American rock 'n' roll songs always dominated their ever-expanding repertoire, the multiformity of their approach is impressive. One scholar broke it down this way: Lennon-McCartney (26 songs), Chuck Berry (14 songs), Eddie Cochran (2 songs), Everly Brothers (6 songs), Buddy Holly (11 songs), Little Richard (12 songs), Carl Perkins (11 songs), Elvis Presley (8 songs), Larry Williams (6 songs), Other rock and roll artists (15 songs), R&B and Motown (18 songs), US pop (15 songs), US girl groups (9 songs), Pre-1945 vaudeville and pop (10 songs), Stage and film musicals (5 songs), UK pop (1 song), "Others" (8 songs).

83 *"I thought of the Beatles"*: *According to the Rolling Stones*, 78.

84 *"Like a lot of my friends"*: As quoted in Stark, *Meet the Beatles*, 203.

84 *"The Beatles were richer"*: Tony Sanchez, *Up and Down*, 1.

84 *"Even in 1965 we Stones fans"*: As quoted in Oldham, *2Stoned*, 284.

84 *"idolizing the authentic legend"*: Kelefa Sanneh, "The Rap Against Rockism," *New York Times* (October 31, 2004).

85 *On more than a few occasions*: The Beatles' press officer, Derek Taylor, described one such spectacle when the group was touring in Australia in 1964: "The routes were lined solid, cripples threw away their sticks, sick people rushed up to the car as if a touch from one of the boys would make them well again. . . . The only thing left for the Beatles is to go on a healing tour." Naturally, the Beatles hated all of this. Eventually they began referring to undesirable hangers-on as "crips." If any of the Beatles were ever annoyed with "outsiders" who were crowding their space—perhaps in a dressing room or a hotel suite—they only had to mutter the word "crips" to one of their aides, and the room would promptly be cleared.

85 *"immature lungs produced a sound"*: As quoted in Spitz, *The Beatles*, 577.

86 *When the band we now know*: Thankfully, they never went with another name that was supposedly bruited about: "Long John and the Silver Beetles." Had they done so, history might not have been the same.

86 *"I had a group"*: As quoted in Jann Wenner, ed., *Lennon Remembers: The Full Rolling Stone Interviews from 1970* (London and New York: Verso, 2000 c. 1972), 133.

86 *(Presumably, this is where)*: This remarkable agreement, which was never legally binding, endured until 1976, when Paul reversed the authors' credits on the Beatles' songs that are featured on his live album *Wings Over America*, so the read "McCartney-Lennon." It did not cause much controversy (and Lennon may not even have known about it).

87 *"He used to follow me"*: As quoted in Geoffrey Giuliano, *Two of Us: John Lennon and Paul McCartney Behind the Myth* (New York: Penguin, 1999), 8.

87 *"that spark [that] we all"*: "Interview," *Playboy* (January 1981).

87 *"had that quality that"*: As quoted in Stark, *Meet the Beatles*, 128.

88 *John was typecast as*: "None of us would've made it alone," Lennon said later, perceptively. "Paul wasn't quite strong enough, I didn't have enough girl-appeal, George was too quiet, and Ringo was the drummer. But we thought that everyone would be able to dig at least one of us, and that's how it turned out."

88 *"We really looked out"*: As quoted in *The Beatles Anthology*, back jacket flap.

88 *"Had those reporters been women"*: Devin McKinney, *Magic Circle: The Beatles in Dream and History* (Cambridge, MA: Harvard University Press, 2003), 51.

88 *For reasons that even psychologists:* The most famous psychologist who was asked to explain the Beatles' unusual appeal was Dr. Joyce Brothers, the American syndicated advice columnist. She observed that the group displayed "a few of the mannerisms which almost seem on the feminine side, such as tossing of their long manes of hair. These are exactly the mannerisms which very young female fans (in the 10-to-14 age group) appear to go wildest over. . . . Girls in very early adolescence still in truth find 'soft' or 'girlish' characteristics more attractive than ruggedly masculine ones." And why? "I think the explanation may be that these very young 'women' are still a little frightened of sex," Dr. Brothers continued. "Therefore they feel safer worshipping idols who don't seem to masculine, or too much the he-man."

89 *"We were actually named after chicks"*: As quoted in David Laing, "Six Boys, Six Beatles: The Formative Years, 1950–1962," in Kenneth Womack, ed., *The Cambridge Companion to the Beatles* (New York and Cambridge: Cambridge University Press, 2009), 23. Also see Miles, *Beatles Diary*, 52–53. Many claims have been made about the origins of "the Beatles." In a 1961

article for *Mersey Beat*, Lennon joked that that the group's name "came in a vision—a man appeared on a flaming pie and said unto them, 'From this day on you are Beatles with a A.'" (Amusingly, Yoko Ono has long insisted that Lennon meant for this quip to be taken literally; she thinks that he really had a hallucination like the one he described.) "The Beatles" may also have been an homage to Buddy Holly's group, the Crickets. After Harrison suggested *The Wild One* might have been the inspiration for the name, Derek Taylor (the Beatles' former press agent, and a good friend of Harrison's) echoed the claim. It was surely Lennon, however, who cleverly proposed the group's name should be spelled "Beatles" instead of "Beetles." "When you said it," he said, "people thought of crawly things; and when you read it, it was beat music."

89 *The Beatles covered nine girl group*: The Beatles recorded "Chains" (by the Cookies), "Boys," and "Baby It's You" (both by the Shirelles) for *Please Please Me*. Two more girl group songs appeared on *With the Beatles*: "Please Mr. Postman" (the Marvelettes) "and "Devil in Her Heart" (the Donays). Live, the Beatles are known to have performed "Keep Your Hands off My Baby" (Little Eva), "Mama Said" and "Will You Love Me Tomorrow?" (the Shirelles), and "Shimmy Shimmy" (the Orlons).

89 *"a male Shirelles"*: As quoted in Stark, *Meet the Beatles*, 129.

89 *"fan favorite"*: Mark Binelli, "Sir Paul Rides Again," *Rolling Stone* (October 20, 2005).

90 *"Should it be"*: As quoted in Braun, *Love Me Do*, 85.

90 *"little trick"*: As quoted in Walter Everett, *The Beatles as Musicians: The Quarry Men Through Rubber Soul* (New York: Oxford University Press, 2001), 108. "We knew that if we wrote a song called 'Thank You Girl,' that a lot of the girls who wrote us letters would take it as a genuine thank you," Paul continued. "So a lot of our songs—'From Me to You' is another—were directly addressed to fans."

An early variation on this formula was "She Loves You," which Lennon and McCartney wrote together in Newcastle in the summer of 1963. McCartney was the one who cleverly suggested that it be put across in the third person. (Here he was influenced by Bobby Rydell, the teen idol who deployed a similar trope in "Forget Him," which was a hit on both sides of the Atlantic.) The result was a song that any teenage girl might identify with. Acting as a go-between for a young couple, the narrator advises the boy in the relationship to apologize to the girl whom he has hurt, and whose love he should be grateful for.

90 *"She was just seventeen"*: Comedian Jerry Seinfeld ribbed McCartney

about the song at a 2010 White House ceremony, where President Barack Obama gave McCartney the Gershwin Prize for his lifetime contribution to popular music. "Sir Paul, you have written some of the most beautiful music ever heard by humans in this world . . . I love you for it," Seinfeld said. "And yet, some of the lyrics, some of the songs, as they go by, can make one *unsure*, even *concerned*, sometimes, about what exactly is happening in song? Songs such as, 'I Saw Her Standing There,' and I quote: 'She was just seventeen/*And you know what I mean*.' I'm not sure I *do* know what you mean, Sir Paul! I *think* I know what you mean!"

90 *And certainly it's difficult*: The bawdy lyrics in "Please Please Me" speak for themselves, but the real giveaway is the tension in Lennon's voice when he sings the call-and-response "come on"s with Harrison and McCartney. "Come on, come on, come on" sounds like a sexual exhortation. (You wouldn't likely exclaim "come on, come on, come on," to someone from whom you only wanted reciprocal emotional affection.) In his 1994 opus, *Revolution in the Head*, musicologist Ian MacDonald claimed that EMI's American outlet, Capitol Records, was at first unwilling to release "Please Please Me" in the US because the song "was widely interpreted as an exhortation to fellatio." But no one has produced evidence proving that. The first critics to describe "Please Please Me" as an "oral sex song" were probably Robert Christgau and John Picarella, writing jointly in the *Village Voice* in 1981.

91 *"the Pill"*: As quoted in Stark, *Meet the Beatles*, 121. At Twickenham Studios in 1964, during the filming of *A Hard Day's Night*, the Beatles took time to answer questions for a televised broadcast. When an attractive young woman plaintively and jokingly asked, "John, why did ya have to get married?" Lennon was clearly rankled. He rolled his eyes and replied, "Because the same reason anyone gets married. I don't want to be slushy-like, but you do it, don't you, when you want to get married. When you got a girl, you got a girl, I always say. Anyhow," he continued (now peering into the camera and using a nasty tone that at he rarely displayed in public), "what's it got to do with you?"

91 *"difficult position"*: As quoted in Pritchard and Lysaght, *An Oral History*, 128.

91 *"Take your pick"*: Larry Kane, *Ticket to Ride: Inside the Beatles' 1964 Tour That Changed the World* (Philadelphia: Running Press, 2003), 77.

91 *Ronnie Bennett was likewise aghast*: Ronnie Spector, *Be My Baby: How I Survived Mascara, Miniskirts, and Madness, or, My Life as a Fabulous Ronette* (New York: HarperPerennial, 1990), 80, 84.

92 *"The only thing they seemed"*: As quoted in Glenn A. Baker, *Beatles Down Under: The 1964 Australia and New Zealand Tour* (Wild and Woolley, 1982), 89.

92 *It is doubtful that most*: One night in 1965, the Stones sat together in a hotel room and tallied how many different girls they'd slept with since the band got together. Charlie hadn't slept with anyone (he was happily married), Keith said 6, Mick counted 30, and Brian said 130. Bill Wyman, an obvious sex addict, and also a loathsome man (who at age forty-eight was carrying on sexually with a fourteen-year-old girl, Mandy Smith), claimed 278 partners.

92 *"We need money first"*: As quoted in Norman, *John Lennon*, 346.

92 *"Count the money"*: http://www.beatlemoney.com/john6063.htm.

92 *"Spend it"*: Beatles Press Conference, Melbourne, June 14, 1964.

92 *"A lot"*: Beatles Press Conference, Kansas City, September 17, 1964.

92 *"Only how to make"*: Beatles Press Conference, Montreal, September 9, 1964.

92 *"More money than"*: Beatles Interview, Doncaster, December 1, 1963.

93 *"If they've got enough rubles"*: Beatles Press Conference, September 3, 1964.

93 *"Somebody said to me"*: As quoted in David Bennahum, ed., *The Beatles After the Break-Up: In Their Own Words* (Omnibus Press, 1991), p. 19.

93 *"We'd be idiots to"*: "Interview with the Beatles," *Playboy* (February 1965).

95 *(It would take more)*: The mathematician who solved the riddle was Jason Brown, using a calculation known as Fourier. With computer software, he was able to identify distinct frequencies that revealed exactly what notes were played on the chord. (Simultaneously, George strummed a twelve-string guitar, John loudly strummed his six-string, Paul played a note on his bass, George Martin hit the piano.)

95 *"This is going to surprise you"*: As quoted in Barry Miles, *The British Invasion: The Music, the Times, the Era* (New York: Sterling, 2009), 68.

95 *"the* Citizen Kane *of"*: See Bob Neaverson, "A Hard Day's Night," in Sean Egan, ed., *The Mammoth Book of the Beatles* (London: Constable & Robinson, 2009), 373.

95 *"a genius of the"*: As quoted in Norman, *John Lennon*, 360.

95 *"anyone who fears the"*: As quoted in Spitz, *The Beatles*, 496.

96 *"He turned on me"*: Melly, *Revolt into Style*, 77. In one of his last interviews, in *Playboy* in 1980, Lennon confirmed that that was really his view: "I thought we were the best fucking group in the goddamn world. . . . As far as we were concerned, we were the best, but we thought we were

the best before anybody else had even heard of us, back in Hamburg and Liverpool."

97 *"Cartoonists had a field day"*: As quoted in Braun, *Love Me Do,* 70.

97 *"We couldn't help it"*: As quoted in Davies, *The Beatles*, 192.

97 *"There's* many *polls"*: Beatles Press Conference, September 17, 1964. "They won it last year too, that one," Lennon added with a chuckle. "You know, I mean, that's *their* poll."

97 *Are you worried about*: See http://www.youtube.com/watch?v=PkFAf6 3FjgY.

99 *"Yes!"*: Ray Coleman, "Rebels with a Beat," in *Melody Maker* (March 14, 1964).

100 *"Tell me, Mr. Coleman"*: Chris Welch, "Obituary: Ray Coleman," *The Independent* (September 13, 1996).

100 *"They look like boys"*: Judith Simons, *Daily Express* (February 28, 1964).

101 *"looked as if they had been"*: As quoted in Wyman, *Stone Alone,* 233.

101 *"I don't know if the people"*: As quoted in Ed Ward, Geoffrey Stokes, and Ken Tucker, *Rock of Ages: The Rolling Stone History of Rock and Roll* (New York: Simon & Schuster, 1986), 283.

102 *"He'd send money orders"*: Marc Spitz, *Jagger: Rebel, Rock Star, Rambler, Rogue* (New York: Gotham, 2011), 25.

102 *"Beatles fans were not"*: Hans Oosterbaan, in *Love You Live, Rolling Stones: Fanfare from the Common Fan* (Springfield, PA: Fanfare Publishing, 2002) 29.

103 *"The Rolling Stones Gather"*: "Rolling Stones Gather No Lunch," *Daily Express* (May 11, 1964).

103 *"imitating the Stones' hairstyle"*: "Beatle Your Rolling Stone Hair," *Daily Mirror* (May 27, 1964).

103 *"American music critic Anthony DeCurtis"*: Fornatale, *Fifty Licks,* 25.

103 *"had to sneak the records and"*: As quoted in Oldham, *2Stoned*, 284.

103 *"Nobody was particularly"*: Richards, *Life*, 166.

103 *"indicated their pleasure or displeasure"*: As quoted in Mark Paytress, ed., *The Rolling Stones: Off the Record* (London: Omnibus Press, 2003), 62.

104 *"an utter disgrace"*: As quoted in Wyman, *Stone Alone*, 238.

104 *"effete posturing"*: As quoted in Wyman, *Stone Alone*, 242.

105 *"Get off my forecourt"*: A forecourt is an open area or courtyard in front of a building's entrance. The term is used more often in England than in the United States.

105 *"Whether it is the Rolling Stones"*: As quoted in Wyman, *Stone Alone*, 306.

106 *"The notion that the Stones"*: Marc Spitz, *Jagger*, 75–76.

106 *Sometimes they claimed they*: In the June 1964 *Rolling Stones Book* (the premier issue), Bill Wyman was asked in a Q&A interview why, before he'd met the Stones, he'd left his job as a retail storekeeper?

"Oh—I had to leave," he said. "Because of my hair. You see, I'd let it grow and grow and people started giving me curious looks. . . . I either had to have a haircut or leave the firm. So I left."

The story is almost certainly not true. In his memoir, Wyman says that before he met the Stones, he looked like an ordinary civilian. In fact, he says that when he was introduced to Jagger, Jones, and Richards at a Chelsea pub in December 1962, he was taken aback by their appearance. They "had hair down over their ears and looked very scruffy—Bohemian and arty," he said. "This was quite a shock: in the pop world I came from, smartness was automatic. I was neatly dressed, *as for work*, with a Tony Curtis hairstyle. My entire demeanor clashed with their unkempt look. People with casual, shabby jackets and trousers were not the sort of people I normally mixed with" [Emphasis added].

106 *"I happen to be particularly"*: Keith Altham, "The Rolling Stones: This Is a Stone Age!" *NME Summer Special* (1966).

106 *"I don't particularly care either"*: "The Hair Stays Long So Hard Luck!" *Melody Maker* (March 28, 1964).

106 *"So what? They"*: As quoted in Massimo Bonanno, ed., *The Rolling Stones Chronicle: The First Thirty Years* (New York: Henry Holt, 1990), 24.

106 *"My hair is not a gimmick"*: "The Hair Stays Long So Hard Luck!" *Melody Maker* (March 28, 1964).

107 *Suggestions that the Stones*: As quoted in Wyman, *Stone Alone*, 170. "Demob suits" was pejorative slang for conventional, unimaginative attire. The phrase comes from the cheap, mass-produced "demobilization suits" that British servicemen were issued after they returned from World War Two, in order to ease their transition into civilian life.

107 *"I'm fed up with people saying"*: *Rolling Stones Monthly Book*, Issue 1 (June 1964), 2.

107 *"Keith and I will talk"*: As quoted in *According to the Rolling Stones*, 68.

107 *("like palm trees in a hurricane")*: As quoted in *Rave* magazine (1964).

108 *"We'd walk into some"*: As quoted in Davis, *Old Gods*, 83.

108 *"The way he performed"*: Peter Whitehead, the filmmaker who shot the Stones' first (and rarely seen) documentary film, *Charlie Is My Darling*, in 1965, said something similar. "Mick was right out there at the front just rubbing up against every single person in the audience, just touching them up, just masturbating them. The boys as well, that was what was ex-

traordinary . . . don't think it was just the girls. The boys were standing at the front weeping! '*Miiick!*'" In 1964, when the Rolling Stones appeared on *The Mike Douglas Show,* the host asked, "Is there one of you five who seems to be more popular with the young ladies than the others?" and Brian Jones chimed in, "Mick's more popular with the men." "He's putting you on!" Jagger protested.

110 *"I was trapped in a field"*: Patti Smith, "Rise of the Sacred Monsters," *Creem* (1973).

110 *"crap," "awful," "full of rubbish"*: As quoted in *Sounds* (October 29, 1977).

111 *"he's my cleaner"*: As quoted in Nicky Haslam, *Redeeming Features: A Memoir* (New York: Knopf, 2009), 142.

111 *"He's great"*: As quoted in Spitz, *Jagger*, 40.

111 *"was crying and shouting at him"*: Marianne Faithfull, *Faithfull: An Autobiography* (New York: Cooper Square Press, 2012), 20.

112 *"famous, plate-throwing"*: As quoted in Carey Schofield, *Jagger* (London: Methuen, 1983), 100.

112 *"Mick would cry a lot"*: As quoted in Norman, *Mick Jagger* (New York: Ecco, 2012), 105.

112 *"growing charisma"*: Oldham, *Stoned*, 47.

112 *"We'd be walking down the street"*: As quoted in Norman, *Mick Jagger*, 105.

112 *"Mick liked to imagine"*: Norman, *The Stones*, 99.

113 *"Mick and I went down"*: *Mod*, insert in *Tiger Beat* (August 1966). A blogger has cleverly speculated that Shrimpton's brass bird might have inspired Lennon's song "And Your Bird Can Sing." Another tantalizing possibility is that Lennon addressed the song to Jagger, after growing weary of hearing him boast about his new relationship with Marianne Faithfull: "bird" was British slang for an attractive female, and Faithfull could indeed sing.

113 *"Later I introduced Mick to Andy"*: As quoted in *According to the Stones*, 79. Emphasis added.

114 *"We were encouraged"*: As quoted in Pritchard and Lysaght, *Oral History*, 170–71.

114 *"multigenerational psychosis"*: As quoted in Norman, *Mick Jagger*, 107.

114 *Fact is that Beatle People*: "Yeah, Yeah, Yeah!" *Daily Mirror*, November 6, 1963. (No byline.)

115 *"An examination of the heart"*: As quoted in Braun, *Love Me Do*, 65.

116 *"I bet that about ten"*: Murray Kaufman, *Murray the K Tells It Like It Is, Baby* (New York: Holt, Rinehart and Winston, 1966), 97.

4: YANKOPHILIA

118 *"The mop-haired singers"*: Murray Schumach, "Teen-Agers (Mostly Female) and Police Greet Beatles," *New York Times* (August 14, 1965).

119 *"We spent weeks drawing"*: As quoted in Danny Somach, Kathleen Somach, Kevin Gunn, eds., *Ticket to Ride* (New York: HarperCollins, 1991), 63.

119 *"You hear that up there?"*: Spitz, *The Beatles,* 577.

119 *It remains one of the*: You can see it in *The Beatles at Shea Stadium,* a 50-minute television documentary that first aired on the BBC in 1966, and then became increasingly widely available, first as a bootleg, then as part of *The Beatles Anthology* DVD series, and now on YouTube.

120 *"I don't envy those Beatles"*: Hutchins, "Prisoners on Floor 33 While Two Stones Went Free," *NME* (August 20, 1965).

121 *At first, they received him*: Oldham had claimed that it was necessary to host the presser on a boat because there wasn't a single luxury hotel in Manhattan that was willing to host the Stones, but that was just another publicity stunt, designed to make the Stones seem more dangerous than they really were.

121 *"That's us . . . We have to be better"*: "The Rolling Stones," *Hullabaloo* (November 1966).

121 *"when we were all"*: As quoted in Ono, *Memories of John Lennon,* 107.

122 *"In the tracks of the Beatles"*: As quoted in Paytress, *The Rolling Stones: Off the Record,* 55.

122 *How do you compare*: YouTube video: http://www.youtube.com/watch?v=j3p2-LkN7EM&feature=watch_response.

123 *Murray the K's Swinging*: As quoted in Pritchard and Lysaght, *An Oral History,* 157.

124 *"Oh, just play the fuckin'"*: Oldham, *2Stoned,* 12.

125 *The Rolling Stones, it is*: Not only is the narrator in "I Just Want to Make Love to You" after sex; he also wants to score with a woman who is otherwise attached. He "knows by the way that [she] treats [her] man" that she'd be a good lay.

126 *Then when Martin introduced*: Wyman, 222.

126 *"some dumb circus act"*: Richards, *Life,* 151.

127 *"sawdust fiasco"*: Oldham, *2Stoned,* 9.

127 *"They would shout across"*: Richards, *Life,* 121.

127 *"I get to meet The Man"*: As quoted in Sanford, *Keith Richards,* 66.

127 *"That throws you a curve"*: As quoted in Bockris, *Keith Richards,* 81.

128 *Muddy Waters grew to have*: Asked about the story in an interview, Marshall Chess said, "No truth in it at all. But Keith maintains to this day that

it actually happened. I've laughed in his face many times as he's insisted he saw Muddy up a ladder with a paint brush in his hand."

129 *the Beatles made headlines*: Years later, Muddy remarked, "The Rolling Stones created a whole wide-open space for the music." He also appreciated that, unlike some other acts, the Stones gave him the credit he deserved. "They said who did it first and how they came by knowin' it. I tip my hat to 'em. It took the people from England to hip my people—my white people—that a black man's music is not a crime to bring in the house."

129 *"I've never seen anything"*: As quoted in Wyman, *Stone Alone*, 232.

129 *"You can buy them"*: As quoted in Dalton, *The First Twenty Years*, 41. Candy floss is known in North America as "cotton candy."

130 *A girl was quoted asking*: Jack Hutton, *Daily Mirror* (June 6, 1964).

130 *"Oldham could not afford"*: Norman, *The Stones*, 136.

131 *"Essentially British—and thoroughly"*: Jones, "The Stones on America," *Rolling Stones Monthly Book* , No. 2 (July1964), 27.

131 *"They had discovered that"*: As quoted in Ono, *Memories of John Lennon*, 11.

131 *It's a well-known phenomenon*: See Daniel Gilbert, *Stumbling on Happiness* (New York: Vintage, 2007). "Beatlemania took its toll," Harrison has said; after a while the Beatles were "no longer on the buzz of fame and success."

132 *"Everybody saw the* effect *of"*: *The Beatles Anthology*, 354.

133 *"After the gig, I remember"*: *The Beatles Anthology*, 227.

133 *"That's it. I'm no longer a Beatle"*: As quoted in Miles, *The Beatles Diary*, 244.

134 *They knew going in*: Incidentally, the Stones also said that they sometimes could not even hear themselves play, but was that really true? A couple days after the first Shea concert, the Beatles played a show in Toronto in front of 35,000. Afterward, George complained that he and John had been out of tune, but they were helpless to do anything about it. "When you get on stage," he lamented, "there's such tremendous noise" that any attempt to adjust the pitch of his strings would only make things worse. "I've been seriously thinking of getting Keith Richard on tour to tune up all of us," he quipped. "He sounds as if he's in tune." Furthermore, when the Beatles talked about how their fans drowned out their music, they often seemed dejected—as if to say, "What a bummer! As a result, we can't play to the best of our ability." When the Stones said that screaming fans overpowered their music, however, it often sounded like they might be boasting.

134 *"They were four musicians"*: George Martin, *All You Need is Ears: Inside the Personal Story of the Genius Who Created the Beatles* (New York: St. Martin's Griffin, 1994), 132.

135 *"[Paul] would say"*: As quoted in Pritchard and Lysaght, *An Oral History*, 192.

135 *"As I could see their talent"*: Martin, *All You Need Is Ears*, 167.

135 *"You don't know us if"*: As quoted in Michael Lydon, *Flashbacks: Eyewitness Accounts of the Rock Revolution, 1964–1974* (New York: Routledge, 2003), 12.

136 *"plastic soul"*: Paul can be heard using the phrase on the compilation album *The Beatles Anthology 2*, after the first take of "I'm Down," which they recorded on July 14, 1965, and was probably inspired by Little Richard. "Plastic soul, man, plastic soul," he says. The Beatles had been kicking around different ideas for the title, and then settled on it after their photographer, Robert Freeman, inadvertently created an elastic effect on one of their photos as he projected it onto a 12" x 12" piece of cardboard.

136 *and it was never that complicated*: In "I Feel Fine," however, the narrator is exuberant about how he can make *her* feel. "She's so glad, she's telling all the world." Another song, "It Won't Be Long" also has an unlikely inversion (coming from a male narrator). They sing "It won't be long, *till I belong to you*." The Stones would have said, "till you belong to me."

136 *Presumably, she's not offering*: It is doubtful whether the Beatles were familiar with Robert Johnson's 1936 song "Terraplane Blues," in which a Terraplane (a model of car made by the Hudson Motor Company) is a metaphor for a woman's body. (The Stones knew it, however.) Regardless, the two songs had different spirits: the Beatles' sentiments were mirthful, and Johnson's were ugly. But the Beatles may well have known Chuck Berry's 1965 single, "I Want to Be Your Driver." ("I would love to ride you," he sings mischievously, "I would love to ride you . . . a-round.")

137 *"the pot album"*: As quoted in Norman, *John Lennon*, 432.

139 *"laughed out of the"*: Richards, *Life*, 143, 172.

139 *"a song with brick walls"*: As quoted in Spitz, *Jagger*, 66.

139 *"Because we'd have had"*: As quoted in Keith Altham, "The Rolling Stones: Neurotic Bird Song," *NME* (February 11, 1966).

140 *"This is actually a child's"*: Oldham, *2Stoned*, 224.

140 *"Everything in the Rolling Stones'"*: As quoted in Wyman, *Stone Alone*, 352.

141 *"Brian played the sitar"*: As quoted in Nigel Goodall, *Jump Up: The Rise of the Rolling Stones* (London: Castle, 2011), 41.

141 *"It means paint it black"*: As quoted in Caroline Silver, *The Pop Makers* (New York: Scholastic Book Services, 1966), 117.

142 *"a big landmark"*: As quoted in Davis, *Old Gods*, 163.

142 *"the time has come to"*: Mike Ledgerwood, *Disc* (April 9, 1966).

142 *"There must have been a"*: *The Beatles Anthology*, 203.

142 *"very cannily worked out"*: Richards, *Life*, 141.

143 *"That was a great period"*: As quoted in Jann Wenner, ed., *Lennon Remembers* (New York: Fawcett Popular Library, 1972), 88.

143 *"We were at the peak"*: As quoted in Miles, *Paul McCartney*, 142.

143 *"didn't get hurt much"*: As quoted in Wyman, *Stone Alone*, 331.

143 *"She was laying into my"*: Keith Altham, "The Rolling Stones: The Stones Hit Back," *NME* (August 6, 1965).

144 *"thundered on"*: Alan Smith, "Second Half," *NME* (May 6, 1966).

145 *"I said to Lennon"*: As quoted in Oldham, *2Stoned*, 320.

145 *"I said they couldn't"*: As quoted in Badman, *The Beatles: Off the Record*, 202.

145 *"I took my life into"*: As quoted in Oldham, *2Stoned*, 320.

145 *"John absolutely exploded!"*: As quoted in Badman, *The Beatles: Off the Record*, 202.

146 *and that turned out to*: They would perform live in England just one more time, on January 30, 1969, on the top of the Apple Building in London. Of course, that concert was not preannounced.

146 *George hid his face behind*: See photo at http://johnlennonbeatles.com/2010/02/john-and-george-go-vinyl-crazy/.

146 *"These are our friends"*: As quoted in Dalton, *The First Twenty Years*, 65.

147 *"Everything we do, the"*: This quote is said to appear in Silver, *The Pop Makers*, although I was not able to find it in that text. Lennon has made a remark similar to this on other occasions, however. In his 1970 *Rolling Stone* interview with Jann Wenner, Lennon said, "I would just like to list what we did and what the Stones did two months after on every fuckin' album."

147 *They were in fact highly inventive*: The Stones' sound and attitude was also a major influence on the Garage Sound phenomenon that spread through the US in the mid-to-late 1960s, and that sowed the seeds of protopunk and later US punk (cf. the New York Dolls, the Stooges). Even some of the era's most distinctive and established artists were influenced by the Stones, as witnessed by Bob Dylan's studio workout around "I Wanna Be Your Man" (i.e., "I Wanna Be Your Lover," unreleased until the 1980s) and The Velvet Underground's intro to "There She Goes Again," which may have been lifted from the Stones' cover of Marvin Gaye's "Hitch Hike" (The intro appears on Gaye's version as well.)

147 *It must have been*: By contrast, you find far fewer mentions of the Stones in the Beatles' authorized biography by Hunter Davies, in McCartney's authorized biography *Many Years from Now*, and in the Beatles' *The Beatles*

Anthology book and film project. Once in an interview, Lennon forgot (or pretended to forget) Bill Wyman's name. "I think Charlie [Watts] is a damn good drummer, and the other guy's a good bass-player, but I think Paul and Ringo stand up anywhere, with *any* of the rock musicians," he said.

148 *"The possibility of the Rolling"*: Keith Altham, "Rolling Stones Have Reached Peak at Home," *NME* (March 25, 1966).

5: POLITICS AND IMAGECRAFT

150 *"That means"*: *World in Action* television program, July 31, 1967.

150 *"You are, whether you"*: As quoted in Simon Wells, *Butterfly on a Wheel: The Great Rolling Stones Drug Bust* (London: Omnibus, 2112), 218.

150 *"We swooped exhilaratingly"*: John Birt, MacTaggart Lecture, 2005. http://www.guardian.co.uk/media/2005/aug/26/broadcasting.uknews.

151 *"like a lost scene"*: As quoted in *Esquire*, Vol. 71 (1969).

152 *"It was not the soft-liberalism"*: William Rees-Mogg, *Memoirs* (New York: Harper Press, 2011), 159. Jagger no doubt made his point, but he used a poor example. (It would, under most circumstances, be a crime against society to kill oneself by leaping out of a window.)

153 *"I'm not a keen protestor"*: Paytress, *Rolling Stones: Off the Record*, 140.

154 *"Musically, they are a near disaster"*: *Newsweek* (February 24, 1964).

154 *"long abide as arbiters"*: Vince Aletti, "Beatles' Albums Divert Course of Pop Music," *San Diego Door* (Jan. 25–Feb. 7, 1968), 4.

154 *"Even those who did not"*: Richard Flacks, *Youth and Social Change* (Chicago: Markham Pub. Co., 1971), 70.

155 *What about this comment*: Kane, *Ticket to Ride*, 38–39.

156 *"But there's not much we"*: As quoted in "Bach Backs Beatles vs. Viet War," *Berkeley Barb* (August 5, 1966), 2.

156 *"We don't like war"*: "Beatles Strike Serious Note in Press Talk," *New York Times* (August 23, 1966).

157 *"We'd heard rumors"*: As quoted in Leo Burley, "Jagger vs. Lennon," *The Independent* (March 9, 2008).

157 *"was an event"*: Geoffrey O'Brien, *Dream Time* (London: Secker & Warburg, 1988), 54.

157 *"With a bit of effort"*: Todd Gitlin, *The Sixties: Years of Hope, Days of Rage* (New York: Bantam, 1987), 210–211.

158 *"were no longer strangers"*: Jonah Raskin, *Out of the Whale: Growing Up in the American Left* (New York: Link Books, 1974), 109.

158 *"the power and audience"*: Gene Youngblood, (Milwaukee) *Kaleidoscope* (Dec. 22, 1967–Jan. 4, 1968), 2.

158 *"At idle moments more"*: Marvin Garon, "And Now, a Word from Our Sponsor," *Berkeley Barb* (February 25, 1967).

158 *"the embodiment of everything we"*: As quoted in Davis, 124.

159 *"I didn't have the slightest"*: Strausbaugh, *Rock Till You Drop,* 16.

159 *By contrast, when the Beatles*: Then again it is doubtful that the Beatles ever got word of the invitation, which was delivered via a fifteen-foot roadside sign that read "The Merry Pranksters Welcome the Beatles."

159 *"rockers, bikers"*: Peter Coyote, *Sleeping Where I Fall* (Washington, DC: Counterpoint, 1998), 163; *Fresh Air* interview with Terri Gross, NPR (April 28, 1998).

159 *"Mick's case had made"*: Sanchez, *Up and Down*, 85–86.

160 *"I just wouldn't be"*: Jones was also quoted saying, "I remember the first time I took [LSD] was on tour with Bo Diddley and Little Richard." That was either a fib, or else the reporters got it wrong. It is true that the Stones toured with Bo Diddley and Little Richard in the fall of 1963, but it's extraordinarily unlikely that any LSD would have been around then. Possibly that is when Brian Jones first smoked cannabis.

160 *"Pop Stars and Drugs"*: *News of the World* (February 5, 1967).

160 *He confidently announced*: As quoted in Wells, *Butterfly on a Wheel*, 86.

161 *Mayfair gallery owner Robert Fraser*: "Michael [Cooper] and Robert [Fraser] were both friends of mine," Jagger later remarked. Fraser, he said, was a bit of "a taste guru" for both the Beatles and the Stones. But Mick also implied that he had the better and more authentic relationship with Fraser, and that the Beatles didn't fit in quite as well in the Swinging London scene. "I think Robert saw the Beatles as a hustle. Everyone did," he said. "They were the richest people in that age group. Very silly with their money, they didn't seem to care. They did very good things, like *Sgt. Pepper*, and did attract good people. But people did target them as a hustle. Robert saw them as a gravy train when he knew that I was not." As quoted in Harriet Vyner, ed., *Groovy Bob: The Life and Times of Robert Fraser* (London: Faber and Faber, 1999), 130.

161 *"This is the tao of lysergic"*: Faithfull, *Faithfull,* 99–100.

162 *"There was the kind of social"*: As quoted in *The Beatles Anthology* DVD, episode 8. For a time, the Beatles also seemed untouchable by journalists. The *Evening Standard*'s pop writer, Roy Connolly, recalled visiting Lennon in November 1968. "Suddenly, a character called Michael X showed up, a real bad guy." (He was a Trinidad-born British black nationalist who would be hanged for murder in Port-of-Spain in 1975.) "He opened up this huge suitcase and took out enough grass to turn on the entire city of

Westminster. Now, I'm a member of the press. Do I mention it? No, nor would John expect me to. That was the deal at the time."

162 *"There's a big knock on the door"*: As quoted in Dalton, *The First Twenty Years*, 98.

162 *That late morsel of a detail*: The irony, Keith later remarked, is that it was a *huge* rug, made of many dozens of rabbit pelts. All wrapped up in it, she was in fact "quite chastely attired for once. Usually when first you said hi to Marianne you started talking to the cleavage."

162 *"'Bang, bang, bang"*: As quoted in Dalton, *The First Twenty Years*, 98.

163 *"Poor Mick—he could"*: As quoted in Norman, *The Stones*, 227.

163 *"Please don't open the case"*: As quoted in Norman, *The Stones*, 228.

163 *When Snyderman skipped*: For a time, Nicky Kramer was briefly suspected as well. After the bust, an authentic East End gangster named David Litvinoff roughed Kramer up in an attempt to get him to confess to betraying the Stones. When Kramer continued to maintain his innocence (according to Richards, even after being dangled outside of a window by his ankles), he was judged to be okay.

163 *"In his right-hand breast pocket"*: Wells, *Butterfly on a Wheel*, 118.

164 *All of this was confiscated*: Snyderman was finally discovered many years later in Los Angeles, working as a small-time television and experimental film producer under the name David Jove. In the early 1980s, he created the show *Night Flight*, hosted by musician Peter Ivers on the then-fledgling USA network. When Ivers was murdered in 1983 (someone bashed his skull with a hammer), Jove was a suspect, but he was never charged. He died of pancreatic cancer in 2004. (Incidentally, his daughter is Lili Haydn, the celebrated violinist.)

164 *"That's what I feel most bitter"*: As quoted in Norman, *The Stones*, 239.

164 *"First they don't like"*: As quoted in Hotchner, *Blown Away*, 251. Of course, the Stones never were offered MBEs. In 2003, however, Mick Jagger received the British establishment's ultimate nod of approval: he was knighted at Buckingham Palace. Keith was angry about it. "I told Mick it's a paltry honor. . . . It's not what the Stones is about, is it?"

166 *"Free the Stones"*: Paytress, *Off the Record*, 132.

166 *"vicious"*: As quoted in Dalton, *The First Twenty Years*, 101.

166 *They promptly announced*: Wells, *Butterfly on a Wheel*, photo insert between 210 and 211.

167 *"The Rolling Stones are"*: As quoted in Paytress, *Off the Record*, 136.

167 *In Britain, it is an*: William Rees-Mogg, "Who Breaks a Butterfly on a Wheel?" *The Times* (London) (July 1, 1967).

168 *"monstrously out of proportion"*: Carey Schofield, *Jagger* (London: Methuen, 1983), 134.

168 *After the* News of the World: "A Monstrous Charge," *News of the World* (July 2, 1967).

169 *"Are we expected to accept"*: As quoted in Wells, *Butterfly on a Wheel*, 218.

169 *"We weren't thinking of the Beatles"*: Spitz, *Jagger*, 106.

169 *"they got twenty billion irresponsible"*: As quoted in Miller, *Flowers in the Dustbin*, 263.

170 *"In each city where I stopped"*: As quoted in Greil Marcus, "Another Version of the Chair," in June Sinner Sawyers, ed., *Read the Beatles: Classic New Writings on the Beatles, Their Legacy, and Why They Still Matter* (New York: Penguin, 2006), 81.

170 *"Everywhere one went"*: Miller, *Flowers in the Dustbin*, 257–58.

171 *"a decisive moment in the history"*: As quoted in Norman, *Shout!*, 331.

171 *"Mick said he'd come"*: Tony Bramwell, *Magical Mystery Tours: My Life with the Beatles* (New York: St. Martin's Griffin, 1996), 195.

173 *"Olympic became the nightclub"*: As quoted in Oldham, *2Stoned*, 354.

173 *"Prior to their arrival the"*: Oldham, *2Stoned*, 344.

173 *"Lennon said, 'Set the mike up'"*: As quoted in Oldham, *2Stoned*, 354.

174 *The two Beatles didn't listen to*: Oldham, *2Stoned*, 344.

174 *Lennon and McCartney's high harmonies*: Because they were signed to different labels, the Beatles and the Stones were not supposed to sing on each other's records. The Stones knew that Lennon and McCartney's appearance on "We Love You" would help sales, however, so they let it circulate as a rumor. In August 1967, when an *NME* journalist asked Jagger point-blank whether John and Paul had sung backup on the song, Mick craftily managed to affirm the rumor while technically denying it. "Don't ask me a question like that—you know we could not do things like that when we work for different labels. That's Keith and I singing—listen . . ." (at which point Jagger humorously tried, and failed, to reach the high harmonies on the record).

174 *"It's just a bit of fun"*: Paytress, *Off the Record*, 140.

175 *"fairies, goblins and elves"*: Norman, *The Stones*, 284.

175 *Their sojourn was cut short*: Beginning in mid-February 1968, the Beatles, their wives and their assistants all got together for an extended stay in the Maharishi's idyllic ashram in Rishikesh, India, where their days were drug-free and devoted to peaceful contemplation. But Ringo couldn't stomach the food, and Paul was put off by the Maharishi's tendency to drench the Beatles in buttery, over-the-top praise—calling them "the saviors of man-

kind" and so forth. So they both left, with polite regrets, before the course was over. John and George, however, claimed they were getting profound (even life-changing) results from practicing Transcendental Meditation. So it was surprising when they abruptly fled the retreat and angrily severed their ties with their spiritual mentor on April 12. To this day, it has never been *precisely* clear what their objection was, but it had something to do with the Maharishi's alleged sexual hypocrisy. After claiming to be celibate, he supposedly made a pass at one of his young female students or was otherwise caught in a compromising position. But Mick Jagger—who was not there—circulated an alternative account of what transpired. In his recently published diaries, Christopher Isherwood recalls meeting Mick on the set of *Ned Kelly*, a motion picture that was filmed in the Australian outback in 1969. "[Mick] told me with amusement that the real reason why the Beatles left the Maharishi was that he made a pass at one of them: 'They're simple north-country lads; they're terribly uptight about all that.' Am still not sure if I believe this story."

175 *"a lovely puddle of psychedelic"*: Steve Appleford, *The Rolling Stones: Rip This Joint: The Story Behind Every Song* (New York: Da Capo, 2001), 55.

175 *"the prototype of junk"*: Keith Altham, "Rolling Stones: Year of the Stones' New Heart," *NME Annual* (1969).

176 *"I can remember"*: *According to the Rolling Stones*, 114.

176 *"You have lost the plot"*: Jim DeRogatis and Greg Kot, *The Beatles vs. the Rolling Stones: Sound Opinions on the Great Rock 'n' Roll Rivalry* (Minneapolis: Voyageur Press, 2010), 19.

176 *"the first psychedelic"*: Jim DeRogatis, *Turn On Your Mind: Four Decades of Great Psychedelic Rock* (Milwaukee: Hal Leonard, 2003), 57.

176 *alluded to LSD's harrowing aspects*: Consider the orchestral crescendo on "A Day in the Life," as well as Love's brilliant 1967 album *Forever Changes* and the Move's 1966 single "Night of Fear."

176 *"I'm quite proud that"*: Jessica Pallington West, ed., *What Would Keith Richards Do? Daily Affirmations from a Rock and Roll Survivor* (New York: Bloomsbury, 2009), 155.

177 *"Even beyond the usual hysterical"*: "Apples for the Beatles," *Time* (September 6, 1968), 59.

177 *"That's why I did it"*: *The Beatles Anthology*, 298.

177 *("When you talk about destruction")*: Lennon and the Beatles recorded three versions of "Revolution." The record described here, which is the public heard first, was actually recorded after "Revolution 1," which appeared on

the so-called *White Album.* On "Revolution 1," Lennon sings "and you can count me out—*in,*" because he says he was unsure how he felt about revolutionary violence. (The record's lyric sheet, however, is unambiguous: it says "you can count me out.") The *White Album* also contained an eight-minute avant-garde montage, "Revolution 9," which many consider the Beatles' worst song ever.

178 *"Cistercian Monk"*: "Uncle Gengis F.," "The Rock Song as Radical Element," (Peoria, Illinois) *The Left Out,* n.d. [circa 1969], 14.

178 *"The more political you are"*: Ralph Gleason, "The Beatles' Revolution," Liberation News Service, No. 111 (October 19, 1968), 10.

178 *"The Beatles aren't just"*: Ralph Gleason, "The Beatles Are More Potent Than SDS," LNS No. 111 (October 19, 1968), 10.

178 *"the seed of the new cultural"*: Roland Muldoon, *The Black Dwarf* (October 13, 1967).

179 *"the inadequacy of [Lennon's]"*: John Hoyland, "Power to the People," *The Guardian* (March 14, 1968).

179 *"Recently your music has"*: John Hoyland, "A Very Open Letter to John Lennon," (Seattle) *Helix* (July 17, 1969), 15.

180 *"I'll tell you what's wrong with"*: John Lennon, "A Very Open Letter to John Hoyland," (Seattle) *Helix* (July 17, 1969), 15.

180 *The feeling's [sic] I've gotten*: John Hoyland, "John Hoyland Replies," (Seattle) *Helix* (July 17, 1969), 15.

180 *"ate the Beatles alive"*: No author, "Beatles Revolution: Two Views," (San Diego) *Teaspoon Door* (November 22, 1968), 8.

180 Village Voice *writer Robert Christgau*: See Wiener, *Come Together*, 60.

180 *"lamentable petty bourgeois cry"*: Richard Merton, "Comment on Chester's 'For a Rock Aesthetic,'" *New Left Review* 59 (Jan–Feb, 1970).

180 *"betrayal"*: As quoted in Wiener, *Come Together*, 60.

181 *"indifference to politics"*: As quoted in Peter Doggett, *There's A Riot Going On* (Edinburgh: Canongate, 2008), 197.

181 *"There is freedom in the"*: Greil Marcus, "A Singer and a Rock and Roll Band," in Greil Marcus, ed., *Rock and Roll Will Stand* (Boston: Beacon Press, 1969), 96.

181 *"However shitty the lyrics"*: James E. Curry, "Dallas" (Madison, WI) *Connections* (February 5–20, 1969), 3.

181 *"more thought and discussion"*: Herman Rumper, "The Beatles Below the Surface," *San Diego Free Press* (Feb 28–March 14, 1969), 7.

181 *"The Beatles' politics are terrible"*: Joshua Newton, letter to the editor, (Detroit) *Fifth Estate* (December 11–22), 1969.

181 *The original record sleeve*: A rumor circulated that the sleeve showed a Chicago police officer brutalizing a demonstrator at that city's 1968 Democratic National Convention, but the picture was actually taken in Los Angeles, during the Sunset Strip curfew riots in late 1966. Today, the record with the original sleeve is one of the rarest of records; some collectors sell it for around $75,000.

182 *"throwing rocks and having"*: Jonathon Green, ed., *Days in the Life: Voices from the English Underground, 1967–1971* (London: Heinemann, 1988), 245.

182 *"Everywhere I heard"*: Amusingly, Tariq Ali threw the original, handwritten lyrics that Jagger had supplied into the wastepaper basket. To hold on to or in any way treasure the lyrics sheet would have contradicted *The Black Dwarf*'s political approach, which opposed the glorification of individuals. It was more important to build group solidarity and create the conditions for collective action.

182 *"I chanted the words myself"*: Jonah Raskin, *Out of the Whale: Growing Up in the American Left* (New York: Link Books, 1974), 119. Actually, "Street Fighting Man" does not contain the lyric Raskin chanted. It goes, "The time is right for *palace* revolution." In all likelihood, Raskin is also the author of an article in SDS's short-lived organ *Fire Next Time*, which lauded the song but similarly misquoted the lyric.

183 *"and what you did here"*: As quoted in sidebar, (Chicago) *Seed* (November 16, 1969).

183 *Greetings and welcome Rolling Stones*: As reprinted in Stanley Booth, *The True Adventures of the Rolling Stones* (Chicago: Chicago Review Press, 2000), 142–143.

184 *"I don't really want to"*: *World in Action* television program (July 31, 1967).

184 *"They must think a song"*: Dave Doggett, (Oxford, MS) *Kudzu* (Feb. 5, 1969), 10.

184 *"America, with its ears turned to its transistors"*: LNS-London, "Beatles, Stones, on Movement," (Hawaii) *The Roach* (February 1–15, 1969).

184 *"he grew rather fond of capitalism"*: Sanchez, *Up and Down*, 121.

184 *"[Jagger] did have a genuine revulsion"*: As quoted in Doggett, *There's a Riot Going On*, 168.

185 *Therefore, culture is war*: As quoted in Miller, *Flowers in the Dustbin*, 272.

185 *In another*: Godard was apparently interested in filming either the Beatles *or* the Stones, and at first he wasn't sure which band was most suitable for his purposes. Later, after Godard made a snide comment about the Beatles' lack of political engagement in *International Times*, Lennon

snapped, "That's sour grapes from a man who couldn't get us to be in the film. Dear Mr. Godard, just because we didn't want to be in the film with you, it doesn't mean to say that we aren't doing any more than you." But Mim Scala, a theatrical agent, said that he persuaded Godard to choose the Stones over the Beatles, and that he had to break that news to Lennon over the phone. He "took it on the chin," Scala said. "I guess he was relieved that this was one more project that the Beatles did not have to worry about."

186 *"I'm beginning to think he's"*: At that point, Lennon did not know that Mao was one of history's greatest mass murderers, but nor could he possibly have believed that Mao was in any way a peaceful man. "Revolution is not a dinner party," Mao had famously said. "A revolution is an insurrection, an act of violence by which one class overthrows another." Interestingly, Mao's remark isn't so dissimilar from Hoyland's line: "In order to change the world, we've got to understand what's wrong with the world. And then—destroy it. Ruthlessly."

186 *"If I were black, I'd"*: Wenner, *Lennon Remembers*, 134.

186 *"it's a very delicate line"*: Ian MacDonald, "John Lennon: *The John Lennon Anthology*," *Uncut* (December 1998).

186 *"The lyrics [in 'Revolution']"*: *The Beatles Anthology*, 299.

186 *"They could own television"*: John Sinclair, (Ann Arbor) *Argus* (Jan 25–Feb 7, 1969), 10.

187 *"I think it may be safely"*: Mayer, "Rock and Revolution" (New York) *WIN* (June 1, 1969), 12.

187 *"For a long time the"*: Francis Moss, "Disengagement and Retreat: Beatles' *Abbey Road*," (Houston) *Space City!* (Nov. 7–20, 1969), 19.

187 *"probably an honest statement"*: As quoted in Mayer, "Rock and Revolution," 12.

187 *"confirmed institutionalists"*: Ron Britain, "A View of the Beatles-Stones," (Milwaukee) *Kaleidoscope* (Feb 14–27, 1969), 21.

187 *"What do you think about"*: Rolling Stones Press Conference, 1969; You Tube. http://www.youtube.com/watch?v=OLC39AfB0Yw.

187 *"I don't dig hero cults"*: Dave Doggett, (Oxford, MS) *Kudzu* (Feb. 5, 1969), 10.

187 *"strive for realism in"*: Jon Landau, "Doing It in the Road," (Atlanta) *Great Speckled Bird* (Feb. 24, 1969), 14–15.

188 *"When you hear a Stones"*: Jon Landau, "If I Thought It Would Do Any Good, I'd Write My Congressman," *Extra!* (December 10–24, 1968) 12.

188 *"The Stones sing to and"*: Mike Kerman, "Class Clash—the Beatles vs. the Rolling Stones," (Detroit) *Fifth Estate* (Feb. 6–19, 1969), 13. Probably the

young writer would have been apoplectic if he knew that around the same time, the Beatles had briefly considered buying a remote Greek island, where they planned to build four hi-tech homes, connected by underground tunnels to a central glass dome with iron tracery.

188 *But the Stones' bloom was*: According to promoters, the steep ticket prices were necessary because the Stones demanded so much money upfront. Most tickets ranged from $4.50 to $6.50, which would amount to between $20 and $33 today. By contrast, tickets for the band's 2005 US tour were $134, and at some shows, prime seats went for $377. Asked about this, Jagger said the band didn't control the ticket prices. He also suggested the question was uninteresting. "We're not really not into that sort of economic scene." On the Stones' 2012 American tour, tickets ranged from $85 to $2,000. "If you really can't afford a ticket, it's sad," Jagger told a journalist. "I feel bad about that. We have some cheap ones that are quite good too. There's a price for everybody, I think."

188 *This was a new thing*: The Beatles' huge outdoor shows in 1966 were the exception. Usually their music was piped through the stadiums' existing PA systems; to the extent that anyone could hear them play, they must have sounded terrible.

188 *"Promoters in almost every city"*: Norman, *The Stones*, 290.

189 *"Unlike the Beatles and"*: "Angry on the Stones," (Chicago) *Rising Up Angry* (July 1969), 6.

189 *To give an example, when the Stones*: "Angry on the Stones," (Chicago) *Rising Up Angry* (July 1969), 6. Abbie Hoffman was one of the "Chicago Seven" (or Chicago Eight) defendants who were charged with plotting to disrupt the 1968 Democratic National Convention. He had been trying for days to get through to the Stones, even going so far as to call the Ambassador West Hotel and impersonating Elvis. ("Yassuh, I jes' wanted to see how Mick an' the boys were doing.") Although Abbie was one of the most visible antiwar activists in the country, a reporter observed that while he was backstage, Mick was the only one to spend time with him. None of the others seemed to know, or care, who he was.

189 *"If the Rolling Stones"*: As quoted in Abe Peck, *Uncovering the Sixties: The Life and Times of the Underground Press* (New York: Citadel Press, 1991), 226.

189 *"[C]lapping hands, cutting up"*: LNS, (Ann Arbor) *Argus* (October 3–17, 1969), 2.

190 *"It would take a little while longer"*: Sanchez, *Up and Down*, 185.

191 *"Just a few decades ago rock"*: Fred Goodman, *The Mansion on the Hill:*

Dylan, Young, Geffen, Springsteen and the Head-On Collision of Rock and Commerce (New York: Vintage, 1998), xi.

191 *"Why does it cost $50,000"*: At the time, most LPs were priced between $5 and $6. The Beatles, however, had negotiated an increase in their royalty rate to 69 cents per album. Before long, record prices went up across the industry.

191 *Why can't rock groups who*: Letter to editor, (Seattle) *Helix* (October 30. 1969), 14.

6: WHEEL-DEALING IN THE POP JUNGLE

193 *"It was simply terrible how lost"*: As quoted in *MOJO's The Beatles*, 293.

194 *"Meditation gives you comfort"*: http://www.youtube.com/watch?v=UhNcGdLyvw0.

194 *"I* knew *that we were in trouble"*: Lennon interview with Jann Wenner, *Lennon Remembers* (audio version).

195 *"In fact, Brian's answer"*: As quoted in Coleman, *The Man Who Made the Beatles*, 263.

195 *"John may have been"*: Tony Barrow, *John, Paul, George, Ringo and Me* (New York: Da Capo, 2006), 49.

195 *"We're going into Decca"*: Richards, *Life*, 179.

195 *("A contract is just a piece")*: As quoted in Klein, *Playboy* (November 1971). Klein continues: "Two parties sign [a contract] in good faith, hoping it indicates what they both want out of a relationship. But situations change, so contracts get renegotiated."

195 *("I mean not over us, he was")*: Richards, *Life*, 179.

196 *"They crumbled and we"*: Richards, *Life*, 179.

197 *"Klein said that"*: Peter Brown, *The Love You Make: An Insider's Story of the Beatles* (New York: NAL Trade, 2002), 227.

197 *"[Epstein] always thought"*: As quoted in Coleman, *The Man Who Made the Beatles*, 265.

197 *"Yeah, well Klein got the Stones"*: As quoted in Brown, *The Love You Make*, 248.

197 *It was a fair question*: Paul: "I complained to Brian. I remember it hurting him, too. It was a learning experience for me: don't do that again. It got to him a bit too much. And he was probably right as well: he had done so much for us and there was me bitching about a penny or two."

198 *"The whole time Allen was"*: As quoted in Oldham, *2Stoned*, 243.

198 *"Allen got very obsessed"*: As quoted in Oldham, *2Stoned*, 206.

198 *"Baby, you're a rich man too"*: George had little to do with "Baby, You're

a Rich Man," which was arranged and recorded at Olympic Studios on May 11, 1967. In fact, it is one of the rare songs from that period that truly was written jointly by Lennon and McCartney. (John had the part of a song that asks, "How does it feel to be one of the beautiful people," and Paul had the part that goes, "Baby, you're a rich man, too." So they wound up combining the two bits.)

199 *"If you wanted a gold-plated Cadillac"*: As quoted in Richards, *Life*, 179.

199 *The Stones eventually launched*: Sue Weiner and Lisa Howard, eds., *The Rolling Stones A-Z* (New York: Grove, 1983), 74.

200 *"We have made numerous"*: As quoted in Wyman, *Stone Alone*, 496.

200 *"We are still awaiting"*: All quotes re: money from Wyman, *Stone Alone*, 505.

200 *"The phone and electricity"*: As quoted in Norman, *Mick Jagger*, 327.

201 *"I didn't trust him and"*: Wyman, *Stone Alone*, 329.

201 *"fat check . . . the biggest"*: Wyman, *Stone Alone*, 330.

201 *"Well, maybe you wouldn't"*: As quoted in *The Beatles Anthology*, 326.

201 *"Mick's strategy in"*: Faithfull, *Faithfull*, 168.

202 *"done them in financially"*: As quoted in Hotchner, *Blown Away*, 201.

202 *"I was equally certain"*: Prince Rupert Loewenstein, *A Prince Among Stones: That Business with the Rolling Stones and Other Adventures* (New York: Bloomsbury, 2013), 68.

203 *Shortly after their song*: John and Mick awkwardly introduce the segment. John calls Mick "Michael" (Jagger's given name) and Mick calls John "Winston" (Lennon's middle name). Mick speaks in a dull accent, somewhat in the style of an American talk show host. "As you know, I've admired your work for so long, and I haven't been able to get together with you so much as I want. Do you remember that old place off-Broadway?" John answers with an apparent non sequitur: "Oh, those were the days, I want to hold your *man*." After a bit more banter, John gets up, hands Mick a bowl of macrobiotic rice that he's been eating, and then sneers as he walks off camera. Mick calls after him: "Yer blues, John." The scene makes absolutely no sense, although it is impossible not to notice that in the end, Mick is left in a subservient position.

An outtake from the film is even more revealing. As the camera rolls, Lennon surprises Mick by pretending to be gay; he pulls at Jagger's jacket from behind and mock-seductively runs his hands over his chest. Once again, Mick seems lamblike in Lennon's presence. The scene was rendered unusable because Lennon's son Julian, age five, can be seen in the background pressing his lips against what is either an unlit, hand-rolled cigarette or (sigh) a joint. "Dad, I've got a little cigar!" he says innocently.

204 *"Allen Klein sat next to"*: As quoted in Davis, *Old Gods*, 279.

205 *"We're in the happy"*: As quoted in *The Beatles Anthology*, 287.

206 *"I remember going [there]"*: As quoted in Doggett, *You Never Give Me Your Money*, p. 53.

206 *"the waiting room of"*: Richard DiLello, *The Longest Cocktail Party* (Chicago: Playboy Press, 1972), 24.

206 *"Mick's home phone number and"*: DiLello, *The Longest Cocktail Party*, 146.

207 *No, not really*: W. Fraser Sandercombe, ed., *The Beatles: Press Reports* (Ontario: Collector's Guide Publishing, 2003), 254.

208 *Of course, they knew Apple*: On January 10, 1969, George Harrison stormed out of Twickenham Studio with the clear intention of quitting the Beatles. Some have speculated that his outburst may have arisen during an argument with Lennon over the *Disc and Music Echo* interview. No one knows for sure, however. In his memoir, *Luck and Circumstance*, filmmaker Michael Lindsay-Hogg said he tried to record Lennon and Harrison's dispute surreptitiously, but the recording was worthless.

208 *"You know this is a small and young"*: Coleman, *Lennon*, 461.

208 *"The day we spoke he"*: Coleman, *Lennon*, 461, 471 (photo insert in the middle).

208 *Why did you want the Beatles?*: Allen Klein, *Playboy* (November 1971), 92.

209 *"[Klein] was so foul-mouthed"*: Brown, *The Love You Make*, 304.

209 *"Klein is essential in the Great"*: As quoted in *MOJO's The* Beatles, 424.

210 *"Sam, I think they're"*: Allen Klein obituary, *The Guardian* (July 5, 2009).

210 *Not only that, he predicted*: Peter Brown remembers Lennon repeating the million-dollar figure while in his office. "I found this quite astonishing, considering that John and Yoko's latest cinematic venture was a long [51 minutes] film of them smiling at each other in soft focus." Some of Ono's other films included *Eye Blink* (a slow-motion picture of a lighted match burning out to its end) and *Bottoms* (consisting only of close-up shots of people's naked bums).

211 *"Yea, though I walk through the"*: As quoted in Norman, *Lennon*, 589.

211 *"He knew every damn"*: Wenner, *Lennon Remembers*, 145.

211 *"He's the only businessman"*: As quoted in *The Beatles Anthology*, 324.

211 *"Please give [Klein]"*: As quoted in *The Beatles Anthology*, 325.

212 *Not only was he gross*: Not long after Klein bought Cameo-Parkway, rumors circulated that his company was about to merge various other companies. One was Merco Enterprises (a giant distribution company that sold other

company's products—in this case 45s and LPs—in racks and bins). The other was Chappell Music Corporation. Cameo-Parkway's stock rose astronomically, from $1.75 a share to $72.

212 *"I didn't want to appear too anxious"*: Allen Klein, "Interview," *Playboy* (November 1971), 94.

213 *"began interrupting everything"*: Brown, *The Love You Make*, 308.

213 *Finally, Eastman*: Klein later claimed that he had practically arranged for that to happen. "It was embarrassing as hell. I didn't mind it for myself—sticks and stones, you know—but for the boys, it was sad. I think everybody saw exactly what was happening and who the Eastmans really were."

213 *"We hadn't been in there"*: Wenner, *Lennon Remembers*, 148.

213 *"advisor"*: Wenner, *Lennon Remembers*, 145.

213 *"Well, he's the only one"*: *The Beatles Anthology*, 324.

214 *It is sometimes claimed*: Prince Rupert Loewenstein says, "It was Mick who introduced Klein to John Lennon a few weeks before I met Mick. After we had spoken he rang Lennon back and said, 'I've rethought it and I've gone to this other person I think you should do the same because I'm not happy about my introduction of Klein.' But it was too late." Beatles assistant Tony Bramwell says that he and Lennon once attended a party at Mick's ornately decorated Chelsea home, at which Mick said to them, "Keep away [from Klein]. He's messed us right up, man." And Peter Swales, an assistant to the Stones, says that Mick once asked him to deliver a handwritten letter to McCartney. "It was a warning, maybe in solidarity with him," Swales said. "It was to the effect of, 'Don't go near [Klein], he's a dog. He's a crook.' "

214 *"We know [Klein] through"*: Miles, *The Beatles Diary*, 334. (The paper was almost certainly *Disc and Music Echo.*)

214 *"I had heard about all these"*: Wenner, *Lennon Remembers*, 141–42.

214 *"We, the Beatles, were all"*: Miles, *Many Years from Now*, 545.

215 *"the first time in the history"*: As quoted in Doggett, Peter, *You Never Give Me Your Money: The Beatles After the Breakup* (New York: HarperCollins, 2010), 70.

216 *"James knew of Klein's"*: Brown, *The Love You Make*, 316.

216 *"a startling blend of bluff"*: Brown, *The Love You Make*, 309.

217 *"I'll play whatever you"*: *Let It Be*, director Michael Lindsay-Hogg (Apple Films, United Artists, 1970).

218 *"We were always wondering"*: As quoted in Doggett, *You Never Give Me Your Money*, 44–45.

218 *"What I thought about the"*: *The Beatles Anthology*, 302. This was in keeping

with one of George's one-liners: "Avant-garde is French for 'haven't got a clue.'"

219 *He got up and*: Lindsay-Hogg, *Luck and Circumstance: A Coming of Age in Hollywood, New York and Points Beyond* (New York: Knopf, 2011), 134.

220 *"There was always a"*: Wyman, *Stone Alone*, 526.

220 *"the prospect of some professional"*: As quoted in Wyman, *Stone Alone*, 464.

220 *"These conversations have not"*: As quoted in Wyman, *Stone Alone*, 465.

221 *"When they went to America"*: Greenfield, Robert, "Keith Richards Interview," *Rolling Stone* (August, 1971).

222 *"I don't really like what the Beatles"*: Mick Jagger Interview with John Carpenter, Part Two, Los Angeles *Free Press* (November 21, 1969), 33.

222 *"Nah. But if we did, we"*: As quoted in Norman, *Mick Jagger*, 415.

223 *"[Mick] is obviously* so *upset"*: Wenner, *Lennon Remembers*, 67.

223 *"Not even McCartney"*: YouTube video, "Keith on the Beatles"—now marked "private" by user.

EPILOGUE

225 *Fans have long debated*: The question is most intriguing if you consider McCartney's *McCartney* and *Ram*, Lennon's *John Lennon/Plastic Ono Band* and *Imagine*, and Harrison's audacious triple LP, *All Things Must Pass,* all of which appeared within fifteen months of one another. (Ringo's first two solo records, *Sentimental Journey* and *Beaucoups of Blues*, both released in 1970, are usually not included in the thought experiment because they both contained cover songs. Still, the Beatles probably would have continued to feature Ringo on at least one song on any subsequent albums they recorded.)

225 *Some have even speculated*: In 1973 all of the ex-Beatles appeared on Ringo Starr's album *Ringo*, although they played different tracks. In 1974, Lennon and McCartney participated in an incredibly sloppy, cocaine-fueled jam session at a Los Angeles recording studio (later released as a bootleg, *A Toot and a Snore in '74*). In 1976, promoter Sid Bernstein ran an advertisement in American newspapers urging the Beatles to reconcile, calculating that a single concert, transmitted around the world, could generate $230 million. Also in 1976, on the television show *Saturday Night Live*, producer Lorne Michaels jokingly offered the Beatles $3,000 if they'd appear on the show. One night, when George Harrison was the musical guest, Paul happened to be visiting John at the Dakota building, and the two of them claim to have actually considered grabbing their guitars and taking a cab to 30 Rockefeller Plaza, which was only two miles away. In 1979, at

Eric Clapton's wedding, Paul, George, and Ringo all played "Sgt. Pepper's Lonely Hearts Club Band" (with Clapton subbing for John). In 1980, Paul attempted to contact John around the time that John and Yoko were working on their *Double Fantasy* LP, but according to Peter Doggett, "that communication had been prevented by a third party" (presumably Yoko). In 1980, Lennon swore in an affidavit that the Beatles were planning a reunion concert, but that was probably perjury—an attempt to bolster the Beatles' case against the producers of the Broadway musical review *Beatlemania.*

225 *John Lennon taped an interview with* Playboy *magazine*: *Playboy* (January 1981).

227 *"run of albums against which"*: Andrew Mueller, "It's Only Rock 'N' Roll," *The Ultimate Music Guide to the Rolling Stones* (from the Makers of *Uncut*), n.d., p. 70.

227 *"a series of roughly perfect albums."*: Crispin Sartwell, "Beatles Versus Stones: The Last Word," in Luke Dick and George A. Reisch, eds., *The Rolling Stones and Philosophy: It's Just a Thought Away* (Chicago and Lasalle, IL: Open Court, 2012), 162.

228 *The only thing that complicates the Stones'*: John Strausbaugh: "In 1978, those of us who had by then been Stones fans for fifteen years took *Some Girls* as a last memento, an aloha from a band entering its sunset years. This was Silver Age Stones, a magnet of instant nostalgia, a last hurrah." A *Rolling Stone* reviewer said, "*Some Girls* brought the Rolling Stones back to life." An *NME* writer observed, "In this album, Jagger suddenly seems interested in what he's doing again." Not everyone was fond of the record, however. In response to a lyric on the title track ("Black girls just wanna get fucked all night / I just don't have that much jam"), the civil rights activist Rev. Jesse Jackson called for a boycott. The Stones responded that the song was merely "a parody of certain stereotypical attitudes."

229 *"As much as Mick professed his love*: Bill German, *Under Their Thumb: How a Nice Boy from Brooklyn Got Mixed Up with the Rolling Stones* (New York: Villard, 2009), 219–220. German continues: "Keith, of course, would have preferred the old way. Throw everything to the air and see where it comes down. Take some risks and embrace the vulnerability. Keith didn't want the show to turn into a predictable greatest hits package . . . [but] Mick felt the band and audience weren't ready."

229 *"What Will They Do With All That Money?"*: See Peter Newcomb, "Satisfaction Guaranteed," *Forbes* (October 1989). Instead of working with legendary rock promoter Bill Graham, who had handled previous Stones'

American tours, the group turned to Michael Cohl, a much less experienced Canadian promoter who guaranteed them a minimum of $70 million. According to the Stones' financial advisor, Prince Rupert Lowenstein, Graham was so livid when he heard about the Stones' decision that he found out about a flight that Mick was taking, booked a seat on the same airplane, and buttonholed him. " 'You're insane,' he shouted. 'Michael Cohl doesn't know how to produce. . . . What have you got against me?' Mick said, 'It's very simple, Bill: not enough money.' "

230 *Depending on how one counts*: In addition to all this, on their website, the Stones peddle apparel for men, women, children, and pets. They sell books and calendars, posters, laminated commemorative tickets, coffee mugs, pendants, tote bags, trading cards, notebooks, and even fiftieth anniversary K2 Rolling Stones downhill skis. (It is unclear whether the skis are being offered up ironically.) A Japanese distillery sells a limited edition, specially blended Rolling Stones whiskey for $6,300 per bottle.

230 *Way back in 1975, Jagger said*: As quoted in Jim Jerome, "The Jaggers," *People* (June 9, 1975). This sentiment—that Mick did not plan to be singing raunchy Stones songs as a middle-aged man—has been frequently attributed to Jagger. In 1978, a *Rolling Stone* interviewer said to Mick, "You once said you didn't want to be singing 'Satisfaction' when you were forty-two," and Mick answered, "No, I certainly won't." According to a quote investigator website, Mick "may have made similar statements on more than one occasion, and he may have specified different cut-off ages."

231 *On average, the Stones charged*: Some prime tickets sold for around $2,000, and some were as cheap as $85.

231 *"All the major blood vessels leaving the heart"*: As quoted in Keith Elliot Greenberg, *December 8, 1980: The Day John Lennon Died* (Milwaukee: Backbeat Books, 2010), 172. It is sometimes said that Lennon was treated by another doctor, David Halleran. Possibly they both worked on him.

SELECTED BIBLIOGRAPHY

BOOKS

Appleford, Steve. *The Rolling Stones: Rip This Joint, the Story Behind Every Song* (New York: Da Capo, 2001).

Badman, Keith, ed. *The Beatles: Off the Record* (London: Omnibus Press, 2008).

Baker, Glenn A. *Beatles Down Under: The 1964 Australia and New Zealand Tour* (Wild and Woolley, 1982).

Barrow, Tony. *John, Paul, George, Ringo and Me* (New York: Da Capo, 2006).

The Beatles. *The Beatles Anthology* (San Francisco: Chronicle Books, 2002).

Blake, Andrew, ed. *Living Through Pop* (London and New York: Routledge, 1999).

Bennahum, David, ed. *The Beatles After the Break-Up: In Their Own Words* (London: Omnibus Press, 1992).

Bockris, Victor. *Keith Richards: The Unauthorized Biography* (London: Hutchinson, 1992).

Bonanno, Massimo, ed. *The Rolling Stones Chronicle: The First Thirty Years* (New York: Henry Holt, 1990).

Booker, Christopher. *The Neophiliacs: Revolution in English Life in the Fifties and Sixties* (London: Plimico, 1992, c. 1970).

Booth, Stanley. *The True Adventures of the Rolling Stones* (Chicago: Chicago Review Press, 2000).

Bramwell, Tony. *Magical Mystery Tours: My Life with the Beatles* (New York: St. Martin's Griffin, 1996).

Braun, Michael. *Love Me Do! The Beatles Progress* (New York: Penguin, 1995, c. 1964).

Bromell, Nick. *Tomorrow Never Knows: Rock and Psychedelics in the 1960s* (Chicago: University of Chicago Press, 2000).

Brown, Peter. *The Love You Make: An Insider's Story of the Beatles* (New York: NAL Trade, 2002).

Buskin, Richard. *The Complete Idiot's Guide to the Beatles* (New York: Alpha, 1998).

Carlin, Peter Ames. *Paul McCartney: A Life* (New York: Touchstone, 2009).

Christgau, Robert. *Growing Up All Wrong* (Cambridge: Harvard University Press, 1998).

Clayson, Alan. *The Rolling Stones: Beggar's Banquet* (New York: Billboard Books, 2008).

———. *The Rolling Stones: The Origin of the Species* (Surrey: Chrome Dreams, 2007).

Cohn, Nik. *Ball the Wall: Nik Cohn in the Age of Rock* (London: Picador, 1989).

Coleman, Ray. *Lennon: The Definitive Biography* (London: Pan Books, 1995).

———. *The Man Who Made the Beatles: An Intimate Biography of Brian Epstein* (New York: McGraw Hill, 1989).

Cording, Robert, Shelli Jankowski-Smith, and E. J. Miller Laino. *In My Life: Encounters with the Beatles* (New York: Fromm International, 1998).

Coyote, Peter. *Sleeping Where I Fall* (Washington, DC: Counterpoint, 1998).

Dalton, David, ed. *The Rolling Stones: The First Twenty Years* (New York: Knopf, 1981).

Dalton, David, and Mick Farren, eds. *The Rolling Stones: In Their Own Words* (London: Omnibus, 1980).

Davies, Hunter. *The Beatles* (New York: W. W. Norton & Co., 2010, c. 1968).

Davis, Stephen. *Old Gods Almost Dead: The 40-Year Odyssey of the Rolling Stones* (New York: Broadway, 2001).

DeRogatis, Jim. *Turn On Your Mind: Four Decades of Great Psychedelic Rock* (Milwaukee: Hal Leonard, 2003).

DeRogatis, Jim, and Greg Kot. *The Beatles vs. the Rolling Stones: Sound Opinions on the Great Rock 'n' Rivalry* (Minneapolis: Voyageur Press, 2010).

Dick, Luke and George A. Reisch, eds. *The Rolling Stones and Philosophy: It's Just a Thought Away* (Chicago and LaSalle, IL: Open Court, 2012).

DiLello, Richard. *The Longest Cocktail Party* (Chicago: Playboy Press, 1972).

Doggett, Peter. *There's a Riot Going On* (London: Canongate, 2007).

———. *You Never Give Me Your Money: The Beatles After the Breakup* (New York: HarperCollins, 2010).

Douglas, Susan J. *Where the Girls Are: Growing Up Female with the Mass Media* (New York: Times Books, 1994).

Egan, Sean, ed. *The Mammoth Book of the Beatles* (London: Constable & Robinson, 2009).

Ehrenreich, Barbara, Elizabeth Hess, and Gloria Jacobs. *Re-Making Love: the Feminization of Sex* (New York: Anchor, 1986).

Epstein, Brian. *A Cellarful of Noise* (New York: Doubleday and Co., 1964).

Epstein, Joseph. *On Friendship* (New York: Houghton Mifflin, 2006).

Evans, Mike. *The Beatles Literary Anthology* (London: Plexus, 2004).

Everett, Walter. *The Beatles as Musicians: The Quarry Men Through Rubber Soul* (New York: Oxford University Press, 2001).

Faithfull, Marianne. *Faithfull: An Autobiography* (New York: Cooper Square Press, 2000).

Flacks, Richard. *Youth and Social Change* (Chicago: Markham Pub Co., 1971).

Fornatale, Peter. *50 Licks. Myths and Stories from Half a Century of the Rolling Stones* (New York: Bloomsbury, 2013).

Freud, Sigmund. *Civilization and its Discontents*, trans. and ed., James Strachey (New York: W. W. Norton, 1961).

Frontani, Michael R. *The Beatles: Image and the Media* (Jackson: University of Mississippi Press, 2007).

Geller, Debbie (Anthony Wall, ed.). *In My Life: The Brian Epstein Story* (New York: St. Martin's Press, 2000).

German, Bill. *Under Their Thumb: How a Nice Boy from Brooklyn Got Mixed Up with the Rolling Stones (and Lived to Tell About It)* (New York: Villard, 2009).

Graham, Bill, with Robert Greenfield. *Bill Graham Presents: My Life Inside Rock and Out* (New York: Da Capo, 2004).

Gilbert, Daniel. *Stumbling on Happiness* (New York: Vintage, 2007).

Gitlin, Todd. *The Sixties: Years of Hope, Days of Rage* (New York: Bantam, 1987).

Giuliano, Geoffrey. *Blackbird: The Life and Times of Paul McCartney* (London: John Blake, 1991).

———. *Dark Horse: The Secret Life of George Harrison* (London: Bloomsbury, 1989).

———. *Revolver: The Secret History of the Beatles* (London: John Blake, 2006).

———. *Two of Us: John Lennon and Paul McCartney Behind the Myth* (New York: Penguin, 1999).

Giuliano, Geoffrey, and Vrnda Devi. *Glass Onion: The Beatles in Their Own Words* (New York: Da Capo Press, 1999).

Goldsher, Alan. *Paul Is Undead* (New York: Gallery, 2010).

Goodall, Nigel. *Jump Up: The Rise of the Rolling Stones* (London: Castle, 2011).

Goodman, Fred. *Mansion on the Hill: Dylan, Young, Geffen, Springsteen and the Head-On Collision of Rock and Commerce* (New York: Vintage, 1998).

"Goodman, Pete" [Peter Jones]. *Our Own Story, by the Rolling Stones* (New York: Bantam, 1965).

Gorer, Geoffrey. *Exploring English Character* (London: Cresset Press, 1955).

Gould, Jonathon. *Can't Buy Me Love: The Beatles, Britain and America* (New York: Three Rivers Press, 2007).

Green, Jonathon, ed. *Days in the Life: Voices from the English Underground, 1967-1971* (London: Heinemann, 1988).

Greenberg, Keith Elliot, *December 8, 1980: The Day John Lennon Died* (Milwaukee: Backbeat Books, 2010).

Greenfield, Robert. *A Day in the Life: One Family, the Beautiful People and the End of the Sixties* (New York: Da Capo, 2009).

———. *Exile on Main Street: A Season in Hell with the Rolling Stones* (New York: Da Capo, 2006).

———. *STP: A Journey Through America with the Rolling Stones* (New York: Da Capo, 2002).

Grunenberg, Christoph, and Jonathan Harris, eds. *Summer of Love: Psychedelic Art, Social Crisis and Counterculture in the 1960s* (Liverpool: Liverpool University Press, 2005).

Haslam, Nicky. *Redeeming Features: A Memoir* (New York: Knopf, 2009).

Hector, James. *The Complete Guide to the Music of the Rolling Stones* (London: Omnibus, 1995).

Hotchner, A. E. *Blown Away: The Rolling Stones and the Death of the Sixties* (New York: Simon & Schuster, 1990).

Hutchins, Chris. *Elvis Meets the Beatles* (London: Smith Gryphon, 1994).

Isherwood, Christopher. *The Sixties: Diaries 1960–1969* (New York: Harper Perennial, 2011).

Kane, Larry. *Ticket to Ride: Inside the Beatles 1964 Tour That Changed the World* (Philadelphia: Running Press, 2003).

Kaufman, Murray. *Murray the K Tells It Like It Is, Baby* (New York: Rinehart and Winston, 1966).

Lapham, Lewis. *With the Beatles* (Hoboken: Melville House, 2005).

Lennon, Cynthia. *John* (New York: Three Rivers Press, 2006).

Lindsay-Hogg, Michael. *Luck and Circumstance: A Coming of Age in Hollywood, New York and Points Beyond* (New York: Knopf, 2011).

Loewenstein, Prince Rupert. *A Prince Among Stones: That Business with the Rolling Stones and Other Adventures.* (New York: Bloomsbury, 2013).

Luci-Smith, Edward. *The Liverpool Scene* (London: Garden City Press, 1967).

Lydon, Michael. *Flashbacks: Eyewitness Accounts of the Rock Revolution, 1964–1974* (New York: Routledge, 2003).
MacDonald, Ian. *Revolution in the Head: The Beatles' Records and the Sixties* (London: Fourth Estate, 1997).
Mansfield, Ken (with Brent Stoker). *The White Book: The Beatles, the Bands, the Biz: An Insider's Look at an Era* (Nashville: Thomas Nelson, 2007).
Marcus, Greil, ed. *Rock and Roll Will Stand* (Boston: Beacon Press, 1969).
Marsden, Gerry (with Ray Coleman). *I'll Never Walk Alone: An Autobiography* (London: Bloomsbury, 1993).
Martin, George. *All You Need Is Ears: Inside the Personal Story of the Genius Who Created the Beatles* (New York: St. Martin's Griffin, 1994).
McKinney, Devin. *Magic Circle: The Beatles in Dream and History* (Cambridge, MA: Harvard University Press, 2003).
McMillian, John. *Smoking Typewriters: The Sixties Underground Press and the Rise of Alternative Media in America* (New York: Oxford, 2011).
Melly, George. *Revolt into Style: The Pop Arts* (New York: Anchor Books, 1971).
Miles, Barry. *The Beatles Diary, Volume One: The Beatles Years* (London and New York: Omnibus Press, 2001).
———. *The British Invasion: The Music, the Times, the Era* (New York: Sterling, 2009).
———.*Mick Jagger: In His Own Words* (New York: Delilah/Putnam, 1982).
———.*Paul McCartney: Many Years from Now* (New York: Holt, 1998).
Miller, James. *Flowers in the Dustbin: The Rise of Rock and Roll, 1947–1977* (New York: Touchstone, 2000).
Milliken, Robert. *Lillian Roxon: Mother of Rock* (New York: Thunder's Mouth Press, 2002).
Norman, Philip. *John Lennon: The Life* (New York: HarperCollins, 2008).
______. *Mick Jagger* (New York: Ecco, 2012).
———. *Shout! The True Story of the Beatles* (New York: Fireside, 2005, c. 1981).
———. *The Stones* (New York: Penguin, 1994).
O'Brien, Geoffrey. *Dream Time* (London: Secker & Warburg, 1998).
Oldham, Andrew Loog. *Stoned: A Memoir of London in the 1960s* (New York: St. Martin's, 2000).
———. *2Stoned* (New York: Vintage, 2003).
———. *Stone Free* (North Yorkshire, England: 2012).
O'Mahony, Sean. *Best of the Beatles Book* (London: Beat Publications, 2005).
Ono, Yoko, ed. *Memories of John Lennon* (New York: HarperCollins, 2005).
Oosterbaan, Hans, ed. *Love You Live, Rolling Stones: Fanfare from the Common Fan* (Springfield, PA: Fanfare Publishing, 2002).

Pallington, Jessica West, ed. *What Would Keith Richards Do? Daily Affirmations from a Rock and Roll Survivor* (New York: Bloomsbury, 2009).

Pawlowksi, Gareth L. *How They Became the Beatles: A Definitive History of the Early Years* (London & Sydney: Macdonald, 1990).

Paytress, Mark, ed. *The Rolling Stones: Off the Record* (London: Omnibus Press, 2003).

Peck, Abe. *Uncovering the Sixties: The Life and Times of the Underground Press* (New York: Citadel Press, 1991).

Phelge, James. *Nankering with the Stones: The Untold Story of the Early Days* (Chicago: A Capella, 2000).

Pritchard, David, and Alan Lysaght, eds. *The Beatles: An Oral History* (New York: Hyperion, 2005).

Raskin, Jonah. *Out of the Whale: Growing Up in the American Left* (New York: Link Books, 1974).

Rees-Mogg, William. *Memoirs* (New York: Harper Press, 2011)

Richards, Keith. *Life* (New York: Little, Brown, 2010).

Riley, Tim. *Lennon: The Man, the Myth, the Music* (New York: Hyperion, 2011).

The Rolling Stones. *According to the Rolling Stones* (San Francisco: Chronicle Books, 2003).

———. *The Rolling Stones 50* (New York: Hyperion, 2012).

Sanchez, Tony. *Up and Down with the Rolling Stones* (London: John Blake, 2011).

Sandercombe, W. Fraser, ed. *The Beatles: Press Reports* (Ontario: Collector's Guide Publishing, 2003).

Sanford, Christopher. *Keith Richards: Satisfaction* (London: Headline Books, 2003).

———. *Mick Jagger: Rebel Knight* (London: Omnibus Press, 2003).

Sawyers, June Sinner, ed. *Read the Beatles: Classic New Writings on the Beatles, Their Legacy, and Why They Still Matter* (New York: Penguin, 2006)

Schaffner, Nicholas. *The British Invasion: From the First Wave to the New Wave* (New York: McGraw Hill, 1982).

Schofield, Carey. *Jagger* (London: Methuen, 1983).

Sevonius, Ian. *The Psychic Soviet* (Chicago: Drag City, 2006).

"Shepherd, Billy" [Peter Jones]. *The True Story of the Beatles* (New York: Bantam, 1964).

Shotton, Pete, and Nicholas Schaffner. *John Lennon: In My Life* (New York: Henry Holt, 1987).

Silver, Caroline. *The Pop Makers* (New York: Scholastic Book Services, 1966).

Solt, Andrew, and Sam Egan, eds. *Imagine: John Lennon* (New York: Macmillan, 1988).

Somach, Danny, Kathleen Somach, and Kevin Gunn, eds. *Ticket to Ride* (New York: HarperCollins, 1991).

Southall, Brian. *Pop Goes to Court: Rock 'n' Pop's Greatest Battles* (London: Omnibus, 2008).

Spector, Ronnie. *Be My Baby: How I Survived Mascara, Miniskirts and Madness, or, My Life as a Fabulous Ronette* (New York: HarperPerennial, 1990).

Spitz, Bob. *The Beatles: The Biography* (Boston: Little, Brown, 2005).

Spitz, Marc. *Jagger: Rebel, Rock Star, Rambler, Rogue* (New York: Gotham, 2011).

Stark, Steven D. *Meet the Beatles: A Cultural History of the Band that Shook Youth, Gender and the World* (New York: HarperCollins, 2005).

Strausbaugh, John. *Rock Til You Drop* (London & New York: Verso, 2001).

Sutcliffe, Pauline. *The Beatles' Shadow: Stuart Sutcliffe and His Lonely Hearts Club* (London: Macmillan, 2002).

Thompson, Elizabeth, and David Gutman. *The Lennon Companion* (New York: Da Capo, 1987).

Thompson, Gordon. *Please Please Me: Sixties British Pop, Inside Out* (New York: Oxford, 2008).

Tremlett, George. *The Rolling Stones Story* (London: Futura Publications, 1974).

Trynka, Paul, ed. *MOJO's The Beatles: Ten Years That Shook the World* (USA & Great Britain: DK Publishing, 2004).

Vyner, Harriet. *Groovy Bob: The Life and Times of Robert Fraser* (London: Faber and Faber, 1999).

Ward, Ed, Geoffrey Stokes, and Ken Tucker. *Rock of Ages: The Rolling Stone History of Rock and Roll* (New York: Simon and Schuster, 1986).

Weiner, Sue, and Lisa Howard. *The Rolling Stones A to Z* (New York: Grove, 1983).

Wells, Simon. *Butterfly on a Wheel: The Great Rolling Stones Drug Bust* (London: Omnibus, 2112).

Wenner, Jann, ed. *Lennon Remembers: The Full Rolling Stone Interview from 1970* (New York and London: Verso, 2000, c. 1972).

———. *Lennon Remembers* (New York: Fawcett Popular Library, 1972),

Wiener, Jon. *Come Together: John Lennon in His Time* (Champagne-Urbana: University of Illinois Press, 1990).

Womack, Kenneth, ed. *The Cambridge Companion to the Beatles* (New York and Cambridge: Cambridge University Press, 2009).

Wyman, Bill. *Rolling with the Stones* (New York: DK Publishing, 2002).

———. *Stone Alone* (New York: Da Capo, 1997).

PERIODICALS

(Underground newspapers available in Bell & Howell's Underground Press Collection on microfilm.)

Argus (Ann Arbor, MI)
The Beatles Monthly Book
The Black Dwarf
Connections (Madison, WI)
Creem
The Daily Express
The Daily Mirror
The Great Speckled Bird (Atlanta, GA)
The Guardian
Helix (Seattle, WA)
The Independent
Kudzu (Oxford, MS)
Liberation News Service (New York City)
Melody Maker
New Left Review
New Musical Express (*NME*)
News of the World
The (London) *Times*
The New York Times
Playboy
Record Mirror
Rising Up Angry (Chicago, IL)
Rolling Stone
The Rolling Stones Monthly Book
San Diego Free Press
The Seed (Chicago, IL)
Teaspoon Door (San Diego, CA)
WIN (New York City)

WEBSITES

www.beatlesinterviews.org
www.beatlemoney.com
www.heydullblog.blogspot.com
www.rocksbackpages.com
www.timeisonourside.com

INDEX

INDEX

INDEX

ABOUT THE AUTHOR

John McMillian is Assistant Professor of History at Georgia State University. He is author of the critically acclaimed *Smoking Typewriters: The Sixties Underground Press and the Rise of Alternative Media in America*, coeditor of *The Radical Reader: A Documentary History of an American Radical Tradition*, *The New Left Revisited*, *Protest Nation: The Radical Roots of Modern America,* and *The Sixties: A Journal of History, Politics, and Culture.* His writing has appeared in scholarly journals, magazines, and major newspapers. He lives in Atlanta, Georgia.